Discrimination, Persecution, Martyrdom:
Following Christ Together

Report of the international consultation
Tirana, Albania, 2-4 November 2015

WIPF & STOCK · Eugene, Oregon

*Because so much of the Christianity
of yesterday and of today
is the history of martyrdom,
each of us and each community
must gather in a glass cup
the tears and blood of the persecuted,
preventing it from being lost
or trampled into the ground.*

Andrea Riccardi, Tirana, 2 November 2015

Convened and Organised by

The Global Christian Forum

Together with

The Catholic Church
(Promoting Pontifical Council for Promoting Christian Unity)
The Pentecostal World Fellowship
The World Council of Churches
The World Evangelical Alliance

Hosted by the

The Orthodox Autocephalous Church of Albania
The Albania Catholic Bishops Conference
The Evangelical Alliance of Albania

Tirana, Albania
2-4 November 2015

Edited by Huibert van Beek and Larry Miller

Introduction by Larry Miller

Wipf and Stock Publishers
199 W 8th Ave, Suite 3
Eugene, OR 97401

Discrimination, Persecution, Martyrdom
Following Christ Together
By van Beek, Huibert and Miller, Larry
Copyright©2018 Verlag für Kultur and Wissenschaft
ISBN 13: 978-1-5326-5365-0
Publication date 3/16/2018
Previously published by Verlag für Kultur and Wissenschaft, 2018

Contents

Introduction: The Tirana Consultation: An Historic Event? iii

Programme xi

Session 1 – Opening Plenary 1
    Welcome to the Consultation 3
    Introduction to the Consultation 10
    Hopes for the Consultation 12
    Keynote Address 20

Session 2 – Voices from Suffering Churches: Part 1 29

Session 3 – Voices from Suffering Churches: Part 2 57

Session 4 – Small Group Discussions 217

Session 5 – Living in Solidarity with Suffering Churches 83

Session 6 – Voices from Churches in Solidarity 115

Session 7 – Voices from Agencies in Solidarity 137

Session 8 – Small Group Discussions 217

Session 9 – Visions of Walking Together as the Suffering Church: Next Steps 167

Session 11 – Next Steps: Walking Together as the Suffering Church 187

Over Lunch Session 203

Summary of Small Group Reports 217

CONSULTATION MESSAGE 241

Participants 245

Acknowledgements

Many heads, hearts, and hands contributed to the creation of the consultation *'Discrimination, Persecution, Martyrdom: Following Christ Together'*: leaders of the four global co-sponsoring bodies and the three Albanian hosting bodies; the churches, organisations, and individuals who contributed financially or in kind, none of whom are here named in respect for those who wish to remain anonymous; and, all consultation participants and presenters, especially those from suffering churches who joined with and ministered to us at personal risk. To all of these, we express our deep gratitude.

Heads, hearts, and hands contributed also to the creation of this report: Huibert van Beek, who did the tedious but foundational work of collecting and transcribing the consultation proceedings; Bruce Barron and Eleanor Miller, who endured the minutiae of English-language copy-editing; Kim Cain, unusually-gifted photographer; Jesse Cain, the designer who adds beauty to content; and the Gebende Hände Foundation (Germany), which has under-written financially and over-seen administratively the publication of this book. To each of these, we express our strong gratitude.

Larry Miller

Global Christian Forum Secretary
Strasbourg, 4 March 2018

Rev Dr Larry Miller, Secretary, Global Christian Forum

Introduction
The Tirana Consultation: An Historic Event?

More than 140 church leaders drawn from 65 nations met in Tirana, Albania, 2-4 November 2015, and called on churches around the world to urgently pray, support, and be in solidarity with those suffering persecution because of their faith. They came from most strands of global Christianity to manifest together their concern for and commitment to Christians who endure discrimination, persecution, and even martyrdom.

The Global Christian Forum convened and organised the event together with the Catholic Church (Pontifical Council for Promoting Christian Unity), the Pentecostal World Fellowship, the World Council of Churches, and the World Evangelical Alliance. It was the first time that these four global church bodies worked together in a common global initiative.

The Orthodox Autocephalous Church of Albania, the Albania Catholic Bishops Conference, and the Evangelical Alliance of Albania hosted the conference, for which the Resurrection of Christ Orthodox Cathedral and Cultural Centre was the primary venue.

It was possibly the first time in the modern history of the church that a gathering consisting of so many streams of global Christianity coalesced around the issue of persecution of Christians. It may have been the first time also that high-level leaders from the widest spectrum of churches acknowledged collectively complicity in discrimination and persecution not only of people of other faiths but also of each other.

This book contains the Consultation proceedings, including the messages and the list of participants. This introduction provides essential context for understanding the proceedings as it describes the sequence of the programme and the spirituality of the event.

The Flow of the Consultation

The consultation programme (see pages xi - xv) was designed in three successive stages, to allow for a pertinent flow of the meeting process from the beginning to the end. The themes for the three days of sessions were (1) Listening to Suffering Churches, (2) Living in Solidarity with Suffering Churches, and (3) Walking Together as the Suffering Church.

On each of the first two days, three plenary sessions were held in the morning and afternoon, with a small-group discussion session in the late afternoon. The evenings were left open for optional meetings and interaction between participants or participating bodies. On the last day, two more plenary sessions took place, along with one session in which the participants of the four global constituencies engaged in the consultation met separately.

The consultation opened with words of welcome from three Albanian church leaders: H.B. Archbishop Anastasios (Orthodox), Bishop George A. Frendo (Catholic), and the Rev. Akil Pano (Evangelical). Rev Dr Larry Miller, Secretary of the Global Christian Forum, also offered introductory remarks. Representatives of the four global bodies expressed their hopes for the consultation; Catholic Kurt Cardinal Koch read a message of greeting from Pope Francis. Dr Andrea Riccardi, founder of the Community of Sant'Egidio, then delivered a keynote address on the theme of the consultation.

During the next two plenary sessions, the participants listened to the voices of suffering churches in Asia, Africa and the Middle East. The afternoon programme on the first day also included a brief introduction to a research project conducted by the International Institute for Religious Freedom (IIRF), on behalf of the Global Christian Forum and the four global constituencies, to collect and verify information on the persecution of Christians.

On the morning of the second day, H.B. Archbishop Anastasios offered biblical and theological perspectives on the consultation theme, and Dr Thomas Schirrmacher and Dr Godfrey Yogarajah addressed issues of human rights and religious liberty. The panellists in this day's plenary sessions reflected on the significance of exercising solidarity with those parts of the global body of Christ that are facing discrimination, persecution and martyrdom. Another IIRF research project, on the language and terminology used when discussing discrimination and persecution, was also presented briefly.

The third day focused on practical actions. The first plenary session included panellists' recommendations as to next steps. In the second session, participants met in groups organised by confessional stream (Catholic, Ecumenical, Evangelical, Pentecostal). The leaders of the four consultation co-sponsors presented the outcome of these deliberations during the final plenary in the afternoon.

Along with these discussions of next steps, the adoption of a consultation message was the primary means of identifying and highlighting ways of moving forward post-Tirana. The planning committee for the consultation, composed of leaders of the Global Christian Forum and representatives of the four global bodies, prepared an initial draft, which was presented and discussed at the morning plenary session on day two. Responses and suggestions were received from the floor, and participants considered the draft in their small-group discussions that afternoon, with some of them submitting additional comments. After a second presentation on the morning of the last day and subsequent revisions, the consultation message was finalized and adopted unanimously at the closing session.

The programme was enriched by two informal sessions, on the second and third days, about the situation of the churches in Iran, northern Iraq and Syria. It was further enhanced by the reception for all consultation participants hosted the final evening in the Presidential Palace by the President of the Republic of Albania, His Excellency, Mr Bujar Hishani.

Most of the consultation presentations were in English, with some in Italian, Spanish, or Arabic, which have been translated into English here. At the consultation, simultaneous interpretation was provided (into English, French, Italian, Spanish, Russian) to assist all participants in understanding.

A Spirit of Prayer

The consultation was heavily embedded in prayer. On the Sunday before the consultation, participants attended the Divine Liturgy celebrated in the Resurrection of Christ Cathedral of the Orthodox Autocephalous Church of Albania. Each meeting day began with a morning prayer time lasting about an hour. On the first and second day, evening prayers were held in the intimate setting of the small groups, which facilitated sharing the richness of the diverse spiritual streams present in the meeting.

As a vivid expression of the three Albanian Christian traditions involved in the preparation and implementation of the consultation, the morning prayers were held respectively in the Orthodox Cathedral, the Albania Christian Centre of the Evangelical Alliance, and St. Paul's Catholic Cathedral, with the host congregation leading the service according to its tradition and providing the preached message. The three speakers, respectively, were H.E. Metropolitan Vasilios of the Church of Cyprus; Pastor Barry Ogden, International Protestant Assembly, Tirana; and Msgr George Frendo, Auxiliary Bishop of Tirana-Durres.

Prayer was also at the heart of the programme in the daily sessions. Each plenary began with a reading from the scriptures in several languages, a time of silence, and the singing of a hymn, according to the tradition of the Taizé community. These moments were animated by

Brother Richard from Taizé and a group of stewards together with some consultation participants. The consultation ended with a closing prayer and a message by Rev. Dr Jerry Pillay, president of the World Communion of Reformed Churches.

Mutual Forgiveness

The conference included a few unexpected but highly significant exchanges that recalled an all-too-unfortunate aspect of the history of persecution of Christians: sometimes Christians have been the persecutors as well as the persecuted. Cardinal Koch addressed poignantly the problem of Christians targeting each other in his message at the first plenary session. He noted that those persecuting Christians rarely make any distinction between confessions or denominations, stating, "It is a sad reflection that those who persecute Christians seem to have understood better than Christians themselves that the Church is one. … While recalling our martyrs of yesterday and today, let us repent of our divisions and mutual harm and ask the Holy Spirit to reunite us in one church, finally visibly reconciled."

Following up on this theme, many interactions and comments during the consultation acknowledged the need for Christian churches to renounce persecuting each other as a precursor to solidarity with each other in facing persecution from other sources. This conviction was incorporated into the consultation message, which states, "We repent of having at times persecuted each other and other religious communities in history, and ask forgiveness from each other and pray for new ways of following Christ together."

David Wells, spokesperson of the Pentecostal World Fellowship returned to this issue of mutual repentance in the closing session. "We know," he stated, "that we must address our own issues, where we have shown arrogance and pride and at times discrimination and persecution, and we appreciate the other bodies of brothers and sisters in Christ expressing similar sentiments to us as well." At the same time, he realistically noted the challenges of achieving reconciliation, pointing out that many Pentecostals still recall experiencing "the pain of being looked down on and at times even worked against systemically by governments and [other] churches".

The Content of the Messages

The messages contained in this book vary considerably in style and content. Some are highly personal and expressed with deep emotion, others more theological. Some describe circumstances that have changed considerably since November 2015. Every message or exchange is important. To facilitate readings, following are some key themes of the consultation and where they appear most prominently.

- One of the most encouraging undertones of the conference involved hearing "what God has done" in Albania, which was an officially atheist state just a quarter-century before we convened in Tirana. The welcoming messages from our Albanian hosts in session 1, the keynote by Dr Riccardi at the same session, and the greeting from Catholic Archbishop Massafra at the beginning of session 3 contain brief but powerful reflections on this transformation.

- Session 1 also features substantive remarks from leaders of the four global bodies and deeply provocative reflections on the meaning of Christian witness and martyrdom today by Dr Riccardi.

- Sessions 2 and 3 contain extensively documented and often heart-wrenching details on the recent experiences of Christians in Myanmar, India, Pakistan, Kenya, Nigeria, Algeria, Syria, Iran, Iraq, Palestine, and elsewhere.

- The urgent need for a unified stance and collaboration among Christian bodies arose repeatedly, such as in open discussions in session 2 regarding Algeria and Kenya; the presentation by an evangelical from the Holy Land in session 3, with a reprise during open discussion in session 6; and a comment from a Bolivian evangelical in session 5.

- The most extensive biblical and theological discussion of the "martyric" church and the nature of self-sacrificial but transforming obedience to Christ was provided by His Beatitude Archbishop Anastasios at the beginning of session 5. His principled, practical articulation of what God expects of those who suffer, how God blesses them, and what God expects of the church today caused the World Evangelical Alliance's Thomas Schirrmacher, the next speaker, to comment, "For some of you who wonder why the Archbishop has the title of Beatitude, I tell you it is because he gives such beautiful speeches."

- The presentations on human rights and religious freedom in session 5 provoked, during the open discussion, lively expression of various perspectives on how practically we should work to secure these desired goals.

- Sessions 6 and 7 shift to the question of how Christians can stand in solidarity with the suffering churches. Two organizations that have extensive involvement with countries where Christians face persecution—Aid to the Church in Need and Open Doors—were among the presenters in session 7. Various strategic issues arose in these sessions, such as the tension between helping Christians to flee from dangerous countries and the desire to maintain a functioning church in those lands, or uncertainty as to whether visits from Western Christians offer helpful support or cause these churches to become more severely targeted. Another important question was how to make common cause with Muslims who also oppose the persecution of Christians and may themselves suffer persecution.

- Among the next steps discussed in sessions 9 and 11 were dedicated prayer, active support for worldwide religious freedom, awareness raising in the West, and providing first-hand visits and teaching support. A Nigerian presenter raised the sensitive question of when Christians should accept suffering and when they should defend themselves. A long time Cuban Christian leader highlighted the value of support "through prayer, presence and resources" received from churches in other parts of the world. Maintaining unity among Christian groups was a prominent concern. A Kenyan respondent expressed concern that promises of solidarity could turn out to be empty without substantive action, urging those bodies that have seats at high places like the United Nations to exercise their influence.

- The best place to find a comprehensive overview of the leading issues and concerns shared by conference participants is the chapter summarizing the outcomes of the small-group discussions. Many frank, perceptive insights are contained therein.

What has Happened Since Tirana?

In the consultation message, participants committed themselves to listen more, pray more, speak up more, do more. They called on all Christians to include more prominently in daily prayers those who are discriminated against, persecuted, and suffering for following Christ daily. They called on all Christian organisations on regional, national and local levels from various traditions to learn, pray and work together in their localities for the persecuted, to ensure that they are better supported. They called on all churches to engage in more dialogue and cooperation with other faith communities.

Have we kept our commitments? Have we pursued the calls? For some of us, the answer may lead more appropriately to confession than to confidence.

What is not in doubt is the continuing need to listen more, pray more, speak up more, do more. Because what is not at all in doubt is that discrimination, persecution, and martyrdom of Christians—and of some other people of faith—continue unabated. Since the Tirana consultation, following Christ together has become no less costly—and no less the call of Christ on all Christians and on all churches.

Programme

Monday, 2 November
Listening to Suffering Churches

09.00 – 10.00	**Morning Prayer** Resurrection of Christ Orthodox Cathedral of Tirana Orthodox Autocephalous Church of Albania
10.30 – 11.00	*Morning Tea and Coffee*
11.00 – 12.30	**Session 1 — Opening Plenary** • Welcome from the Albanian churches • Introduction to the consultation • Hopes for the consultation • Keynote presentation: Discrimination, Persecution, and Martyrdom in the 21st Century
12.30 – 14.00	*Lunch and networking*
14.00 – 15.30	**Session 2 — Plenary** • Voices and Data Research: Introduction • Panel: Following Christ Together in Discrimination, Persecution, Martyrdom — Voices from Suffering Churches (I) • Conversation with the panel and one another
15.30 – 16.00	*Afternoon Tea and Coffee*
16.00 – 17.30	**Session 3 — Plenary** • Panel: Following Christ Together in Discrimination, Persecution, Martyrdom — Voices from Suffering Churches (II) • Conversation with the panel and one another
17.30 – 17.45	*Brief Break*
17.45 – 19.15	**Session 4 — Small Groups** • Learning to know one another: telling personal and ecclesial stories related to the theme • Discerning together: responding to the presentations and panels • Praying together: evening prayers
19.30 – 21.00	*Dinner and networking*
21.00 – 22.00	Optional evening meetings: stories, reports, information by consultation participants

Tuesday, 3 November
Living in Solidarity with Suffering Churches

09.00 – 10.00	**Morning Prayer** Albania Christian Centre Evangelical Alliance of Albania
10.30 – 11.00	*Morning Tea and Coffee*
11.00 – 12.30	**Session 5 — Plenary** • Keynote presentation: Biblical and Theological Perspectives • Keynote presentation: Human Rights and Religious Liberty Perspectives • First Consideration of a 'Consultation Message'
12.30 – 14.00	*Lunch and networking*
14.00 – 15.30	**Session 6 — Plenary** • Reflection on Language Research: Introduction • Panel: Following Christ Together in Discrimination, Persecution, Martyrdom — Voices from Churches in Solidarity • Conversation with the panel and one another
15.30 – 16.00	*Afternoon Tea and Coffee*
16.00 – 17.30	**Session 7 — Plenary** • Panel: Following Christ Together in Discrimination, Persecution, Martyrdom — Voices from Agencies in Solidarity • Conversation with the panel and one another
17.30 – 17.45	*Brief Break*
17.45 – 19.15	**Session 8 — Small Groups** • Discerning together: 　- Responding to the presentations and panels 　- Considering a 'Consultation Message' • Praying together: evening prayers
19.30 – 21.00	*Dinner and networking*
21.00 – 22.00	Optional evening meetings: stories, reports, information by consultation participants

Wednesday, 4 November
Walking Together as Suffering Church

09.00 – 10.00	**Morning Prayer** St. Paul's Cathedral Catholic Church in Albania
10.30 – 11.00	*Morning Tea and Coffee*
11.00 – 12.30	**Session 9 — Plenary** • Panel: Visions of 'Walking Together as Suffering Church: Next Steps' • Second Consideration of a 'Consultation Message'
12.30 – 14.00	*Lunch and networking*
14.00 – 15.30	**Session 10 — Confessional Groups** (Catholic, Ecumenical, Evangelical, Pentecostal) • Discerning together: next steps for ourselves and with others
15.30 – 16.00	*Afternoon Tea and Coffee*
16.00 – 17.30	**Session 11 — Plenary** • Panel: Next Steps Walking Together as Suffering Church – Leaders of the Catholic Church, PWF, WCC, WEA, GCF and suffering churches • Conversation with the panel and one another • Third Consideration of a 'Consultation Message'
17.30 – 17.45	*Brief Break*
17.45 – 19.15	**Session 12 — Closing Prayer**
19.30 – 21.00	*Reception held by the President of Albania*

Theme and Goals of the Consultation

(1) Provide opportunity for exchange in a safe space among leaders of churches suffering discrimination, persecution, and even martyrdom

(2) Better listen to, learn from, and accompany churches suffering discrimination, persecution, and martyrdom

(3) Inform one another of our activities in solidarity with churches in these situations

(4) Seek a common understanding of the facts of the situations of suffering as well as a more common framework and language for the development of appropriate Christian responses to them

(5) Encourage the churches and agencies to speak and work together in response to these situations

(6) Pray for the flourishing of God's kingdom in the midst of discrimination, persecution, and martyrdom

Nature of the Consultation

(1) Voices of suffering churches — The voices of suffering churches should be lifted up as much as possible.

(2) Working consultation — This will be a gathering not only for listening, but also for discerning and deciding how to move forward together.

(3) Spirituality of the consultation — While this is a working consultation, it is also a time for spiritual discernment and prayer, considering what it means to follow Christ together in a world of discrimination, persecution and martyrdom.

(4) Inter-church — The uniqueness of the consultation is its breadth of representation of Christian churches and organisations. This aspect will be lifted up wherever possible. At the same time, the consultation must address the real tensions between churches in relation to situations of discrimination, persecution, and martyrdom.

(5) Global Christian Forum culture — A foundational element of GCF gatherings is building relationships and recognizing marks of living faith in Christ in one another. May this consultation have a similar culture.

(6) Non-public — The consultation will have low public visibility in order to provide a safe space for all participants and for honest exchange between us.

Potential Outcomes

(1) During the consultation, participants will have heard from and discerned with the full spectrum of global Christianity the call to 'follow Christ together in discrimination, persecution, and martyrdom'.

(2) By the end of the consultation, each participant and each participant body will have articulated potential 'next steps' in response to this call — next steps for themselves and next steps with other participants and participant bodies. Existing initiatives may be strengthened. New initiatives may arise.

(3) At the end of the consultation, participants may issue a joint message to the churches.

(4) After the consultation, participants will receive materials (news releases, photos, videos, a comprehensive report) from the organisers, enabling them better to share the experience with their own churches, organisations, and communities.

H.B. Archbishop Anastasios, Orthodox Autocephalous Church of Albania

Session One – Opening Plenary

Moderator:

Rev Nicta Lubaale, General Secretary, Organisation of African Instituted Churches, Global Christian Forum

Welcome from Albanian Churches:

His Beatitude Archbishop Dr Anastasios, Orthodox Autocephalous Church of Albania

Bishop George Anthony Frendo, Catholic Archdiocese of Tiranë-Durrës

Rev Akil Pano, Evangelical Alliance of Albania

Introduction to the consultation:

Rev Dr Larry Miller, Global Christian Forum

Hopes for the consultation:

Rev Dr David Wells, Pentecostal World Fellowship

Bishop Ephraim Tendero, World Evangelical Alliance

Rev Dr Olav Fyske Tveit, World Council of Churches

Cardinal Kurt Koch, Pontifical Council for Promoting Christian Unity, Catholic Church

Message from His Holiness Pope Francis

Discrimination, Persecution and Martyrdom in the Twenty-First Century

Dr Andrea Riccardi, Catholic Church

Welcome to the consultation

Welcome from the Orthodox Autocephalous Church of Albania

His Beatitude Archbishop Dr Anastasios of Albania

It is a particular joy to welcome and greet in the love of Christ all the distinguished participants of the Consultation on "Discrimination, Persecution, Martyrdom: Following Christ Together", organized by the Global Christian Forum in collaboration with the Christian communities of Albania.

Albania faced many serious trials during the course of the twentieth century. The persecution against all religions throughout the whole country had two phases. In the first phase, from 1944 to 1967, it was similar to the other forms of persecution that Christians experienced in the Soviet Union and other communist countries. The second phase, from 1967 to 1990, was an absolute persecution that destroyed every expression of religious life. The Hoxha regime imposed a constitution that prohibited every form of religious expression. In all of world history, no other state has had this type of law. Every ecclesiastical structure was demolished and the clergy persecuted; many died in exile or in prisons, together with devoted laypersons. Most monasteries and churches were destroyed, or their use was changed to become cinemas, stables, storehouses, etc. The Orthodox Church was completely destroyed.

After the changes in the Soviet Union and the fall of many communist regimes, Albania in 1991 embraced religious freedom and has fostered peaceful coexistence between religious communities, but also with those who do not belong to any religion. The change did not happen by any revolution but by changes of roles in the political parties.

When I arrived in Tirana in 1991, I was greeted at the airport by a small group of elderly and anguished people who led us to the ruined cathedral, which for decades had been used as a gymnasium. From that very first moment, I wanted to define the essential message of my mission. So I asked everyone to take a candle and asked how they say the words "Christ is risen" in Albanian. I proceeded to light the candle, chanting "*Krishti u ngjall!*" One after another, the faithful few who were present lit their candles and responded in tears with the words "*Vërtetë u ngjall*" (Truly, he is risen). Since then, the phrase "Christ is risen" has become the motto with which we have carried on all these years. It illumined the heavy autumn melancholy and dark cold winter that followed. During your stay in Tirana, you can see some of the signs of the resurrection and growth of the Orthodox Church that has happened during these last 23 years.

May the Lord bless our meeting and help us to examine more deeply our theme and propose new forms of support for persecuted Christians around the world. May he strengthen our fraternal relations and give us new enthusiasm to face discrimination, persecution and martyrdom while following Christ together. Surrounded by countless martyrs of the Church, with eyes fixed on Christ, we run towards the final goal, not discouraged. We know on whom we have placed our hope (2 Tim 1:12) and face each adversity looking forward in faith to the crucified and resurrected Lord, with the certainty that the resurrection does not come after the Cross, but actually is located within the Cross.

Welcome from the Catholic Church in Albania

Bishop George Anthony Frendo, O.P., General Secretary, Episcopal Conference of Albania and Auxiliary Bishop of Tiranë-Durrës

On behalf of the Catholic community in Albania, I welcome you, while I express my desire that this meeting be for all of us an expression of faith, hope, and charity.

First of all, it is an expression of faith. The slogans of the secular city, according to Harvey Cox, are love, fraternity, solidarity, peace, justice, freedom, human dignity, human rights, etc. These, Cox says, are all basically Christian values. But they remain just slogans and can never become concrete and directive values unless they are inspired by that faith which enlightens us in such a way that we see the face of God in the face of every man. That is why Mother Teresa shook the foundations of the society of anonymity. One cannot ask what she did without asking also why she did it. She did it because she believed in him who said, "Whatever you have done to the least of my brethren, you have done it to me." And this is what distinguishes Christian love from philanthropy.

Second, it is an expression of hope. Salvation history teaches us that there is no evil from which the almighty God cannot draw something good. Jacob's sons, driven by envy towards their brother Joseph, sold him to the Egyptians. Later on, when the Pharaoh appointed Joseph as his deputy, Joseph's brothers were obliged to go to Egypt to buy food. When they noticed that Pharaoh's deputy was their brother Joseph, they all feared that he would take revenge on them. Yet Joseph said to them, "You did me harm, but God turned it into something good as you can see. … Do not be afraid! I will take care of you and your children" (Gen 50:20–21). In Revelation 6:10, the souls of the martyrs cry out to God, asking how long it will be before he vindicates them. Such a desire (and refusal to be driven to despair) shows total trust in the power and will of God: "I know whom I have believed, and am persuaded that he is able to keep that which I have committed unto him against that day" (2 Tim 1:12).

And finally, it is an expression of charity, which translates itself in love and solidarity with the victims of persecution and with their families. As a young person, I shared the ideas of the young people who, in the 1960s, were reacting against the status quo of contemporary society. I remember the beatniks and the interesting life pattern that they adopted in California, far from the maddening crowd of the cities; their lifestyle was a clear message to that society. I remember the students' revolts in many European cities in 1968. I too shared those dreams at that time. I too imagined that society was badly in need of a radical change of its structures. But I think that what the world has passed through, especially in the past twenty years, has only convinced us that this is far from true. What the world needs is not a change of structures, but a change of hearts. Only love can change hearts. I remember a song that was very popular in my childhood: "Love makes the world go round." May our love be always an expression of our deep conviction that only love can change the world.

"God is love." This is how St John has defined God. Consequently, no war can ever be waged in the name of God.

Welcome from the Evangelical Alliance of Albania

Rev Akil Pano, General Secretary, Evangelical Alliance of Albania

I am honoured to bring warmest greetings and brotherly love from the Evangelical Church of Albania in your presence today. Over two years ago, I was representing the Evangelical Church of Albania in the Orthodox-Evangelical initiative organized by the Lausanne movement here in Albania, and I had the privilege to meet Dr Larry Miller. He shared with me about this gathering, which was still being planned at that time. When I was told that the Global Christian Forum was considering Albania together with two other locations for this event, I gave my brother all the reasons why such an important event had to take place in Albania at this time.

The first reason is the history of the Christian church of Albania and the apostolic tradition of faith. The Gospel was brought to our territory by the early Christians.

The second reason is the perseverance of the saints in this land. We have a history of persecution lasting 500 years, having been under the Ottoman Empire from the fifteenth to the twentieth century, followed by a severe communist dictatorship that by its constitution changed Albania into the only truly atheist country in the world.

But there is another reason why Albania is a proper country to host such an important event. In Albania, God has favoured us to experience the rise of his church. Here we can witness his word to be true that indeed he brings out beauty from ashes. The story of Albanian Christianity continues with the church after its centuries of persecution. Holding this event in such a place is important because in this context we all can understand that there is life after death. We all can comprehend that the old dead bones can still live when God's word is being proclaimed with the power of the Holy Spirit. We can see a little teenage boy fight a mighty giant and win. God wants to show us that he is leading his people through the rough places of life. Sometimes he is allowing the storm of discrimination, persecution and martyrdom to bring us to the place of total surrender, to sanctify us and to help us to change the manmade universe with ourselves at the centre. These are the times when we can see the cross of Christ inviting us to fellowship with Christ and in his sufferings. But I believe that this is a reminder of God's faithfulness.

Many years ago on the battlefield, after they had suffered defeat, Israel pleaded with God for help and he granted them a miraculous victory. Their priest and leader, Samuel, set up a monument to remind them of God's strong hand in their triumph. Samuel named the pillar Ebenezer, saying, "Thus far the Lord has helped us." This stone pillar called God's people to recall the many times when God turned events from bad to blessing.

"I will utter hidden things, things from ancient times", the psalmist said—things we have heard and known, things our ancestors have told us, to help you remember God's power, to give you trust and confidence in him, to teach you to lean on him to be your Ebenezer for as long as you live on this side of heaven.

This morning in my home I remembered the two discouraged disciples walking confused and alone on their road for reasons that we today may know. They were not aware of the fact that the Lord Jesus Christ was walking with them on that road. The very Christ was walking with them! He was speaking to them, but they were too loaded with the burdens, pressures and fears of this life so it was not possible for them to see the reality of his presence. Only when he ministered to them the bread did something unusual happen: their eyes opened.

It is the same with the Church today but with a little difference. Although we know and proclaim that Christ is risen and is alive forevermore, many times we miss him as he is walking with us on the roads of this life. The same pressures, burdens and fears of life don't allow us to acknowledge that he is indeed with us. But when he breaks his bread, our eyes are opened and we can see him. We have fellowship with Christ, partake of the emblems of his covenant, and stay connected to him. Allowing him to minister to us his divine word will give us all power and all encouragement to finish our race faithfully and humbly. May the risen Christ minister to us as we stay close to him these days.

May he give us his living bread to feed our faith and open our eyes to see him as he walks together with us on the roads of this life. And if it happens that someday you feel discouraged and dismayed, remember these days in Albania. Remember the rising again of the Church here and God's faithfulness. God who turned the ashes into beauty in Albania can do the same thing for you in your country.

Now to him who is able to keep you from all stumbling and to present you blameless before his glorious presence and with great joy, to the only God our Saviour through Jesus Christ our Lord be glory, majesty, power and authority, before all ages, now and forevermore! Amen (Jude 24–25).

Introduction to the Consultation

Rev Dr Larry Miller, Secretary, Global Christian Forum

Our journey to this consultation began four years ago in Indonesia. At the second global gathering of the Global Christian Forum, participants said, "It is time for the Forum to take up the second part of its purpose: to create space for the widest possible spectrum of the churches of the world to address common challenges together.

What are the challenges that all churches face today? One of the first answers to that question came in Rome a few months later, during the annual meeting of the Global Christian Forum international committee. More precisely, it came from Father Mikhail, representative to the committee from the Russian Orthodox Church (Moscow Patriarchate). "The persecution of Christians", said Father Mikhail, "is once again a growing challenge to all churches. We must address it together."

In the months that followed, consultation with leaders of a broad spectrum of churches at the global and continental levels confirmed Father Mikhail's conviction. It also showed that discrimination, persecution and martyrdom can be a source of tension between churches. Understandings of the situations diverge. Words used to describe the phenomenon differ. Our responses to the suffering are sometimes incompatible with each other. Discrimination, persecution and martyrdom of Christians have not always inspired Christian unity; they have also provoked fraternal conflicts or at least mutual suspicions. Yet awareness of this fact only reinforced the conviction that the time had come for us to address the challenge together. The World Evangelical Alliance, the Pentecostal World Fellowship, the World Council of Churches, and the Catholic Church agreed.

But what in fact is the challenge? The first name for this initiative was "Discrimination, Persecution, Martyrdom: Facing the Challenge Together". In an early planning visit to Tirana, His Beatitude Anastasios challenged that name. The church, he said, is always a suffering church—or it is not the church. It is always the church of martyrs, or it is not the church of Jesus Christ. And in the next planning group meeting, Father Mikhail added, "The challenge, the real challenge, is to follow Christ. It is to follow Christ even in discrimination, persecution and martyrdom—and, most of all, to do so together."

Together. Is that not the key word for us these days? We are here not only to follow Christ more closely; we are here to do so together. For these few days, we together form one visible community of faith.

Who is this community? Who are we? We are churches who suffer discrimination, persecution, even martyrdom. We are churches and organizations who want in some way to bear the burden with those who suffer. We are Christians who are called to take the next steps together.

You have received this morning a list of our names, our countries, our churches, our organizations. Treat it with care. Use it to know one another. Use it to nurture one another. Use it to build unity with one another. Use it to take the next steps together on our common journey with Jesus Christ.

Hopes for the Consultation

Rev Dr David Wells, Executive Committee, Pentecostal World Fellowship

We have gathered from different traditions with different labels, but united as the body of Christ to reach out with compassion to members of our Christian family who are experiencing discrimination, persecution and martyrdom because of their faith in our Lord Jesus Christ.

The Pentecostal World Fellowship sees it as vital that the body of Christ stands together with our persecuted brethren in prayer and fellowship and to see how to render practical assistance that would encourage and strengthen their faith.

The apostle Paul says, "The body has many different parts, not just one part. If one part suffers, all the parts suffer with it, and if one part is honoured, all the parts are glad" (1 Cor 12:14, 26). He also says, "Be happy with those who are happy, and weep with those who weep" (Rom 12:15).

What a glorious day that will be, when the Lord returns to hear Him say, "Come, you who are blessed by my Father, inherit the Kingdom prepared for you from the creation of the world. For I was hungry, and you fed me. I was thirsty, and you gave me a drink. I was a stranger, and you invited me into your home. I was naked, and you gave me clothing. I was sick, and you cared for me. I was in prison, and you visited me. ... I tell you the truth, when you did it to one of the least of these my brothers and sisters, you were doing it to me!" (Matt 25:34–36, 40).

My prayer is that this Consultation will result in the discovery of affirmative and helpful ways in which the universal church can address the plight of our suffering believers. May the wisdom of the Holy Spirit guide us in our deliberations in the days here in Tirana.

Bishop Efraim Tendero, General Secretary, World Evangelical Alliance

Persecution and martyrdom are all too familiar in the history of Christianity. In the very early chapters of Matthew's gospel, we read the tragic story of Joseph, Mary and the young Jesus fleeing from Herod to Egypt, followed by the massacre of the infants. There are many in this room who themselves know the fear and trauma of running from persecution; we have heard or seen in the media the horror of massacres.

As Christians, we follow a Lord who was crucified as a criminal. The good news that Jesus brought was a threat both to civil and religious powers of his day, so it should come as no surprise to us that persecution will likely follow for those who follow Jesus. And yet we come together because the gospel also says NO to persecution.

It is a privilege and a joy for the World Evangelical Alliance to be part of this historic gathering. The struggle for religious liberty has been part of the WEA's history since its very beginning in 1846 and continues to be central to our identity and mission.

Despite the differences that separate some of our communities of faith, the current crises around the world demand that together we collaborate for those who suffer persecution and martyrdom. Building on the ground-breaking work we did together in the production of "Christian Witness in a Multi-Religious World", this consultation is a major step towards showing our joint solidarity for those who are persecuted and our deep desire to strengthen the witness of the church all around the globe.

For more than twenty years, I served as national director of the Philippine Council of Evangelical Churches. We are glad to have full freedom of religion and expression in our country. It does not mean, however, that we are free from our share of violation of human rights and a dose of manmade human sufferings.

We had increased numbers of extra-judicial killings and enforced disappearances. At one point, eighteen pastors from one mainline denomination were killed in a single year.

But as a church from different traditions, we worked together for the common good. I initiated dialogue with the president of the Philippines, the bishops of the PCEC and the National Council of Churches in the Philippines. Such dialogue resulted in the formation of the Church Police Military Liaison Committee, which met regularly and within a year reduced by 90 percent the cases of extra-judicial killings.

We also initiated the Philippine Ecumenical Peace Platform that advocates for the pursuit of the peace process between the Philippine government and the National Democratic Front of the Philippines.

Moreover, we actively participated in interfaith dialogues in the Philippines. Among the items on the agenda are the peace-building efforts in the southern Philippines between the Moro National Liberation Front and the Philippine government.

I count it a great privilege and solemn responsibility to have been elected as Secretary General of the WEA starting in March of this year. We are glad that the WEA has several units that address the issue of persecution and help people who are suffering for their religious convictions.

At the forefront is our Religious Liberty Commission, which engages in education, advocacy and lobbying, legal aid, and research. We also have the International Institute for Religious Freedom, which produces research and publications on this issue. We helped to initiate the religious liberty partnerships and the refugee highway partnerships. We have instituted the International Day of Prayer for the Persecuted Church. Recently, we established a task force on the refugee crisis. Along with all these initiatives, we have consultative status with the United Nations

Religious freedom is a principal element of the Universal Declaration of Human Rights. Among the major themes of our Christian teaching are to uphold the dignity of every person, since all persons are created in the image of God, and to pursue the mission of Jesus who gave His life on the cross so everyone may have life in all its fullness.

May we then in solidarity, with all humility and full dependence on the almighty God, collaborate with one another to help the suffering churches be delivered from their miseries and enjoy the fullness of life for the glory of God the Father, the Son, and the Holy Spirit. Amen!

Rev Dr Olav Fykse Tveit, General Secretary, World Council of Churches

An increasing number of churches and Christians are going through challenging times at this moment. During my recent visits to countries in the Middle East, but also in Africa and Asia, I have been deeply impressed and saddened by the harsh realities, the violence and the suffering of so many people because of tensions and conflicts between religious and ethnic groups or oppression by dictatorial regimes. The situation of people who have to leave their village, town or country, because they are afraid of losing their lives is heart-breaking. The number of refugees has increased beyond imagination. They have lost hope for a good future in their own country. They want to give their children opportunities for a life without fear and violence.

This consultation on "Discrimination, Persecution, Martyrdom: Following Christ Together" is therefore timely. It is very much needed that we come together as Christians from different confessional families and discern how we can work together in supporting those sisters and brothers who are experiencing challenging times. St Paul wrote to the Corinthians, "If one part suffers, every part suffers with it; if one part is honoured, every part rejoices with it" (1 Cor 12:26). The suffering of so many people, Christians as well as adherents of other religions, makes all of us sad and vulnerable. In a way, we are all coming together here in this consultation around the cross of Christ. Reflecting on Christ's suffering, we seek to understand God's message of hope for our world today. Can our faith in the risen Christ guide us in discerning practical ways of solidarity with those who are suffering today? Can we as Christians from different parts of the world, from different realities, become beacons of hope through our support for one another?

From my experience in the World Council of Churches, I have become convinced that even in times of conflict and oppression, we need to hold on to an inclusive approach. It will not help us if we think in terms of Christians over against the "others". In many countries, not only Christians are suffering under discrimination, persecution and violence. Also, other religious and ethnic minorities go through difficult times. Similarly, it is not helpful to generalize in accusing a particular religion of causing troubles. Today, almost all religions struggle with tendencies towards radicalism within their own constituencies. In some cases, this leads to outbreaks of violence in the name of a particular religious conviction; in other cases, it leads to violence against religions. For this reason, the executive committee of the World Council of Churches asked me to give specific attention to religion and violence and to find ways in which the Christian family can follow Christ in bringing peace and hope. The tenth assembly in Busan, in 2013, called us to embark together as churches on a pilgrimage of justice and peace.

It is encouraging that so many responded positively to the invitation to come to this joint consultation. I am extremely happy that we are starting by listening to those of you whose churches are going through challenging times right now. All of us need to learn from the voices of those among us who experience on a daily basis the reality of discrimination and persecution. We need to listen to those of you who know how *marturia*—witness—and martyrdom are closely interrelated and inter-connected. You need to help all of us to understand what we can do jointly to support one another in following Christ.

I hope that this consultation will go beyond sharing stories and help us to move from reflection to action. At the World Council of Churches, we are engaged in practical work to support the churches. New plans are underway to support churches in Syria and Iraq to see how we can work with the churches and the international community to develop safe spaces in the future. With the ACT Alliance, we are engaged in humanitarian assistance in many parts of the world. However, the uniqueness of this consultation is that we are here together as representatives of the Catholic Church, evangelical and Pentecostal churches and the ecumenical family. This vivid expression of Christian unity in solidarity has not taken place before. It shows the urgency of the problems that we want to address, but also the readiness to move forward together.

Finally, I want to thank the Global Christian Forum, especially its secretary Rev Dr Larry Miller and the planning group of this consultation, for bringing us together. I pray that we will use this God-given opportunity to find ways of supporting one another in the way Christ has taught us. May the Holy Spirit guide us in our work!

Cardinal Kurt Koch, President, Pontifical Council for Promoting Christian Unity, Catholic Church

On behalf of the Catholic Church and the Pontifical Council for Promoting Christian Unity, I am pleased to extend my fraternal greetings to the distinguished participants gathered here in Tirana, in this splendid conference centre where we are graciously welcomed by our Orthodox brothers. I warmly greet those of you who represent persecuted communities from around the world, as well as those representing churches in solidarity and those from different organizations and agencies working in support of Christians in need. In a special way, I wish to greet the organizers and the hosts of this consultation: those representing the Global Christian Forum as well as those representing the Christian churches in Albania. I feel most privileged and honoured to be a part of this unique gathering, which represents a meaningful illustration of global Christianity today and a significant expression of universal Christian solidarity that goes beyond denominational or confessional boundaries.

Discrimination, persecution and martyrdom constitute a painful challenge that all churches and ecclesial communities face today somewhere in the world. Christians of different traditions experience various forms of hostility from governments, organized groups and individuals merely as a result of their faith in Jesus Christ. They are driven out from their villages and towns while their houses and possessions are confiscated, their places of worship are destroyed, and the symbols of their Christian affiliation are removed from public view. They are kidnapped, imprisoned, tortured and murdered only because they bear the name of Christians.

Once again in the course of history Christians of different traditions are facing discrimination, persecution and martyrdom, yet probably never before have they felt so close to each other as they do today. Indeed, the most convincing form of ecumenism is the ecumenism of blood and suffering. In situations of shared suffering, we rediscover each other as brothers and sisters journeying alongside one another on the pilgrimage of faith. We learn to trust our fellow pilgrims, putting aside all unwarranted suspicions and unjust prejudices that over time have contributed to isolating us from one another.

At the same time, it is a sad reflection that those who persecute Christians seem to have understood better than Christians themselves that the church is one. Indeed, the persecutors do not make any distinctions between churches, confessions or denominations. For them, all Christians belong to the same community of the followers of the Nazarene.

May our gathering together here in Tirana be an embodiment of how we can and even must transform this tragic experience of common suffering for Christ's sake into an unexpected moment of grace—a divine *kairos*—and an opportunity to strengthen and deepen the personal bonds of unity between us, the participants in this consultation, and between our churches and ecclesial communities around the world. While recalling our martyrs of yesterday and today, let us repent of our divisions and mutual harm and ask the Holy Spirit to reunite us in one church, finally visibly reconciled.

In the face of hostilities against our Christian brothers and sisters, we cannot remain indifferent. May this consultation become an opportunity to call once again the attention of the international community to the fate of persecuted Christians and other religious minorities. Hostilities must stop and proper protection must be accorded by national governments and international organizations throughout the world.

Jesus teaches his followers to love their enemies and pray for those who persecute them (cf. Matt 5:44). Revenge or vengeance can never be a Christian response to persecution. We cannot continue the circle of violence. Christianity is a religion of universal love. We must be ready to forgive and to open the way to reconciliation and peace among religions, ethnic groups, peoples and nations.

Drawing closer to one another during this consultation, let us pray for each other, listen to each other, learn from each other and seek with each other a common understanding and a proper response to the demanding challenge of following Christ together in the world today.

> At this end of his speech Cardinal Koch read a message of greeting from *Pope Francis*.

I extend greetings to you and all those participating in the Global Christian Forum consultation, to be held in Tirana from 2 to 4 November 2015, as you reflect on the theme "Discrimination, Persecution, Martyrdom: Following Christ Together." In a particular way, I wish to greet our brothers and sisters of different Christian traditions who represent communities suffering for their profession of faith in Jesus Christ, our Lord and Saviour. I think with great sadness of the escalating discrimination and persecution against Christians in the Middle East, Africa, Asia, and elsewhere throughout the world. Your gathering shows that, as Christians, we are not indifferent to our suffering brothers and sisters. In various parts of the world, the witness to Christ, even to the shedding of blood, has become a shared experience of Catholics, Orthodox, Anglicans, Protestants, Evangelicals and Pentecostals, which is deeper and stronger than the differences that still separate our churches and ecclesial communities. The *communio martyrum* is the greatest sign of our journeying together. At the same time, your gathering will give voice to the victims of such injustice and violence, and seek to show the path that will lead the human family out of this tragic situation. May the martyrs of today, belonging to many Christian traditions, help us to understand that all the baptized are members of the same body of Christ, his church (cf. 1 Cor 12:12–30). Let us see this profound truth as a call to persevere on our ecumenical journey towards full and visible communion, growing more and more in love and mutual understanding.

From the Vatican, 1 November 2015,
    FRANCISCUS PP.

Keynote Address:

Discrimination, Persecution and Martyrdom in the Twenty-First Century

Dr Andrea Riccardi, founder of the Community of Sant'Egidio and Professor of Contemporary History at the University of Rome

The West has had little awareness of the martyrdom of Christians. Western culture has nurtured a sense of guilt over the responsibility of Christians and the violence perpetrated by them in their history. This consciousness (which has its reasons) has concealed an important reality, which continued throughout the twentieth century: the persecution of Christians. Christian communities, closed in on themselves or self-centred, do not hear the question and the cry that come from a world of men and women of faith, humiliated and persecuted. They do not feel the searing memory of the history of the twentieth century. This insensitivity and ignorance of the past intertwine.

We are in Albania, a land steeped in pain and in the blood of many Catholics, Orthodox Christians and Christians of other confessions, persecuted since 1945. Beginning in 1967, they were forbidden to participate in any acts of worship, because the country became the first atheist state in the world. A French diplomat in Tirana in 1967 has left an account of the last church service at the Catholic cathedral, between the screams of the groups of the Communist Party. Father Kurti was the celebrant of the last mass of Tirana. In 1972, he was accused of clandestinely having celebrated the baptism of a child. He was sentenced to death. He was 70 years old.

I was in communist Albania in the mid-eighties, a country that appeared dominated by silence and fear and without hope. The last Albanian martyr, Father Gruda, accused of being a priest in secret, died of exhaustion in a detention camp in 1989. And the Wall was falling.

Significantly, today we are speaking in the Cathedral of the Resurrection, rebuilt by Archbishop Anastasios, by whom I have the honour of being considered a friend and whom I admire so much. The primate of this Church has thought, since the time when there were ruins, that there might be a resurrection. The old Orthodox cathedral was in our hotel, and it had been destroyed to build the International Hotel. It is meaningful to speak of martyrdom today in the Cathedral of the Resurrection of Jesus. Jesus is the model of the Christian martyr, with his choice not to flee but to stay in Jerusalem with his disciples in the temple every day among the people. But here we encounter the gospel of the resurrection, represented by this building, symbol of a resurgent church. Here, the gospel of the resurrection gives us an appointment in Galilee: "But go, tell his disciples and Peter that he goes before you into Galilee", says the angel to the women (Mk 16:6).

Galilee was a periphery for the city of Jerusalem. It is a message for us as well: we must meet Jesus in the peripheries of the world, humiliated and persecuted in the limbs of many Christians. For Jesus identifies himself with the persecuted ("Saul, Saul, why do you persecute me?" says Acts 9:4), and he also recognizes himself in the poor, as we learn from the parable of the kingdom in Matthew 25. Very often, churches and Christians have refused to meet him in the living body of the humiliated brothers, because they were of another Christian denomination, because they were of a different nationality, because they were distant or it was inconvenient. To those we could apply the words of Jesus in the parable of the kingdom: "Depart far away from me, you cursed, into the eternal fire prepared for the devil and his angels, because I was persecuted and humiliated and you did not welcome me." So Jesus said to those who do not recognize him in his little persecuted brothers.

I am glad to see this conference in the Cathedral of the Resurrection, with many friends of different Christian communities. Jesus is alive and suffering in our earth, and we encounter him so little. This is why we are so divided.

Christians today, in many parts of the world, suffer discrimination and persecution. In recent years, especially after September 11, 2001, we have discussed the persecution of Christians as a result of the clash between Islam and the West. This is an ideological thesis on the clash of civilizations. But the suffering of Christians is not the result of a clash of civilizations and religions, but something much deeper, certainly mixed with history. There is something deeper to understand with regard to the history, to be welcomed with veneration, of the first witnesses of the Word of God.

The martyrs are not asking for vengeance or inciting confrontation. The persecution of Christians is not suitable for ideological or political purposes. These are painful human stories of Christians, discriminated against, expelled, forced to leave their country, forced to be greatly restricted in their worship or even to give it up and—let us not forget!—imprisoned and killed.

Persecution must be studied carefully, as every story is different. We must also understand the intentions and attitudes of persecutors or regimes that discriminate. This is why, in 2000, I published a book on the persecution of Christians in the twentieth century. I thought I knew at least a little about the history of contemporary Christianity, but to do this research on modern martyrs, as I studied the various instances of martyrdom, I felt as if I was descending into the catacombs of history. For me, it was an introduction to a different history from the known one! So much of the Christianity of yesterday and of today is the history of martyrdom. Writing on the past century of martyrs, I realized that each of us and each community must gather in a glass cup the tears and blood of the persecuted, preventing it from being lost or trampled into the ground.

The century of martyrdom

John Paul II, who had experienced persecution in communist countries after 1945, said as the twentieth century closed, "At the end of the second millennium, the church has again become a church of martyrs." He was right. Today more than a triumphant Christianity, we have a Christianity humiliated and tortured. For Pope John Paul II, martyrdom was not just about the Catholics; there were Orthodox martyrs, Anglicans, Evangelicals and Pentecostals. Rather, he said, "Ecumenism of the martyrs, the *communio sanctorum* (communion of saints), speaks louder than any division." Again he was right. Orthodox, Evangelicals, Catholics and Pentecostals have suffered together in Nazi concentration camps and in the communist gulag. There, everything united them and little divided them. So wrote a witness to the life of the Solovski Islands gulag in the Soviet Union in the 1920s:

> *Joining together in the effort of vigorously pushing the load were a still young Catholic bishop and an emaciated, gaunt old man with a white beard, an Orthodox bishop, ancient of days but strong in spirit. ... Those of us who will have the good fortune one day to return to the world will have to witness to what we see here now. And what we see is the rebirth of the pure and authentic faith of the first Christians, the union of the churches.*

In the twentieth century, Christians have suffered together, in the same places, at the hands of the same persecutors whose single design was to eradicate Christianity. Martyrdom brought them together in unity. The martyrs go ahead of us, and we must listen to them and contemplate their stories. John Paul II said, "We are united against the background of the martyrs; we cannot but be united."

For this reason, their stories should not be lost; they must be retrieved and stored. You have to invest in memory, collecting their tears and their blood in the cup of memory. The Community of Sant'Egidio in Rome, after 2000, inaugurated a memorial to the new martyrs of the twentieth century. It is at the Basilica of St. Bartholomew on the Island in Rome, built in memory of a martyr of the beginning of the past millennium, Saint Adalbert, a basilica visited by Patriarch Bartholomew. Benedict XVI, on a pilgrimage to the basilica, stated that the new martyrs "may seem humanly to be the losers of history." The disciples of the cross believe that there is a force of love and salvation among the losers.

The Russian Church endeavoured to study the many martyrs of the Soviet period. It canonized many Christians killed during that time, such as the Patriarch of All Russia, Tikhon, who died in 1925 under mysterious circumstances. The Catholic Church has granted the honour of beatification of many martyrs of the twentieth century, such as Franz Jägerstätter (a farmer killed by the Nazis for his refusal to serve in the German army during the war) and the Armenian Catholic Archbishop Msgr Maloyan, assassinated during the massacres of

Armenian and Syrian Christians in 1915 in the Ottoman Empire. This year is the centenary of these events, a great moment for Christians.

In the twentieth century, the concentration camps created by totalitarian regimes were the place par excellence of the persecution of Christians. But elsewhere, Christians have also fallen as missionaries in every continent. Great persecutions took place in secular and anti-clerical Mexico, as well as during the civil war in Spain. Independent Africa recorded the murder of many Christians due to ethnic strife in Rwanda and Burundi. Throughout the twentieth century, there have been martyrs who were opposed to violence, oppression, domination, intrusive criminal organizations and acts of terrorism. But why are Christians still dying in this millennium?

The new martyrs of the third millennium

To answer this question, we must retrace the many stories of persecution, which show that the twenty-first century is a new time of martyrdom. The millennium opened with cases such as the murder of a Roman priest, Andrea Santoro, in Turkey, under mysterious circumstances in 2005. After him, three Evangelicals who published Bibles in Turkish were killed in the same country. Why are Christians murdered? Because these figures, with their humanity and their actions, represent a different way of living that is unacceptable to the prevailing fanaticism or to the dark interests that aim to control society. Christians cannot be subject to the logic of conflict; on the contrary, they seek spaces of dialogue and coexistence, they educate the young generation in a responsible way of life, they do not cooperate with criminal or repressive powers, they are friendly and human, and they communicate their faith. Despite their weakness or minority status, without using any armed force, Christians represent a meek alternative to the prevailing ideology or power. For this reason, they will be put aside, silenced, eliminated.

Very often, these Christians, even when threatened, did not abandon their place, feeling that the preservation of their lives was not worth more than their service to others. This is the story of Annalena Tonelli, a physician, an Italian volunteer in Somalia, who was killed in 2003. She bore witness to a generous and peaceful life in the violent and degraded Somali environment. "Our task is to live on earth," she wrote, "and life is certainly not sentencing, the law of war, prosecution, revenge." Although Tonelli saw the violence of criminal gangs and radical groups—kidnappings and genital mutilations—she refused to fight back with violence. Her hospital was a human space in the barbaric situation of Somalia. Despite the threats, she did not flee.

I also want to remember the American sister Dorothy Stang, who served in Brazil. At age seventy-three, she was killed in 2005 in the Brazilian state of Para. Threatened for years, she went public with her stories of intimidation. Her commitment to the landless led to clashes with landlords, who saw in her an obstacle to the exploitation of precious woods. Two gunmen stopped her and asked her if she had weapons. Sister Dorothy displayed a Bible, saying, "Here is my only weapon." She was found murdered and bent over her Bible.

I should also mention the stories of my two brothers of Sant'Egidio. In the Congo, Floribert, a young director of customs, despite bribery attempts and threats, refused to allow rotten food on the market. He resisted in the name of faith and was assassinated. Another young Christian in El Salvador, William, working alongside poor children, was threatened and asked to join a criminal gang. He refused and continued his service in this dangerous spot until he was killed. These have fallen unknown to the world, but I think that they have not been forgotten by God.

Christianity continues in the twenty-first century to produce people who are generous and faithful in serving others in a disarming way. These people are obstacles to evil projects, which are carried out through threats, impositions and terrorism. In impoverished lands and among peoples in grave difficulties, these Christians and their communities are resources for humanity.

An atlas of the crosses

Entire Christian communities are persecuted. In Mosul, Iraq, under the rule of the so-called caliphate, Christian religious services can no longer be held, after having been celebrated for nearly nineteen centuries under all kinds of regimes. The houses of the few remaining

Christians are marked with an N, the first initial of *Nassarah*, or Nazarene in Arabic, the Muslim way of saying *Christian*.

Christians in Syria are held hostage by radical Islamic rebels and by dictatorial power. Aleppo, where Christians and Muslims live together, besieged by fundamentalists and defended by the government, illustrates the condition of the Syrian Christian hostages. Aleppo was a city of coexistence between Muslims and Christians. Of over two million inhabitants, the Christians numbered 300,000. Two bishops of Aleppo, the Syrian Orthodox Mar Gregorios Ibrahim and the Greek Orthodox Paul Yazigi, disappeared a few years ago along with two priests from the city. They are my friends. Two hundred Assyrian Christians are caught in the hands of ISIS, and other Christians do not care about them. We pray for them.

In the Middle East, twenty centuries of Christian presence are ending with the destruction of churches and symbols of faith. A tragic terrorist attack took place at the Syrian village of Ma'lula, where the Christian community was still speaking Aramaic, the language of Jesus. The destruction and desecration of churches symbolize the eradication of Christianity. The Arab, Mongolian and finally Turkish occupations in Syria allowed Christians to survive in these places, which have been inhabited by Christians to this day without interruption. Is our time even more aggressive towards Christians than all the previous difficult centuries?

The persecution of Christians is often under the pressure of totalitarian Islam, which does not tolerate the existence of other belief systems. One thinks of the incredible situation of Christians in Saudi Arabia, an entirely Muslim land, where every act of Christian worship is forbidden. Although there are a million Christians among the immigrant workers there, they are a ghost community that cannot legally exist. Or one thinks of the dramatic situation in the north of Nigeria and the terrorist actions by the Boko Haram Islamist organization that affect not only the Nigerian Christians, but also Muslims and educational institutions. The Nigerian military can do very little. For Christians to participate in Sunday worship is an act of courage because of the attacks of Boko Haram on the churches in the north of Nigeria, where, the journalist Domenico Quirico writes, "to be Christian is a sin that deserves death."

Another difficult situation is that of Christians in Pakistan, who are the poorest part of the population. I will be going to Pakistan next month to visit the Community of Sant'Egidio located there. In 2011, a terrorist commando killed the Pakistani Catholic Shahbaz Bhatti, minister for minorities, engaged in seeking to protect those who are discriminated against and Christians who live under the threat of the charge of blasphemy with serious penalties. Many Christians are still in prison, having been summarily charged with blasphemy. I met Bhatti during his visit to Sant'Egidio in Rome and I still remember his serenity. I received his Bible; he was a man of prayer.

Shortly after the killing of Bhatti, the governor of Punjab, a Muslim was assassinated. His name was Salmaan Taseer, and he had come out against the blasphemy law. Sometimes discrimination against Christians finds, among adherents of other religions, people who are sensitive to human rights. Thanks be to God, righteous people do exist. In fact, religions are not destined to clash in wall-to-wall confrontation, as if the gene of conflict were present in their chromosomes.

The weak force

When we open the atlas of persecution today, we are carried away from our own communities and called to step out both with our hearts and our minds. And so we meet worlds that seem impossible, like that of communist North Korea, totally oppressive, which destroyed all the Christian communities. In many parts of the world, it seems that Christianity is destined to disappear. Will there be a defeat of Christianity in the twenty-first century? We could say that. But in the martyrs there is a meek power, both humiliated and hidden. The patriarch of Constantinople, Athenagoras, in 1968, when Christianity seemed to be ending in Russia, said, "Russian Christians were victorious over totalitarianism in their country. They won with their faith, with their prayers, with the suffering of their confessors and martyrs." We must not look only at the surface of history. Athenagoras added, "Still we do not see their victory. Many heavy things are slow to surface in history, while they have already made a change in the depths."

The martyrs, humiliated and defeated, show the strength of the weak and meek Christianity. The apostle Paul writes in his second letter to the Corinthians, "Therefore I take pleasure in infirmities, in reproaches, in necessities, in persecutions, in distresses for Christ; when I am weak, then I am strong" (2 Cor 12:10). This is the power of Christianity: "When I am weak, then I am strong." In this sense, the martyrs reveal to us the heart of Christianity and the mystery of faith; they evangelize us. Strength is not in the economic resources of the churches, nor in its wealthy supporters; it is not in dealings with governments, nor in organization. Rather, its strength is in weakness—like the weakness of this church of Albania, which had been crushed for years, her leaders and facilities destroyed, but today bears witness to the resurrection.

Finally a personal question remains—at least, I feel it directed at me from so many examples of faithfulness to Jesus even to death. We are contemporaries of the martyrs. We have known them. We have also shared their table and we have been their friends. I think of the times I was at table with brother Christian de Chergé, prior of a monastery in Algeria, killed because he remained to witness to the Gospel in that country. I remember the Syriac bishop of Aleppo, kidnapped because he was a generous believer. We are contemporaries of the martyrs. How can we remain always the same? How can we remain closed up in our institutions and communities? I think that the power of their witness can transform our lives, so that we may live out the gospel in this century of martyrdom, "surrounded by so great a cloud of witnesses" (Heb 12:1).

Left to right: Mrs Connie Kivuti (Kenya), Rev Dr Ibrahim Wushishi Yusuf (Nigeria), and Pastor Nordine Benzid (Algeria).

Session Two –

Voices from Suffering Churches: Part 1

Moderator:

Dr Teresa Francesca Rossi, Associate Director, Centro Pro Unione, Italy

Introduction to data and voices research:

Rev Dr Thomas K. Johnson, World Evangelical Alliance

Panel members:

Bishop John Saw Yaw Han (Catholic, Myanmar)

Rev Dr Richard Howell (Evangelical, India)

Rev Dr A. R. Hasmat (Pentecostal, Pakistan)

Mrs Connie Kivuti (Evangelical, Kenya)

Rev Dr Yusuf Wushishi (Protestant, Nigeria)

Pastor Nordine Benzid (Protestant, Algeria)

Introduction to the Voices and Data Research Project

Rev Dr Thomas K. Johnson, Advisor to the Theological Commission and the International Institute for Religious Freedom of the World Evangelical Alliance

Good afternoon, dear brothers and sisters in the Christian faith. The International Institute for Religious Freedom was commissioned by the Global Christian Forum and the four pillar bodies to look at the documentation regarding the persecution of Christians. The concerns were whether there were mistakes in documentation and reporting, whether some parts of persecution were better reported than others, whether any discrepancies existed between Evangelical and Roman Catholic reporting, etc. The good news we have discovered is that there is a very high level of coordination and cooperation across the different parts of the Christian world about our reporting on discrimination. We did not find any significant biases against each other in this process.

We are in contact with researchers and scholars from around the world. And with God's blessing, we hope that continuing research by our team of scholars will lead to better responses to persecution of Christians. But there are always limits to what anyone can know from a distance. There is always something very important about persecution of Christians that is known only to local people. And sometimes we do not understand people who belong to other churches as well as we understand the members of our own churches. We want feedback to what we have been doing from Christians from around the world. We need your help!

We have put together country profiles or country reports about the 50 countries where we think the persecution of Christians is the worst. You will receive this report during this meeting. The information came from two good sources: the World Watch List, which is managed by our friends from Open Doors, and the Religious Freedom in the World Report from our friends at Aid to the Church in Need. From these sources, we can learn a lot about the situation of persecuted believers in many countries. We can also begin to see global patterns, such as how commonly persecution arises from Islamic extremism or from other types of religious nationalism or from totalitarian governments.

We sent questionnaires to you, asking for your help and input into two large areas: reporting about persecution, and your statements to the church and the world. We received some very good responses, but perhaps some of you could not write this kind of thing in an email. So please help us now. You may still write an email, but you may also write something on paper and give it to us at the IIRF booth, or to me personally. We have translators available, so you may write in English, Russian, Arabic, Chinese, Korean, Spanish, or French, as well as other major languages. Please write clearly. Again, we need your help in two areas: reporting and statements.

Reporting: Please read the report about your country and tell us what you think. Is there something missing that we need to know? Is some part of the report not quite what it should be? Do we have something wrong? What should we change or add? We need you to write something back to us. Our friends who write these reports are constantly upgrading, so this is your time to help them.

Statements: We also want to receive your statements. These are your interpretations of your situation and your responses to persecution and discrimination. God has given gifts of wisdom and knowledge to many people in many churches. In the questionnaire we asked big questions, such as "What do you expect from the global church concerning your situation?" "If your church or Christian organization has valuable ideas about how Christians from around the world can work together better in response to discrimination, persecution and martyrdom, please share them with us"; and "Could you give us your message to the global church in a few sentences? This can be a spiritual message, a fact, a plea or a request."

I hope you can tell us something important that will significantly improve our global response to the persecution of Christians. Please write something for us.

To encourage you to write something, let me read a few words we have already received:

From Archbishop Antonio Audo of the Chaldean Church in Syria and president of Caritas-Syria:

(1) As Christian communities in the Middle East, and especially in Syria, we absolutely want an active and lively Christian presence. This presence is rooted in Christian history and should mean a lot for each and every church in the world.

(2) These oriental churches have been enculturated in the Arab and Muslim reality since the beginning of Islam. Despite all the difficulties and, surely, the persecutions during history, we have been able to live and be witnesses for Christ.

(3) Moreover, these Oriental churches of the Middle East have been, at each moment in history, agents of initiative, opening up the sciences and philosophy (cf. the Omayyad period, the Abbasids, and the Renaissance of the nineteenth and twentieth centuries). Today an approach stemming from the social sciences can become a link for reflection and dialogue.

(4) In our context and that of the West, one should not only focus on the dangers of persecution that come forth from Islamic extremists, but one should rather think about how the Muslim world is debating with the modern world.

(5) For us, as the church, it is necessary to insist on freedom of conscience, inter-religious dialogue, and ecumenical dialogue. The West should not present itself as a military force of humiliation, but rather as a force of respect for human dignity on all levels.

From Nigeria we received the following:

The churches in Nigeria have a number of ways by which they try to respond to the situation. These responses differ from region to region. Preference has always been given to dialogue, to being watchful, using preventive measures, and to discouraging reprisals. The churches also try to put pressure on the government to increase their efforts to guarantee people's security. On a more spiritual level, churches pray for an improved situation.

There is a need to continue to speak out on what is currently happening in Nigeria. Such a voice from the global church can be heard by powers that knowingly or inadvertently, maybe surreptitiously, lend support to and encourage the persecution and discrimination being experienced. Unfortunately, there are people within and outside the country who financially sponsor the terror groups and who produce the arms that are used in the persecution of Christians, not just in Nigeria but all over the world. It does appear sometimes that there is an interest in sustaining the persecutions by some groups for ulterior motives.

In Nigeria, there is a need to place reconciliation at the centre of any work to overcome discrimination and persecution. There is a lot of mistrust between north and south, Muslims and Christians, on account of events of the past. There is a need for the government to actively encourage education and inter-religious courses in the universities and other institutes of learning.

And we received this prayer request from Iraq:

We need prayer to move this cloud in our country, and to encourage all Christians to stay in Iraq. There have been Christians in Iraq (Mesopotamia) from the first century and we have a rich patrimony (three of our cities are mentioned in the Bible: Ur of the Chaldeans, Nineveh of the Assyrian empire and Babylon). Our church supplied many of the martyrs.

If you have a statement about persecution, please give it to us so that we can share it with Christians around the world. We will print the final results and send copies to everyone. And be sure to tell us if we may mention your name and role in the church, or if you want keep your name, job, or country private.

Bishop John Saw Yaw Han, Catholic Auxiliary Bishop of Yangon, Myanmar

My country, Myanmar (Burma) is in south-east Asia, bordered by Bangladesh, India, China, Laos and Thailand. The capital city is Naypyidaw and its largest city is Yangon. The country population is 51 million according to the 2014 census, of whom 80% are Buddhists, 7% Christians, 6% adherents of Burmese folk religions, 4% Muslims, 2% Hindus and 1% other.

The majority of Buddhists are generally very good and kind, generous and ready to help others. They coexist and work with people of other religions. Sometimes they are even ready to help Christians in their evangelization and ministry. It is possible to learn, to eat and even to pray together with leaders of different religions, for peace and for the country's development. Occasionally, Christians, Buddhists and Muslims represent our country at international conferences and meetings.

Of course we experience religious discrimination, especially from the authorities:

(1) For non-Buddhists, it is hard to join the army or to get a job in the government, which are the main routes to success in the country.

(2) Those who are called the Myanmar-Portuguese are Christians born in Myanmar, and if they manifest themselves as Christians they will have difficulties getting citizenship, because of not being Buddhist.

(3) Sometimes it is difficult to build Christian churches in Myanmar. Sometimes constructions have to be stopped. It is easier to get permission to build a factory than to build a church, so sometimes we build a factory to hold our worship.

(4) Christians churches are not allowed to run schools, but Buddhist monasteries are. They have the so-called "Baka schools", established and managed by Buddhist monks and administered by the Ministry of Religious Affairs.

(5) In some parts of the country, some places of worship belonging to religious minorities (Christian or Muslim) have been attacked by the religious majority.

(6) Buddhist monks also have the right to import expensive cars tax-free through benefactors, whereas other religious groups do not have this right.

Nowadays, we have some extreme nationalist Buddhist monks who are afraid that their religion will be undermined by other religions. They have pressured the government into enacting four discriminatory bills. The government, on the other hand, uses religion for political benefits, to gain the people's favour in upcoming elections.

The four bills to which I refer are the Religious Conversion Law, the Buddhist Women Special Marriage Law, the Population Control Healthcare Law and the Monogamy Law.

(1) The Religious Conversion Law aims to establish a system by which individuals who want to change their religion must apply to a state-governed body, which will review their application and decide whether to approve it and issue a certificate of conversion. Only people who have reached the age of 18 are permitted to apply for religious conversion. The law also contains provisions prohibiting the following:

- conversion with an intent to insult, degrade, discriminate or misuse religion;
- compelling conversion through bonded debt, inducement, intimidation, undue influence or pressure;
- preventing, interfering in or hindering people from converting.

(2) The Buddhist Women Special Marriage Law establishes provisions to be observed by a non-Buddhist man but no similar or any rules or obligations are placed on the wife. The law states that a non-Buddhist husband of a Buddhist wife must not insult Buddhism in word or writing or through visible representations or gestures with the intention of causing bitter feelings in the Buddhist woman. With regard to

custody of the children, the law does not make the interests of the child the primary consideration, because it automatically grants a Buddhist woman married to a non-Buddhist man guardianship of all children in the event that the couple should divorce.

(3) The Population Control Healthcare Law imposes a required three-year gap between births for a married woman.

(4) The Monogamy Law punishes those who have more than one spouse or who live with a different partner from the one they married. The legal punishment can be more than six years of imprisonment.

We want to live together in a peaceful existence. We are trying together to work for peace and harmony in our country with the Buddhist monks and people who are broad-minded.

Rev Dr Richard Howell, General Secretary, Asia Evangelical Alliance and Evangelical Fellowship of India

India is a sovereign, socialist, secular, democratic republic governed by an excellent Constitution that came into effect on January 26, 1950. It has a parliamentary form of government, federal in structure, with unitary features. The Constitution of India assures justice (social, economic and political), liberty (of thought, expression, belief, faith and worship), equality (of status and opportunity) and fraternity (protecting the dignity of the individual and the unity of the nation) to all citizens. The fundamental rights embodied in the Constitution of India include the right to freedom of religion—to profess, practice and propagate any religion—along with the freedom to manage religious affairs and to own, acquire and administer property for religious or charitable purposes.

India is on the road to becoming a very important economic player in the world. However, for development to take place, it is essential for the country to have peace and stability. This is now increasingly being threatened by the rise of violent Hindu nationalism. The world needs to take notice of this violent trend in India. The President of India, Mr Pranab Mukherjee, has repeatedly warned the nation of rising intolerance. The Prime Minister, Mr Narendra Modi, has chosen to remain silent, thus emboldening those perpetuating the ideology of hatred.

India is one of the most religious nations in the world, but it is also a nation where non-state and state actors have increasingly attacked freedom of religion. The Pew Research Forum ranks India very high on its social hostilities index regarding religion.

Freedom of Religion Acts

Seven states of India have enacted freedom of religion bills. However, in only five states have these laws been implemented. Instead of promoting religious freedom, as the name might suggest, these bills curb freedom of choice by making it mandatory for a convert to receive permission from various government authorities before converting to worship according to his or her own free choice. People converting from Christianity or Islam to Hinduism require no such permission. In addition, the Dalit who converts to Christ is denied the benefits extended to those who worship Hindu gods and goddesses. Why this discrimination?

Rise of Violent Hindu Religious Nationalism

In an interview before his election as prime minister of India, Mr Narendra Modi declared that he was a Hindu nationalist. The ideology of Hindu religious nationalism is "One Nation, One Culture and One People", which is the kind of Hinduism promoted by RSS [Rashtriya Swayamsevak Sangh, the Hindu nationalist organization that predates Mr Modi's political party]. By this definition, all minority communities, Muslims and Christians are considered anti-national. The question is one of identity. Christians are urged to call themselves Hindu Christians.

Recent incidents targeting minorities, in addition to the killing of rationalist thinkers and human rights defenders by Hindu nationalist groups, show that using violence as a tool to promote religious nationalism is on the rise and becoming mainstream while being referred to as "essential" for India.

As observed by representatives of civil society and social scientists in their recent report on the first 365 days of the new government and its impact on minorities, "The administrative, legal, scientific and educational structures created during the past sixty years have either been demolished or tempered. India's cultural DNA of pluralism and diversity is being threatened. The meddling with the judicial system at the highest level threatens to foreclose the one option that is left to the citizens to challenge, stop and reverse this trend."

The RSS's campaign to malign, isolate, criminalize and target Christians and Muslims, inciting mobs to commit violence against them, has generally been overlooked by central and state police forces. Never in free India has the public discourse been so poisoned by MPs and ministers of the elected ruling alliance. All too often, police have been complicit in the violence.

According to the partial list available from the Evangelical Fellowship of India, there were 147 incidents of violence and hate against the Christian community in 2014. In 2015 so far, the number of incidents has already exceeded 130. Reports by civil society groups have recorded at least 43 deaths in over 600 cases of violence, 194 of them targeting Christians and the rest Muslims, between 26 May 2014 and 13 May 2015. This is a worrisome trend.

The government's efforts to reassure minorities have fallen well below the mark. Instead of investigating the violence, the government has sought to trivialize these incidents by its explanations of several incidents that got international attention. No politician or Sangh activist has been punished.

The church in India is constantly being targeted by physical and organized social violence. Church buildings are attacked, prayer services disrupted, priests and pastors beaten, nuns raped, and some even murdered while false cases against Christians are being registered at an alarming rate throughout the country.

In the central state of India, Chhattisgarh, more than 60 village councils have passed resolutions outlawing Christianity and attacks are being reported with alarming regularity from the area.

The situation is getting worse in the neighbouring state of Madhya Pradesh, which has also reported many attacks since last year. Attacks and instances of discrimination are also being reported from the north-eastern states of Arunachal Pradesh and Assam.

Within the past month, at least 23 incidents of attacks on Christians have been reported from Madhya Pradesh, Punjab, Uttar Pradesh, Jharkhand, Chhattisgarh and Gujarat. Christians praying even in their own homes, in private worship, are no longer safe as they are being targeted by right-wing extremists who seem to be drunk on political power and support. Children, sometimes even as young as six months old, are being arrested and detained in police lock-ups.

Physical and social persecution is also being coupled with structural persecution as Christian institutions have been targeted on frivolous charges. Laws are being selectively used against Christians on the ground. Nearly every week, three or four incidents are reported in which pastors and Christian lay people are charged either under the various Freedom of Religion Acts or under certain sections of the Indian Penal Code.

Persecution has drawn the church closer together in unity, and Christians in the grassroots are more aware and ready to pay the cost that it will take to follow Christ.

The National United Christian Forum, composed of the Catholic Bishops Conference of India, the National Council of Churches, and the Evangelical Fellowship of India Council of Churches, addressed the issue in "The National Consultation on Upholding Constitutional Rights of Minorities, with Special Reference to the Christian," held on 17 March 2015 in Delhi. The church needs to be equipped in order to stand strong in the midst of this onslaught.

International advocacy assists in securing the rights of the minorities in India. This must continue. The global church must pray and speak out for their sisters and brothers in India even as many churches across the country are bearing the brunt of anti-Christian violence and experience discrimination, persecution and even martyrdom. Christians have been killed, nuns have been raped, churches have been burnt.

They try to divide Christians, saying "Only the Pentecostals and Evangelicals are the trouble-makers, you are all right." But that is not the case. Every denomination in India is facing the challenges. But praying and walking together, working together makes a difference.

Rev Dr A. R. Hashmat, Chairman of the Assemblies of God in Pakistan

It is a privilege for me to share about Pakistan, because Pakistan is a needy country at the moment. It is the second-largest Muslim country in the world, and every day something happens. Pakistan has become the land of fanatics, extremists and terrorists. We Christians always pray for the revival of love and tolerance in Pakistan, but the fanatic religious spirit of groups moving around all over the country has resulted in great hatred and biased thinking towards minorities in Pakistan.

I want to tell you about the current situation of suffering and some incidents that have happened in Pakistan.

Penal Code Sections 295 B and C

The Pakistan Penal Code, sections 295 B and C, prohibits blasphemy against any recognized religion, providing penalties from a fine to death. From 1987 to 2014, over 1,300 people have been accused of blasphemy. The vast majority of the accusations were lodged for desecration of the Quran. Over 50 people accused of blasphemy have been murdered before their respective trials were over, and prominent figures who opposed the blasphemy law have been assassinated (Salman Taseer, former Governor of Punjab, and Shahbaz Bhatti, the Federal Minister for Minorities). Since 1990, 62 people have been murdered as a result of blasphemy allegations. The laws became particularly severe between 1980 and 1986, when a number of clauses were added by the military government of General Zia-ul Haq to "Islamicize" the laws and deny the Muslim character of the Ahmadi minority. Prior to 1986, only 14 cases pertaining to blasphemy were reported.

There are some well-known cases of blasphemy against Christians:

- Martyr **Shahbaz Bhatti**, a politician and elected member of the National Assembly who became the first Federal Minister for Minorities Affairs in November 2008. He raised his voice against 295 C and was assassinated on 2 March 2011 in Islamabad.

- **Rimsha Mashi**, a girl who was arrested by the police in August 2012 on blasphemy charges for allegedly desecrating pages of the Quran.

- **Asiya Bibi**, a woman who was convicted of blasphemy by a court and sentenced to death by hanging in November 2010. She had been involved in an argument with a group of Muslim women with whom she had been harvesting berries. The women got angry with her for drinking from the same water as they, and they subsequently accused her of insulting the Prophet. She denies the charge. If executed, she would be the first woman in Pakistan to be lawfully killed for blasphemy.

- **Shama and Shahzad Mashi**, a couple who were beaten up and burnt alive by a Muslim mob in November 2014 in the brick kiln where they were working, for allegedly desecrating the Holy Quran according to the police. The incident took place in Kot Radha Kishan, some 60 kilometres from Lahore.

Discrimination

- **In education**: the government has allocated 5% of available places for minorities but unfortunately the quota is not being observed.

- **In employment**: in a recent ad, the Punjab government indicated that only non-Muslims can apply for cleaning jobs.

- **In the Constitution**: the positions of President and Prime Minister are only for Muslims.

Persecution

Many incidents are happening. I will share a few.

- **Shanti Nagar**. On February 6, 1997, Muslim extremists burnt down 850 houses of Christians in Shanti Nagar just because they found some burnt pages of the Quran near these houses.

- **Gojra**. On 2 August 2009, an angry mob marched towards a village of a rival community in Tehsil Gorja District where fierce clashes erupted. Six Christians, of whom four were women, were burnt alive and dozens were wounded. A church and 40 houses were burnt down over the alleged desecration of the Holy Quran in the town.

- **Murdan**. On September 21, 2012, St. Paul Lutheran Church in Murdan was burnt down by an angry mob protesting against an anti-Islam film. Several thousand people broke into the church compound and destroyed everything.

- **Badami Bagh**. On March 9, 2013, an enraged mob torched dozens of houses in Joseph Colony, Badami Bagh, a Christian-majority neighbourhood of Lahore, after allegations of blasphemy against a Christian man. The man was booked under Section 295 C.

- **Peshawar**. On September 22, 2013, a twin suicide bombing took place at All Saints Church in Peshawar; 127 people were killed and over 250 injured. It was the deadliest attack on the Christian minority in the history of Pakistan.

- **Lahore**. Fifteen people were killed and more than 70 injured when Taliban suicide bombers attacked two churches during prayers in the Youhanabad neighbourhood of Lahore, home to more than 100,000 Christians.

Martyrdom

- Pastor **Sajid William** of the Assemblies of God was shot and killed by unidentified masked gunmen on January 17, 2008. Age 29, he was on his way to his home in the city of Peshawar.

- On July 6, 2013, two church policemen of the Assemblies of God were killed by unknown bikers while they were on duty at the gate of the Assemblies of God church in Swati Gate, Peshawar.

- Other incidents that have affected the Assemblies of God were the jailing of two laymen because of open evangelism and the capture of Pastor Bernard by a group of Taliban when he was on his way to preach. Miraculously he was released.

What would you like to say about this situation to the global church? (Here Rev Hashmat, like some of the following panel members, was repeating and responding to one of the questions from the Data and Voices Project.)

- The global church must support us with their prayers;

- It must support us physically when this type of situation arises;

- It should raise its voice against the persecution of Christians in Pakistan at the world level, especially in the UN;

- As the global church is opening its doors for Syrian refugees, it should do the same for us;

- The global Church should support us in education and employment and give us opportunities to work.

From your perspective, what are the next steps that churches around the world must take if we are to walk together as the suffering church?

- We should pray together;

- We must show solidarity at the world level when any church faces persecution;

- Every church must be prepared for persecution, as it is written in the Bible that we will face persecution when spreading the good news;

- We should support each other by all means.

Pakistan is at the top of the list of countries where violence, terrorism and fanaticism are growing and there is a lot of discrimination; therefore, Christians are not feeling secure and more and more Christians are fleeing to Sri-Lanka, Thailand and Malaysia.

Mrs Connie Kivuti, General Secretary, Evangelical Alliance of Kenya

Background

Kenya is 80% Christian. Another 12% are Muslim and the remainder are persons of other religions. The majority of the Christians are nominal; few are devout, born-again Christians. Kenya was the first country in the Eastern and Central African region to introduce Islamic banking, a decade ago, and the first fully Sharia-compliant insurance company was registered in 2011 in Kenya.

Most churches in Nairobi and other cosmopolitan areas in Kenya have been forced to hire private security services. Every Sunday, the worshippers are searched or frisked for improvised explosive devices (IEDs) or other similar bombs.

What is the situation of suffering—discrimination, persecution, martyrdom—that your church is facing?

In regions where Islam dominates—northern and north-eastern Kenya and the coastal strip—there exist subtle persecution and social ostracism. Christians are prone to insults of their physical characteristics, e.g. hair texture and skin colour. They cannot own a business or are excluded from owning real estate or property in some of these regions. Churches experience obstruction from buying land to put up a church building. With the exception of the Coast province, which is cosmopolitan, there are no cemeteries where Christians can be buried. Cultural practices such as dress code are enforced, e.g. women must cover their head and wear long dresses. Some Islamic preachers ridicule or discredit the Bible and criticize Christianity.

With regard to terror attacks against Christians, it has been said that it is simply terrorism, but for us it is terrorism directed at Christians. To highlight a few of the incidents:

- In 2010 a prayer meeting was bombed; 13 worshippers died and more than 100 were injured.
- In 2011 an East Africa Pentecostal Church (EAPC) in Garissa was attacked, and 3 people died.
- In April 2012 in Mtwapa, along the coast, 3 Christians were killed.
- In July 2012, at an African Independent Church in Garissa, 17 Christians died.
- In 2013, a pastor was killed in Kisauni while on his knees praying, and another pastor was shot dead along Mombasa-Kilifi Road and his body thrown in the bush.
- During the West Gate attack in September 2013, those who could not recite Quran verses or the Shahada were targeted.
- In October 2013, the Salvation Army church in Majengo, Mombasa, was burnt down and in December 2013 a church in Likoni suffered the same fate.
- In March 2014, at the Joy Jesus church in Likoni, 6 Christians were killed.
- In June 2014 in Lamu County, 78 Kenyans died, most of them Christians, and in November of the same year 28 were killed at the Mandera massacre.
- In April 2015, at a prayer meeting, 147 Christian Union students were massacred, a real nightmare for us.

Kenya has been a haven of peace, but it has not been able to provide that peace for the Christians.

What would you like to say about this situation to the global church?

At the beginning of this year we had the Trans-Africa Conference in Nairobi, from 27 February to 3 March, organized by the Barnabas

Fund, to deal with the dramatic increase in conflict in certain areas of both West and East Africa. As extremist militant groups are gaining control of entire regions, the purpose was to formulate coordinated and appropriate responses to the challenges facing the church as a result of this instability.

Second, in the wake of the attack in which 147 Christian students were killed, a consultation among heads of churches and Christian umbrella bodies was held on 15 April 2015, to look at how we as Christians should respond to terrorism.

Another meeting bringing together about 20 senior Church leaders took place on 7 May 2015, to discuss the state of the nation after the massacre of Christian students. A task force was set up to report on planning a way forward.

Under the auspices of the Association of Evangelicals in Africa (AEA), the General Secretaries of the national alliances of the AEA held a pre-General Assembly special seminar on Christian-Muslim relations on 27 June 2015 at Harare, Zimbabwe. This seminar looked at the Islamic agenda in Africa and how Christians should respond.

What do you ask of the global church?

John 15:18–21: "If the world hates you, you know that it hated me before it hated you. If you were of the world, the world would love its own. Yet because you are not of the world, but I chose you out of the world, therefore the world hates you. Remember the word that I said to you. … If they persecuted me, they will also persecute you … because they do not know Him who sent me."

This is nothing new; it was predicted, and it is happening. But the issue is how we can strengthen the Church towards a new way of carrying out the affairs of the Kingdom of God.

Persecution is something that we should expect. We have been called to the ministry of reconciliation, so how do we keep our focus on our core call with all that is going on around us, knowing that these things must come to pass? How do we design discipleship programs and Bible study materials to make them appropriate for targeted age groups and geared towards apologetics?

Some of our youth in Kenya are being drawn to Islam for the financial gains promised to them. How can we build the capacity of Christians and church leaders in the areas of economic development and sustainability, so that they can have a holistic paradigm enabling them to address some of these real social issues that people are going through?

As the church, we ought to have institutions where Church leaders are trained about legal rights and advocacy and are prepared to provide relief and first aid to all who are suffering, even as we carry out research which is very important.

From your perspective, what are the next steps for churches around the world to walk together as the suffering church?

First of all, we need to be each other's keepers. We need to amplify the global Christian voice. In a few days, the Pope will be in Kenya. After that, we will have a visit from the president of the World Evangelical Alliance. We need to amplify those voices on what is happening to the Christians in Kenya. We need unity in voice, action and sharing. We must have a united voice, we must act together, we must share together. And we must also have a rapid response in voice, action and sharing. We need:

- Ongoing research and dissemination of information;
- Strategic global prayer and intercession;
- Building capacity for preparedness and response, a tool kit in cases of persecution, and safe houses to host refugees or persecuted persons;
- An emphasis on child evangelism and discipleship;
- Theological colleges and other Bible teaching institutions that offer sound theological training without compromising our core beliefs;
- Training on economic development and initiating Christian banks, insurance systems, etc.;

- Building the capacity of church leaders and individual members on how to engage with the government in development issues (contextual sensitivity);
- To engage politicians and the government towards accountable governance;
- To monitor the legislature and drafting of bills;
- Resource mobilization and facilitating of resources;
- Security—intelligence gathering, pre-empting threats.

Let us all be busy for the Kingdom, for night will surely come and then we will not be able to work. For behold, He who is coming is coming soon and will not delay. Maranatha, God bless you.

Rev. Dr Yusuf Wushishi, General Secretary, Christian Council of Nigeria

I bring you warm greetings from the Christian sisters and brothers in Nigeria. I wish to thank the leadership of the GCF for organizing this important global consultation. I wish to begin this short speech by affirming that I find the theme of this consultation quite inspiring and reassuring. The theme asserts our collective aspiration, as members of the body of Christ and through our faith in our Lord Jesus Christ; the realization of our unique connectivity even in suffering; and the willingness of the global church to share from the challenges of other parts of the body. It also conveys to us, who are experiencing the tragedies of conflict and insecurity in our countries, the assurances of your prayers and solidarity.

Permit me to state here that since the inception of Nigeria as an independent nation in 1960, the nation's security has never been stretched to its limit as we are experiencing right now. The country has experienced many forms of conflict, such as ethnic, religious and tribal conflicts, especially in the north. Northern Nigeria is ethnically, religiously and culturally diverse. It is home to hundreds of people groups of varying sizes and cultural distinctives. Generally, Islam is the dominant religious group in northern Nigeria.

Most people of northern Nigeria share certain similarities, with the result that people in the south have a hard time distinguishing who are Christians and who are Muslims; hence, the tendency in the south is to erroneously refer to all northerners as Muslims. The heterogeneous nature of the northern population and its cultural diversity appear to be among the causes of inter-communal, ethnic and religious conflicts in the area. The minority Christians spread across northern Nigeria have suffered severe hatred, discrimination, persecution and martyrdom due to their faith in Christ Jesus. In some areas, especially in the far north, Christians are not allowed to secure property for church building; some are denied employment and/or promotion in their places of work, even if they are qualified. Some are treated as second-class citizens in their fathers' land. They are criminals because they are Christians. The northern Christians have learned to live with the situation for a very long time.

In recent years, the activities of the terrorist group of Islamic militants known as Boko Haram, whose proclaimed intention was to create an Islamic state in northern Nigeria, have worsened the situation in the north, as thousands of people have been killed, many places of worship and properties worth billions of niaras belonging to Christians have been destroyed, and many young girls and women have been abducted, including the abduction of over two hundred Chibok school girls that sparked a global outcry. Women are made widows, many children are orphaned, villages have been looted, and people are left traumatized. The sect's attack on and abduction of school girls was an assault on female child education, and the forced conversion of the girls to Islam against their wish was an assault on religious freedom. We are deeply saddened by what has befallen these innocent girls and other women who have been abducted, and we continue to agonize over their condition and fate.

The activities of this sect have caused the widespread internal displacement of over 1.5 million people in Nigeria. Most of them are of the Christian faith. Although Boko Haram's desire to inflame religious war between Muslims and Christians failed, there is a mutual suspicion among the population due to lack of clear understanding of who is sponsoring the shadowy group. It is true that at the beginning Boko Haram targeted mainly Christian communities, churches and Christian schools, while also engaging in indiscriminate killing of Christians in the streets and in their homes, and that they enjoyed the sympathy and goodwill of some Muslim groups. But it has now become clearer that they spare no one. Anyone who does not subscribe to their ideology is an enemy. However, the military's recent successes against the insurgents have given us hope that the dark days may soon be over, and signs of hope are growing.

The church has not been deterred in responding to the situation. The suffering and persecution of Christians especially in northern Nigeria has rekindled the collective awareness of all that, no matter what adversity we face, God's promise in Hebrews 13:5–6 stands. Through His death and resurrection, our Lord Jesus Christ taught us the meaning of God's love in suffering. The call for Christians to pray for their enemies is still valid as it was in those days, though very difficult, but we have to follow the hard way. The church and other parts of civil society have risen to the challenge by engaging in activities that promote peace and religious harmony in Nigeria. The Christian Council of Nigeria, a coordinating body of the member churches of the World Council of Churches in Nigeria, has keyed in to the World Council of Churches' pilgrimage of justice and peace, a journey meant to promote peace and religious harmony. Hence the Council's commitment to join in the formation of an interfaith documentation centre, to be jointly managed by the Christian Council and Jama'atu Nasril Islam, an umbrella organization of the Muslim community in Nigeria. The centre, which is expected to begin operations in the first quarter of 2016, is jointly supported by the World Council of Churches and the Royal Aal al-Bayt Institute for Islamic Thought, in Jordan. The primary objective of the centre is to conduct and promote education with the aim of preventing and transforming inter-religious conflict in Nigeria. There are so many responses from the church towards achieving inter-religious harmony. The church alone cannot make peace without identifying people from the other camp who share the same concerns, so that we can join together in the pilgrimage of peace.

What can the global community do? Let me use this medium to call on the church not to allow the way we are mistreated to define who we are in society. Rather, our responses to the tragedies we experience ought to glorify God and bring hope to the ugly situation. Therefore as Christians, we cannot do without prayer. We appreciate your prayers and your solidarity. We ask again: pray for us, pray for God's grace for the Christians in northern Nigeria, for courage to remain faithful to the faith, no matter the situation. We need your solidarity and support for initiatives that are geared toward promoting peace and harmony in the affected countries. Peace is not a commodity that can be imported from one country to another, but we can learn the best practices of peace building from other countries and regions. Experience has shown that local peace-building initiatives are more likely to succeed than an imported peace process. Therefore, we need the support of all to build the capacity of our church to respond to the new challenges we are facing today.

Pastor Nordine Benzid, General Secretary, Association of Protestant Churches of Algeria

It is a privilege and an honour to be here with you. As Christians in Algeria, we are one body, and I bring you greetings from the whole church in Algeria, in particular from Mr. Haddad Mamout who is the president of the Association of Protestant Churches in Algeria. This is a legal, national Christian association, recognized by the government in July 2011. It is the first time that authorities in a Muslim country have recognized Muslim-background Christians. And that is for us a grace of our Lord Jesus Christ and a gain that we have to preserve. I would like to thank also all those who have made it possible for me to be here.

Algeria is a country in North Africa. Ninety-eight percent of the population is Muslim. Our church in Algeria is a young church, only 25 years old. It came into being in 1993–1994, and today there are about

50 congregations, of which 43 have legal status through this Association of Protestant Churches of which I am the general secretary. The church in my country is facing difficulties every day, in all sectors of society: social, educational, professional. How can I describe the situation of suffering of our church today in Algeria? I can list some challenges.

There is the problem of acceptance of Christians who have converted from Islam; we Algerian Christians of the church to which I belong we are all Muslim-background Christians. I was a Muslim, and now I serve the Lord since I accepted Jesus as my Saviour and my Lord. The problem is that the Quran anathematizes such persons as renegades who deserve death. Many leaders of churches in Algeria have been facing death threats. I myself have received death threats several times.

There is also the challenge of the laws inspired by sharia that disadvantage Algerian Christians, such as the laws on marriage, forced divorce and inheritance, as well as loss of employment and persecution by one's family and sometimes by society. Laws passed in 2006 prohibit evangelization and the building of churches. Legal provisions against Christians were reiterated in 2012, incriminating the act of proselytism and prohibiting the construction of places of worship. Of the 43 churches in our Association, only 45% have a place of worship. All the other churches worship in private houses or in the fields.

As Algerian Christians, what would you like to say about this situation to the global church?

The global church should be sensitive to the difficult situation of the church in Algeria and in the Muslim world. It should manifest actively its solidarity with this part of the body of Christ, because "when one member suffers, the whole body suffers with him".

From your perspective, as church of Algeria, what are the next steps for churches around the world to walk together as the suffering church?

Churches should multiply opportunities for sharing and information, establish programs of prayer for the persecuted church, create networks of assistance and support for the benefit of the suffering church, and where applicable appeal to organizations that are active in the area of human rights to put pressure on states that persecute.

We have experienced this in Algeria. It is thanks to the prayers of the global church and to the pressure exerted by international organizations that the government accepted us in 2011. We did go through very difficult times in 2006 and 2008, when several Christians were taken to court. All the churches were asked to close, but thanks to your prayers and to the pressure of international institutions, in the end we won, by the grace of our Lord Jesus Christ. May God bless you.

Comments and Questions from the Floor

Bishop Panti Filibus Musa (Lutheran Church of Christ in Nigeria) addressed a question to Pastor Nordine Benzid. He asked if, in spite of the difficulties and challenges, the Association of Protestant Churches had strategies to assist new converts from Islam, which is also a common challenge in his country, Nigeria. Pastor Benzid acknowledged that it is not easy to take care of all the people being converted because of the revival. At each worship service, he said, tens of converts give their lives to Christ. The Christians are not allowed to preach outside the church; people come to the church. The only strategy that the Association has is to organize camps and conferences, to help converts to deepen their faith and their understanding of the Bible. Pastor Benzid said that the best way to reach the Muslims is to live the gospel in our daily lives, in words and acts.

The second question also dealt with the Algerian situation. **Archbishop Basilos Georges Casmoussa (Syrian Catholic Patriarchate)** asked what was the origin of the converts, and how Pastor Benzid viewed conversions to the Catholic Church. After repeating that Algeria is the only Muslim country in the world accepting Christians of Muslim background, Pastor Benzid recalled that Islam is the state religion according to Article 2 of the constitution. The majority of the converts come from the Kabyle people. Few of them are Arabs. Kabylia is known for being a more tolerant region. The Association has ten churches in the Arabic-speaking area, and it is trying to send pastors and missionaries who speak Arabic. It is not easy to be a Christian there, but thanks to the Association which plays the role of intermediary between the authorities, the churches and the people, it has been possible to establish churches in the Arabic-speaking regions.

The Association has fraternal contacts with the Catholics, Methodists and Anglicans, the so-called Western or foreign churches. According to the law, it is forbidden to have relations in Algeria with churches made up of Christians who are not Algerian. "We can be accused of being spies or traitors", Pastor Benzid said, "so we try to protect our churches and at the same time to keep good relations with our Catholic and other brothers and sisters."

Dr Thomas Schirrmacher (World Evangelical Alliance, Germany) addressed a question to Ms Kivuti. He asked, "The incidents in your country are fairly recent. What is the feeling of the churches, and what is the level of solidarity among the churches?" Ms. Kivuti replied as follows:

"Kenya is a Christian nation in essence, but this comfort is slowly but surely eroding. Although Muslims form 12% of the population, they have been systematically removing the bricks from the Christian house of comfort, in the political arena and in business, using the issue of violence in pressing their point. There has been a systematic deterioration of the influence that Christians had in the nation. Whereas it may seem that the incidents are particular and not necessarily organized, there is a bigger plan to drive the Christians out. When there is an incident, we hold a press conference, we condemn, and immediately after that there is another one. Press statements are not doing much. Attacks on our position in society are gradually increasing for the body of Christ.

"The other element is that in the past we have not had a concerted effort to deal with the issue. The main reason for this is that most of the churches which have been attacked are evangelical. The mainline churches—Catholic, Methodist, Anglican—have not been targeted. So there is a wedge that is dividing the church. There is a feeling that it is the evangelicals, not us, and that we are safe. But the question is how long that safety will last. We came together last May and formed a task force, as I mentioned. We have yet to come back together again. The hierarchical way of doing church business is our undoing. By the time an order from a high level is approved, a lot of damage has been done. This reduces the confidence in any coming together that may have taken place. We are imploding as a church because we have not been able to look at the bigger picture. To engage in a certain area, we need consensus at a higher level in order to move on as a body, as a unit. The question is how we can re-address our own undoing.

"The fact that some of the mainline churches think that they are strong enough is a disadvantage to the unity of the whole body. When some of the churches are limping, this means that the whole body is not well. How can we strengthen these churches, so that the whole body is well enough to be able to deal with the issue? We have been trying to deal with it corporately. Even if 80% of the population is Christian, the constitution has locked us out. We have a constitution that talks more about the Muslims than the Christians. It is just a matter of time before Muslims will trample on Kenya and we will hear, God forbid, that Kenya is a Muslim country. … We are trying to do what we can at our level."

Mrs Rosangela Jarjour
(Syria/Lebanon)

Session Three –

Voices from Suffering Churches: Part 2

Moderator:
Mrs Esme R. Bowers, Evangelical Alliance, South Africa

Greetings:
Archbishop Angelo Massafra,
Catholic Bishops' Conference of Albania

Panel members:
Mrs Rosangela Jarjour (Protestant, Syria/Lebanon)

Bishop Azad Marshall (Anglican, Iran and the Gulf States)

Bishop Basel Yaldo (Catholic, Iraq)

Archbishop Shahan Sarkissian (Orthodox, Syria)

Rev Dr Munir Kakish (Evangelical, Palestine/Israel)

Evangelical leader (Africa)

> Prior to the panel, ***Archbishop Angelo Massafra*** of Skoda, President, Catholic Bishops' Conference of Albania, shared a greeting as follows.

Greetings, dear friends from many nations, gathered to discuss the persecution, martyrdom and discrimination still suffered by many Christians in various nations. I am not able to be here throughout this three-day forum in Tirana because I will be elsewhere celebrating the courage of the Catholic Church in this very context of persecution.

I would like to give you a photograph with a cross, which I will explain shortly. As has already been mentioned this morning, in 1967 the Albanian dictator absolutely prohibited every faith, Christian and Muslim alike; prohibited every public or religious gesture; prohibited even the sign of the cross. And although persecutions, homicides and shootings had already started back in 1945, in 1967 Albania became in fact the first atheist state. Despite these prohibitions, priests vowed to celebrate the sacraments clandestinely in jail, as in many other parts of the world, with a drop of wine and a piece of bread, just as they celebrated holy mass secretly in homes. They gave communion to prisoners while being prisoners themselves.

But on 4 November 1990, which will be 25 years ago the day after tomorrow, after the fall of the Berlin Wall, there was a different atmosphere. A priest, along with others, challenged the state and celebrated the first mass in the Catholic cemetery in Scutari; that is, he held a holy mass that had been prohibited like all other liturgical acts in 1967. It was the first public liturgical act, a very courageous act, and the police somehow allowed it. As many people were afraid to attend the eucharistic celebration that day, a belated recognition of All Souls' Day was held on 2 November when we Catholics commemorate all the departed.

Don Simon Jubani, who was celebrating the eucharist, had come to an agreement with the two other Franciscan priests. He said, "If they kill me, you continue with the mass." Therefore they were quite committed, even if there was much fear. What was that fear? The police certainly knew that they were going to celebrate the mass, because every breath was under their control. So some trap could have been set up: "Let them celebrate their mass in public, then let the Catholics who have survived and who are strong come out into the open, then we will imprison them and kill some of them." This strong fear inhibited many people on that 4 November. But after that mass was conducted without incident, on 11 November some thirty, forty, perhaps fifty thousand Catholics brought statues to the cemetery for a solemn mass attended by Orthodox, Catholics and Muslims. On 16 November, Muslims took possession of their mosque after many years, and therefore they too are celebrating their 25th anniversary now.

It is because of these celebrations that we are unable to be with you for all these days, which saddens me, but unfortunately I do not have the gift of being in two places at once. So while I am able to be with you today, I have to return. I have already mentioned to the Cardinal, who will be coming for the homily, that on the 4th while we will be celebrating our 25th anniversary, in Tirana another conference will be lifting up their prayers against the discrimination and persecution of Christians, and that we will be in the communion of prayer with you on that day.

This cross that I am giving you is the idea of a photographer who has placed in many locations a photograph of the many, many martyrs who have been killed or imprisoned by communism. As a Catholic diocese, we have commenced the canonical process for 38 martyrs of communism. We are now at the concluding phase of this process. We have submitted the *positio* (2,500 pages) to the Congregation for the Causes of the Saints in Rome. We have been told that the Theological Commission will give its response by Christmas. If it is positive, as we hope, next year will bring the beatification of these martyrs for the faith and for faithfulness to Christ and to the homeland. Most of those who were killed shouted at their deaths, "Long live Christ the King, long live Albania, long live the Pope." Father Simon Jubani, who spent over 30 years in jail and who was liberated in 1989, recounts in his book *My Prison* that when he was called by the police, they presented him with an image of the Madonna, telling him to spit on it in order to be rewarded with his release. Father Simon replied, "The Madonna has done me no harm; it is you who have imprisoned me. And therefore I will never spit on the Madonna," after which they kicked him. He was faithful, always. Once freed, he had the immense courage to celebrate this first mass whose 25th anniversary we commemorate the day after tomorrow.

Our beautiful church in Albania has deeply suffered, but we also have a great honour, Catholics first but also the Orthodox and Muslims, because at Scutari we sent a shock wave through the communist system that had by decree committed itself to eliminating God from the land of Albania. God never retreated, nor did Jesus Christ. Many people remained truly faithful to Christ, praying the holy rosary, praying in silence, undercover and even unto death for our Lord Jesus. This is our witness. Therefore, when we heard a year or two ago that ISIS had emerged in Iraq, together we Catholics, Orthodox, Muslims and Evangelicals in Albania prepared a joint declaration, sending a letter to the Cardinal which stated that we Albanians understood their sufferings and joined them in solidarity, praying that no person would be killed for any reason whatsoever, that every person would have the right to pray and that no one would be expelled from the homes in which they were born and where they had parents and relatives. This solidarity is the beauty of our church and our Albanian people, who may be divided in faith but who love the Lord and strive to do what is best.

I will invite you when our martyrs are beatified. But in the meantime, take this souvenir. You have visited a poor but beautiful nation, a martyred nation that will have its freedom, and that with Mother Teresa as our guide commits itself in the world to being the bearer of the value of freedom as well of peaceful co-existence among people.

Mrs Rosangela Jarjour, General Secretary, Fellowship of the Middle East Evangelical Churches

Although I represent the Fellowship of the Middle East Evangelical Churches, which is a regional church body, I have been asked to speak about one country only: Syria. So I will limit myself to that country, in the hope that the others who have come from Syria and other parts of the Middle East and are not a part of this panel will feel comfortable contributing.

As I stand here saying these words, I would like us all to visualize how Jesus lived the way of the cross, how he was betrayed by Judas, how he was denied by Peter, how he was humiliated by the soldiers, how he was made to bear the heavy cross alone, and how he was the object of ridicule, fury and abuse by the jeering crowds.

- From the Christian quarters of al Hamidiya and Bustan el Diwan in the old city of Homs, the city where I spent my childhood and teenage years, more than 80,000 Christians were forced from their homes in early 2012, and their homes were occupied by the militant rebels (Al Farouq brigades).

- Eight kilometers away from my parents' village lies Saddad, a peaceful town that was mentioned twice in the Bible. The townspeople there lived peacefully for decades until late October 2013, when both the Free Syrian Army and Al Nusra Front attacked Saddad and brutally murdered 53 civilians, including an entire family of six who were blindfolded, shot in the head, and thrown in a well.

- The hundredth anniversary of the Armenian genocide was commemorated in Aleppo with the Islamic factions' leveling to the ground of seven buildings in the Al-Suleimania Christian neighborhood of Aleppo on Good Friday (April 10, 2015). Twenty-nine Christians lost their lives and 56 were injured. Easter Sunday became a day to mourn the dead family members and relatives as the whole town was in deep shock.

- Only three weeks before that, 179 Christian families lost shelter and all possessions after Al Nusra Front stormed the city of Idlib. Of these families, 85% were able to flee with women wearing Islamic robes and hijabs, but the others faced an unknown fate.

- The daily mortar and missile attacks by the so-called moderate rebels on Meharda and the Christian neighborhoods of Damascus and Aleppo have claimed hundreds of innocent Christian civilians' lives, among them many children victimized by attacks on schools and nurseries.

- The Christian population of 400,000 in Aleppo, many of Armenian descent, had already been reduced to an estimated 45,000 or fewer by March 2015.

- In the north, 30 Christian Assyrian villages were attacked and wiped out. Many were massacred and the rest either became internally displaced persons or left the country altogether. As of today, 200 families are still held hostage by ISIS.

For many Christians in Syria, it has become a daily happening that Islamic extremists, whether ISIS or the rebels, storm Christian neighborhoods, towns and villages; destroy their churches, tear down their crosses and deface their icons and murals; kidnap Christians for ransom or murder them; and kidnap or murder their priests and pastors. Those Christians, who chose to live peacefully on their ancestors' land, are now being eradicated by merciless militants for no reason other than they are followers of the Christian faith. Meanwhile, the Western world has mostly remained silent and even reluctant to listen to their voices or respond to their intense suffering.

It is deeply saddening that, in a world with such systematic disinformation, many Westerners have unknowingly become promoters of violence, bloodshed and war. It has come to sound acceptable for them to overthrow regimes with terrorism, to kill hundreds of thousands of Muslim and Christian civilians under the name of peace, to displace millions from their homes for a "better future", and to send terrorists to kill for democracy. Furthermore, media hypocrisy has succeeded in making innocent Christians the culprits and terrorists the victims. Christians were cunningly accused of standing against demands for freedom and the will of the Syrian people. Contrary to that, Christians are firm believers in participatory democracy, the rule of law, and human rights. However, for these Christians, chaos, violence, bloodshed and destruction of our law, order, history and heritage cannot be appropriate means to produce any change, especially unpredictable change that compromises their rights and threatens their mere survival.

Unfortunately, peace is a long shot as long as the instruments of war continue to flow into the Middle East, as long as arms manufacturers are making billions of dollars in profits every month, and as long as these manufacturers and dealers have influence over statesmen and the media. Some countries, which have been supporting, funding and arming Jihadi brigades in Syria, have purchased weapons worth tens of billions of dollars each year throughout the crisis from Western allies, even though both sides know that some of the weapons are used to commit the worst of atrocities against Christians, other minorities, and moderate Muslims. In a gentle rebuke to the U.S. Congress last month, Pope Francis said, "Why are deadly weapons being sold to those who plan to inflict untold suffering on individuals and society? Sadly, the answer, as we all know, is simply for money: money that is drenched in blood, often innocent blood. In the face of this shameful and culpable silence, it is our duty to confront the problem and to stop the arms trade." In May, Pope Francis referred to the weapons industry as the industry of death and argued that powerful people do not want peace because they live off war.

Christian suffering is on the rise all over the globe, and Christians have never been as defenseless as they are now. Christians should create a niche in the world of media to influence public opinion. Churches should raise their young people's awareness and encourage them to take part with their older counterparts in reporting and publicizing incidents of Christian suffering. Churches should form lobbies to influence politicians. Western churches should get firsthand information from the victim churches and communities, not from media reports. It is strange that any incident of an assault on a non-Christian goes viral, whereas the murder of 53 civilian Christians in Saddad and the massive Christian cleansing in Homs have been completely ignored. Does it require the coinage of a special term, or the creation of a complete system to publicize Christian suffering?

Today we stand as witnesses to the pain inflicted on our brothers and sisters in Christ in Syria. We think of innocent families hiding with their children in their homes behind the doors, trembling with fear as they hear calls for jihad or chants and threats against the infidels. I am referring to several that are being targeted these days that need your prayer. For that reason, His Holiness Patriarch Mor Ignatius Aphrem II had to head back and take a detour. He was in Zurich and then headed back to Syria to be with these very people. We should think of those who became Dhimmis, those who are facing trials that may lead to their death, and those who have been martyred. We should also remember the tens of thousands of families who were displaced from their homes only with their clothes on, and who have been impoverished by the war and the ensuing economic woes.

Almost all Christians in Syria have lived the various stations of the way of the cross, from betrayal to condemnation, to crucifixion. Some have already been martyred and some have survived, but many are weak, cold, hungry and thirsty. Will we deny them and remain silent as they are forced to walk along their way of the cross? Or will we help them endure and survive the cup?

Christians in Syria and Iraq need your support to survive. Christians across the Middle East need your support to remain and live peacefully on their land. Failing to help Middle East Christians who remain in their land is like sounding the death knell for ancient Christianity. It is an appeal from the Christian community that has carried the message of the risen Christ to the whole world from the very beginning. It is not just our duty; it is our responsibility and our mission in a troubled world.

Bishop Azad Marshall, Anglican Diocese of Iran and the Gulf

Following Christ together is a wonderful theme, as some of us have a very lonely walk. Finding so many of us who are in the same boat, with the same challenge and the same aspiration, makes it wonderful to be here this morning. I have been the Anglican bishop in the diocese of Iran for the last eleven years. Previous to that, I was bishop of the Gulf, a responsibility that I still carry.

For me, life in Iran, Pakistan, Afghanistan or the Gulf countries is not about suffering. It is not about discrimination; it is not even about living in societies that are hostile to the gospel. It is about submission to the command of Christ: "If they persecute me, they will persecute you also." It involves a sense of preparedness to be able to face that. It is a willingness to say that with all our weaknesses, we will continue as the ambassadors of Christ in those dark societies.

Eleven years ago, when I went to Iran, I had no priests in my diocese. I will give you a perspective on discrimination and persecution through some brief stories. One priest was in prison, and he was told when he was released that he cannot even come near that compound. I tried to contact him, saying, "You are the only one, can we work together?" He said no, but after my long insistence, he invited me over. When I went to see him, he cried like a baby. This 69- or 70-year-old priest was crying like a baby.

He said, "You are my bishop; I have to listen to you. But I will not be allowed. The government will not allow me. But anyway, come, I want to show you my chapel." I said, "You have a chapel?" (He was sharing a house with his extended family.) He took me to a small room, ten by ten feet, maybe a storeroom that he had converted. On a small table he had his Bible and his prayerbook. And then on one side he had his cassock hanging, and on another side he had the pictures of the old church where he was serving as a priest, which he built, and on another side he had an old tape recorder. He said, "This is my chapel. I come here every day and act like a priest and pray for Iran." Then I knew that there was hope for that country.

Before I went to Iran, one of the things I was told was not to go there because they kill bishops. And that is what happened to one of my predecessors. He was attacked and shot at. Thank God, he was saved, but later on his son was killed. The church in Iran has seen every difficulty, every persecution; the priests had to flee. And even in those circumstances, I have seen faithful people in Iran who are willing to take up their challenge and the commandment of Christ, and to accept his words that "They persecuted me so they will persecute you also, so be prepared, and be willing to stay here and be the light in the darkness." So meeting this priest was a great experience for me, because it encouraged me that I am not alone in this work.

My friend Rev. Hashmat has already talked about Pakistan, and he did a good job. I just want to add that the majority community who are of the Islamic faith in Pakistan have institutionalized discrimination and persecution, discrimination that leads to persecution. We started out in Pakistan as a democracy, but due to the majority community's pressure, in 1948, one year after Pakistan's creation, the so-called "objectives resolution" was passed. That resolution says that no law can be passed by the Parliament which is against the Islamic injunctions, against sharia. And that is where our troubles started. The blasphemy law was mentioned this morning, and a lot of people know about that and pray for us. Please remember it and pray for us, because that is the worst example of such a practice. It is completely discriminatory, and minorities are clearly the target of such a law. Because it really brings you down to nothing, you can not do anything. People are accused of all kinds of things, even their promotions are blocked, and they are threatened under the blasphemy law.

Shabaz Bhatti was mentioned as having been killed. He was the federal minister for minorities. He was a brave man, but he was killed for really standing up for the rights of the minority. Our governor Salmaan Taseer was killed because he did the same thing. The Talibanization of that part of the world is alarming. But again the good thing is that in Youhanabad, where the suicide bombers tried to kill a majority of the Christians, they were stopped by one man who was on guard—not by the police, but by one Christian man who was guarding the church.

He realized what was going to happen, and he knew he was going to die, but he said "I am going to save my congregation." And he did. The interesting thing is that the following Sunday, the church was full. People were saying, "No one will go there, people are afraid," but that's the story of our church. The church is resilient, but they need support and they really need our prayers. They need people who will follow them all along, who will go along with them and show them their solidarity, that they are not alone.

Today I want to mention one more country, and that is Afghanistan. There, you cannot be a Christian. If you are a follower of Christ, you have no identity. Because of our close proximity to Afghanistan and our relationships in the last thirty years with a number of people, and because both the diocese of Iran and the diocese of Peshawar are their neighbors, I know that there are many who have decided to follow Christ. Who will support them? Who prays for them? Who is really concerned about those situations? When the constitution was being framed, many Afghan believers who cannot openly declare begged of their American or Western friends: please, when you are forming the new constitution, leave a little space for those who may want to have another faith and want to live peacefully in this country. But nothing was done, there is no provision.

My time is up, but I just want to tell you about one Afghan Christian that I know of. He was a teacher, and one day the Taliban came to him and they slapped him and said, "We know you have become a Christian. We are going to kill you. You are not a teacher, you are actually teaching people about the Christian faith." He realized that was the end. So that day, he gathered all his family and his friends, and he told them the story of the cross. He told them what it means to follow Christ, and he fell down and died. And there are many who are faithfully following Christ and paying a huge price. Let us not forget them.

Bishop Basil Yaldo, Auxiliary Bishop of Baghdad, Chaldean Catholic Patriarchate of Babylon, Iraq

On behalf of His Beatitude Mar Louis Raphael Sako, our Patriarch, I would like to thank all the members of the Global Christian Forum for this consultation and for the invitation.

What is the situation of suffering—discrimination, persecution, martyrdom—that your church is facing today?

All Iraqi people are suffering from the current situation, but those suffering the most are Christians, because they are a minority in the country and have no power or authority in this state. Therefore the migration of Christian families leaving Iraq has spread over different parts of the world. We have families in Jordan, Syria, Lebanon, Turkey, etc.

Since 2003, after the fall of Saddam's regime, the Christians in Iraq have suffered serious persecution: threats, kidnapping and even death itself. The Christian community, which has been deeply rooted in this country since the beginning of the first century, is now reduced in number to less than 400,000. More than 800,000 left the country; many were killed or died in the explosions. Fifty-three churches were attacked. Christians are afraid to stay in Iraq. All the people want to leave Iraq, but especially the Christians, to save their lives.

Neither the government nor the international community has done enough for the Christians in Iraq. For example, after the conference of Pope Benedict XVI, in September 2006 in Germany, there were strong reactions by radical Muslims. They bombed the Patriarchate of the Assyrians in Baghdad and attacked many churches, including the Church of the Holy Spirit in Mosul. They kidnapped many Christian girls in Baghdad. I myself was kidnapped by a fanatic group at that time. The Rev Paul Alexander of the Syrian Orthodox Church in Mosul was beheaded, and many other clergy were martyred, such as my friend Father Ragheed who studied in Rome for five years with me. They killed our Bishop of Mosul, Msgr Faraj Rahho. There was also the attack by Al-Qaida against the Syrian Catholic Church in Baghdad, in which they killed 57 people and two priests during the Sunday prayer in Our Lady of Salvation Church. Bishop Casmoussa who is here with us was kidnapped. He was the first one in Iraq.

You know what was done in northern Iraq in August 2014 by ISIS, called the state of the Islamic Caliphate. More than 120,000 Christians fled in one night from Mosul and the plain of Nineveh at the risk of their life, forced to choose between death, conversion to Islam or registering and paying a tax that equals one year's salary. Most Christians fled to northern areas of Iraq, to Kurdistan. Many of them now live in a small room or in vans or tents! It is not easy from a psychological point of view; the feeling of concern for their homes and cities, for jobs lost and a dark future for their children is evident.

What would you like to say about this situation to the global church?

We encourage our people to stay in Iraq, because we believe in our mission to witness to the gospel. We must remember that not all Muslims are ISIS. God created us different. God has his plan for our presence in this land, and invites us to carry the message of love, brotherhood and tolerance, as Christ did.

But we need your help, support and especially your prayers to stay in our land—Mesopotamia, the land between two rivers. We have been here from the end of the first century. According to tradition, the apostle Thomas was the first to evangelize this region, on his trip to India. So we were there before the Muslims came in the seventh century. We have in this blessed land three famous cities that are mentioned in the Holy Bible: Ur of the Chaldeans in the south of Iraq, Nineveh of the Assyrian Empire in the north of Iraq, and Babylon, very close to Baghdad in the center of the country. We need to save this rich patrimony.

So what are the next steps that churches around the world must take in order to walk together as the suffering church?

(1) First, we ask you to help Iraqi Christians through your prayer and solidarity, by visiting our refugee camps. Many churches have come to visit the Christians. That gives us courage.

(2) We ask you to put pressure on the international community for the liberation of the Christian villages in Iraq. All 24 villages around Nineveh, the biggest city in Iraq after Baghdad, are now occupied by ISIS.

(3) We ask your churches to promote the voice of our martyrs in the world media, to encourage other Christians to testify for Jesus Christ.

(4) Finally, we ask your churches to help with the necessary goods for refugees, like food, medicine and education.

Shahan Sarkissian, Archbishop of Aleppo, Armenian Apostolic Church.

(As Archbishop Sarkissian was unable to leave Aleppo, Rev Housig delivered his message.)

I would like to thank the organizers of the Global Christian Forum for this very timely and needed global consultation. I could not ask for a better Christian forum to describe the discrimination and persecution that my church is suffering from today. Indeed, it comes at a time where martyrdom, at least where I come from, has changed its course and objective.

I am sure that the organizers had in their mind the purpose, plan, vision and the realization of Christian soteriology (salvation) through Christ's supreme example. This is in fact an invitation to follow the challenging path, but with a special emphasis on our unified and strengthened expedition. Moreover, I would add two indispensable quotations from the New Testament. The first is from Hebrews 12:2–4:

> *Looking unto Jesus, the author and finisher of our faith, who for the joy that was set before him endured the cross, despising the shame, and has sat down at the right hand of the throne of God. For consider him who endured such hostility from sinners against himself, lest you become weary and discouraged in your souls. You have not yet resisted to bloodshed, striving against sin.*

The second is from 2 Timothy 3:10–12:

> *But you have carefully followed my doctrine, manner of life, purpose, faith, longsuffering, love, perseverance, persecutions, afflictions, which happened to me at Antioch, at Iconium, at Lystra—what persecutions I endured. And out of them all the Lord delivered me. Yes, and all who desire to live godly in Christ Jesus will suffer persecution.*

The message that I have tried to relay is certainly common to all Christians, and as such we will always be persecuted, but never abandoned by the Lord. Therefore our persecution is somehow a natural course, which constitutes part of our identity and the existential testimony of belief for humanity. Consequently, we will bless and pray for those who persecute us, similar to the prophets, and most importantly similar to our Savior of mankind, Jesus Christ.

Throughout history, the Middle East and its immediate surroundings have been and continue to be the stage for various conflicts. In this respect, let us remind ourselves of the past century of genocides, and in particular the Armenian genocide—the genocide of my people and church in historical Armenia and Cilicia, currently situated in Turkey. The Armenian genocide, as well as the Syrian, Chaldean and Greek genocides and similar atrocities of the past, and along with the current widespread violent practice of discrimination, persecution and martyrdom of my church and followers in Syria, constitute the reason why we are holding this forum today.

The Middle East and in particular the situation in Syria are significantly more dangerous than before. Racial and cultural discrimination on one hand and religious radicalism, extremism and intolerance on the other are endangering our existence as Christians. In fact, this is no longer a matter of democracy, development or social justice for underserved people, but a mixture of thirst for strategic political and economic gains, and regretfully the victims are human diversity and minorities. Consequently, the world is witnessing, though taking no action to stop it, obvious collective persecution, ethnic cleansing and genocides.

The country where I come from, Syria, as you all know has been mired in civil war for the past four and a half years. Why and how the war started may have different explanations. However, it resulted in hundreds of thousands of dead people regardless of their ethnic or religious background, plus millions of refugees and internally displaced persons and ruined cities, villages and infrastructure.

The Middle East, the region where Christianity and its churches initially spread, has become a less safe area for its inhabitants and in particular for Christians. The current, greatly diminished numbers of Christians remaining in these lands and operating churches speak volumes. For example, the once peaceful land of Syria, where Christians and Muslims used to co-exist, has become the world's most dangerous place, a destroyed and terrorized country, with most of its Christian believers either waiting in queues in front of embassies to emigrate or taking the deadly path across the Mediterranean, hoping for a better life anywhere in Europe or North America.

In an attempt to answer the five questions raised by the organizers of this conference, I can state the following:

What is the situation of suffering that our church is facing today?

The situation of our church in Syria is dramatic. We have experienced, and continue to experience, the worst forms of discrimination, hatred and threats, including oral, written and physical aggression. In Aleppo, persecution, discrimination and martyrdom have become the normal course of life. Churches, schools, neighbourhoods, residences and workplaces have been shelled, looted, burnt and destroyed because Christians or Armenians owned them. The city of Aleppo is dependent on a very fragile supply route, often challenged by non-state armed groups and closed for days as it is today. Electricity is provided one or two hours a day, and water supply is almost non-existent, given the fact that the non-state armed groups manage the water pumps of the city, by way of blackmail or pressuring the government. Christian minorities have become targets for kidnapping, forced deportation and violent extermination.

Today, only one-quarter of the Armenian community (including Orthodox, Catholic and Protestant Armenians) continues to exist in Syria. Amongst the 11 Armenian schools, only five are now partially open. The Orthodox Armenians have five churches in Aleppo, of which the Forty Martyrs Cathedral (the diocese's central church), at least 500 years old and the most ancient church in the city, is closed. St George Church was the victim of a violent confrontation and was burnt to ashes. St Gregory the Illuminator Church is located at the demarcation line between the rivals and is at the mercy of the unmerciful snipers. St Jacob Church cannot be used because of its unsafe location. The only church currently open to worshippers is the St Mary Theotokos Church. The once vibrant cultural, social and community life is totally paralyzed. The only active body today within the Armenian community is the newly organized Syrian Armenian Relief and Restoration Committee, along with its four sub-committees.

What kinds of challenges are we facing?

Our key challenge and fear is extermination. Our existence is at stake. It is obvious that if the current situation continues or international political and diplomatic efforts fail, only handfuls of Christians will remain in Syria. This is neither pessimism nor exaggeration. It is happening now under our watch.

What can we draw from our experience?

- The Christian church remained divided and was only weakly reactive to existential events in Syria, rather than adopting a proactive approach. Moreover, our lobbying and advocacy efforts need to be revisited. The lack of a strong Muslim counterpart ensuring co-existence and condemning radical Islam was obvious. Subsequently, there is a need to strengthen and tackle the dangers of isolation, discrimination and extremism.

- Based on its principles, Christianity as a religion is fragile or brittle.

- We must initiate practical steps to strengthen our relationships between us and others.

- We must have representation (or a representative body) within international organizations such as the United Nations and acknowledge the same right for other religions.

What do we expect from the church?

- More coordinated and effective political advocacy and protection efforts for minorities in danger. Stronger engagement with the Muslim world.

- In the current situation, we ask for vocal messaging and communication of our suffering to the international community, along with unconditional solidarity, permanent assistance and help by all possible means for those in crisis.

- Humanitarian and financial assistance.

- Collective and permanent prayer for suffering people in particular churches currently under existential threat.

What are our vision and expectations?

In general, the church needs to be dynamic and reactive to the current reality; fight all sorts of extremism and terrorism; educate the new generation with new approaches to strengthening human values and dignity; and find dignified and fair solutions for refugees and internally displaced people. Only through these approaches and collective efforts can we follow our Lord Jesus Christ.

I strongly suggest having a reference to Aleppo and Syria and its dangerous situation in the concluding statement of this significant conference.

Rev Dr Munir Kakish, Chairman, Council of Local Evangelical Churches in the Holy Land

What is the situation of suffering—discrimination, persecution, martyrdom—that your churches are facing?

The churches in the West Bank, as well as the churches in Israel and Jordan, are seeking recognition and to obtain civil rights, such as recognition of marriage certificates, funerals, being able to have bank accounts for the church, and being able to purchase land and register it in the name of the church. We are equated with the Jehovah Witnesses and experience discrimination for that reason. We also have problems because evangelism is discouraged, even about the teachings of Jesus, baptism, and St Mary. This comes in addition to persecution by Muslims. The basic issue is religious intolerance. There is dialogue between different groups, but evangelicals are not invited to attend. Furthermore, we have problems due to Israeli authorities restricting our travel and not issuing permits for travel to Jerusalem and holy sites during religious holidays. Currently, I spend a lot of time obtaining permits for our pastors and church congregations to visit the holy sites in the Galilee area as well as in Jerusalem.

What would you like to say about this situation to the global church?

Pray for us and for peace in the Holy Land. Be respectful of all peoples. Influence the historical churches to recognize the evangelicals and let the people worship where they feel a connection to God.

From your perspective, what are the next steps that churches around the world must take to walk together as the suffering church?

Have a greater voice in the political arena. Exert pressure on governments to stop persecution of Christians and minorities and resolve conflicts.

(At this point, Rev Kakish continued with a PowerPoint presentation. His words have been edited to make his message clearer for readers who do not have access to the PowerPoint slides.)

I chose as my theme Jesus' words, "Blessed are the peacemakers," because my presentation might be a little bit different from others. I'm asking you today to become a bridge of peace as you listen to my brief presentation.

I have been asked to describe the situation of the churches in the Holy Land, Israel and Palestine. Some of the things I will say also apply to Jordan. I have also been asked what our message to the global church is and how all of you can help.

I believe that the threat of ISIS is growing and that we all have a problem with radical Islam. I believe that the goal of ISIS and extremist Islamists is to wipe out Christians from the Middle East, where we have about 12 to 16 million Christians. I believe that the answer for this world lies in Jesus Christ. And as you come to the Holy Land, I pray that you will be able to visit the living stones in our area, not just our present churches.

In Israel, we have a council with five different denominations or groups working together along with parachurch organizations. Our problem with the Israeli authorities in the West Bank is that they do not give us permits for pastors to be able to travel into different areas and towns in that area. They do give to a few pastors, but we are still struggling to leave the West Bank in order to go to Israel and this is very important for our ministers.

The churches in Israel are also seeking legal recognition for their synod to be recognized legally in terms of its civil rights, the ability to give marriage certificates, and also to register the land of the churches in the name of the church instead of personal names.

In Israel there is also discrimination from the Jewish community. Several churches in Jerusalem and Galilee have been burned and damaged. The latest one was burned by the Sea of Galilee—the church at the place where we believe that Jesus fed the five thousand.

Pray for the churches in Israel. They need legal recognition. Also, pray that persecution will be reduced and that there will be safety.

Now we will turn to the West Bank, which includes East Jerusalem. Since the war in 1948, which affected the working class, many Christians and pastors have left the area. This has been a setback for the evangelical church. In spite of this, the Arab churches in the West Bank, East Jerusalem and the Gaza Strip are moving forward. We have established our Council uniting most evangelical churches and organizations or parachurch bodies, to present a united front to the Palestinian authorities.

The Palestinian Authority and other churches have seen the credibility, accountability, unity and organizational stability of this Council in the West Bank, including Gaza. The Council provides us with one voice; it has a constitution (or *dastour*) and standardized procedures. The Council is gaining recognition as the voice of the evangelical churches in Palestine.

In Israel, we have messianic Jews and Palestinian Christians meeting together. We have a fellowship together at the Garden Tomb in Jerusalem. We have a Bible college in Bethlehem and supply aid to the refugees in Jordan.

We also have outreach ministries to Muslim communities throughout the Holy Land. Many of these are underground for fear of reprisal.

Our main problem in the West Bank is that we are seeking recognition for our Council. The Palestinians are not recognizing us at all. We need the same thing as in Israel and in Jordan: to register our marriage certificates and to register land in the name of the church.

The evangelical body in the West Bank and Gaza also would like to be invited by the Christian authorities on matters that have to do with churches, as is done with other Christian church leaders. We would really appreciate your help in this area.

Now I would like to turn to Gaza. Gaza is a huge ghetto in which the Christians have been confined. The Christian population of Gaza has declined. Today I believe they are less than 1,000. Years ago there were many, many thousands. The Christians are trying to leave that area because of many problems.

Our brothers and sisters in the Gaza Strip are facing the threat of annihilation from the wars. Many Christians and Muslims leave when they have the possibility to emigrate to another country. Christians there must deal with Hamas and other factions and have been mistreated by Muslims. They have been asked to convert to Islam. The ones who suffer the most are families and children. There are still Christian churches operating in the Gaza Strip, along with a Christian school. They need your prayers for their safety and survival.

Our message to the global church is that the Holy Spirit is still working through the churches in Israel, the West Bank and the Gaza Strip.

We still are training youth, as they are the future of the church. We continue furthering the Kingdom of God as united evangelicals. We continue to have outreach to Muslims. Much more is going on but we do not have time for everything. We continue to be a bridge for making peace. We continue to help the Iraqi and Syrian refugees in Jordan. We continue to be peacemakers. We are actively trying to stop the war, to end suffering and to allow the current flow of refugees to return to their own countries.

Pray for peace in the Holy Land. Pray that we can be respectful of all people. Pray that the historical church will recognize the evangelicals and we can all worship where we feel a connection to God.

What can you do? Exert pressure on the Israeli government to recognize the evangelical churches in Israel. Exert pressure on the Palestinian Authority to recognize the evangelical churches in Palestine and the Gaza Strip. Educate your people and tell them that there are committed Christians in Israel, Palestine and the Gaza Strip. We are all one in the Lord Jesus Christ!

We ask you to be active peace makers. Do what you can to end the suffering in the Arab world and to end the wars. Pray for the Palestinians and the Jews, and for peace and justice. This is the place where Jesus was born, suffered, died and rose on the third day and where He will come back to the Mount of Olives to rapture the church.

I would conclude with a quote attributed to Einstein: "The world is a dangerous place to live, not because of the people who are evil, but because of the people who don't do anything about it."

Evangelical Leader, Africa.

I would like to start by telling you a brief story about myself. Then I will answer the questions proposed by the organizers.

Two years ago, security forces came to my house in my absence, searching everything, asking my wife and children about my whereabouts. My family did not know where I had gone, so the security forces searched the house and took whatever served their purpose, including my passport and my other documents. I stayed in hiding while they were searching for me for two months. When the time came that I could not continue in hiding, the elders, my family and my relatives advised me to leave the country. I left the country. During my time of hiding in my country, they repeatedly called my wife to their office. When they did not get anything, after a week they took her to prison. She was held for a month because of me. Finally she was asked to pay a fine and then they released her. Now my family is not able to leave the country and I cannot go back to my country.

What is the situation of suffering, discrimination, persecution and martyrdom that the church is facing?

The government issued a decree that all evangelical churches should close their worship places and stop gathering. Since then, the churches have started to worship underground in cell groups. As the Bible says, "I will strike the shepherd and the sheep will be scattered" (Mark 14:27). One year after the closure of the churches, church leaders were arrested. They are still in prison, except one who was released because of serious illness. And these people have not been allowed to see or communicate with their loved ones. One of the ministers, whose wife passed away while he was in prison, was not allowed even to attend her funeral.

Since the decree was issued, the President and other top authorities have been harassing Christians as if we are a threat to them and the country as a whole. In their view, Christians are considered agents of the CIA and sympathizers with other governments which are the enemy in their view. As a result, they have tried to stir up the society against us, but thanks to God the society has not followed their evil plot. Here are some of the things the authorities have been doing or saying about Christians.

Authorities have been heard saying in public that "HIV-AIDS and we are the same and we will fight them."

The activities of the church being underground, whenever Christians are found assembled for prayer and Bible study, they are arrested and taken to remote areas where it is very difficult to live. Some of them are locked up in ship containers and are not even allowed to go out for nature's call except at six in the morning or six in the evening.

Bibles, musical instruments and choir uniforms are heaped up and burned in the church compound. Church buildings have been confiscated, and every group has reported that whatever seemed valuable to them was confiscated.

Even our children who are in high school and college are always intimidated and often arrested whenever they are found talking about their faith in small groups.

Female university students were arrested and sent to remote areas simply because they refused to dance on National Liberation Day. The last of them were released after seven years of imprisonment.

There are Christians who have been beaten to death and others who passed away due to their inhuman treatment by the regime.

There are hundreds of believers and ministers who are still in prison and almost half of them are women. There is no legal processing and nobody knows when he or she might be released.

Everyone knows what his or her wedding day should look like. In our case, matrimonial ceremonies are not public. They are always in hiding. Only six to eight individuals attend the ceremony. The participants are not told the hour and the place until the day comes. It must be early in the morning or late in the evening. When it is done, they walk out separately, wearing ordinary clothes. We had an instance when the bride and groom and all the wedding guests were taken to prison because they sang songs in the hall they had rented for their wedding celebration.

Because of the extended time of persecution, believers are forced to migrate and leave the country in an illegal way to find a safe place to practice their faith freely. But some are falling into the hands of kidnappers and are being sold to other abductors, and some have drowned while crossing the Mediterranean Sea.

What would you like to say about this situation to the global church? Or what do you ask of the global church?

First, I would like to thank you for inviting me and giving me this opportunity to share with you the calamities my brethren are experiencing. Second, on behalf of my church I would like to thank Open Doors for the consistent help they have been giving since the time when the persecution started. I ask the global Christian community, as members of the body of Christ, to feel our pain and call for global, fervent and consistent prayer; to look for any possible means to bring an end to the injustice and the suffering of Christians; and to take practical measures to encourage Christians who are experiencing suffering so that they may persevere and remain faithful to their faith and calling.

What are the next steps that churches around the world must take to walk together as the suffering church?

(1) To create awareness globally so that believers may pray persistently;

(2) To set a global day of prayer for the churches who are suffering;

(3) To help the leaders of the suffering churches by giving training to continue working for the Kingdom of God despite the suffering they are encountering;

(4) To give the leaders of the suffering churches an opportunity to share their experience and edify each other;

(5) To practically show your solidarity by trying to respond to the needs of those who suffer;

(6) Lastly, to send a signed appeal to the president for the release of Christians and freedom of worship.

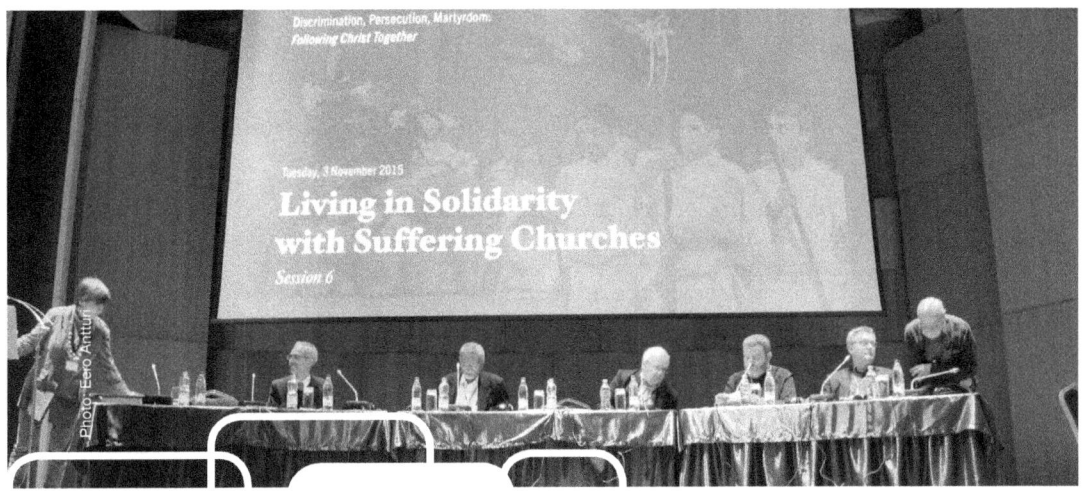

Panel session.

Session Five –
Living in Solidarity with Suffering Churches

Moderator:

His Eminence Metropolitan Dr Gennadios of Sassima, Ecumenical Patriarchate of Constantinople

Biblical and Theological Perspectives on Discrimination, Persecution and Martyrdom:

His Beatitude Archbishop Dr Anastasios, Orthodox Autocephalous Church of Albania

Human Rights and Religious Liberty: Perspectives on Discrimination, Persecution and Martyrdom:

Dr Thomas Schirrmacher, World Evangelical Alliance

The Biblical Basis for Religious Freedom:

Dr Godfrey Yogarajah, Evangelical Alliance Sri Lanka

Biblical and Theological Perspectives on Discrimination, Persecution and Martyrdom

His Beatitude Archbishop Dr Anastasios, Orthodox Autocephalous Church of Albania

In the last century, during the relentless atheistic persecution which brought Albania into a deep spiritual darkness, the discrimination against Christians and martyrdom reached its high point.

I remember a distinctive instance. Fr. Jorgios was an Orthodox priest in a village in the South. He was a teacher and also an agriculturist. When the communist persecution broke out, he was forced to leave his priestly duties and to labour as a road construction worker. One day, when he stopped to take a break from the gruelling work and hot sun, a friend of his, a faithful Christian from another village, approached and whispered to him Christ's words, "In the world you have tribulation." Fr. Jorgios raised his eyes calmly and continued the verse: "But be of good cheer, I have overcome the world" (John 16:33). Another time, fanatical followers of the communist party engraved a big cross in the middle of the road and compelled him to step on it. He devoutly kneeled, spread out his hands on the cross and embraced it.

Deception and slander have always existed as a prelude in the drama of persecution. Subsequent actions such as exiles, hardships, long-term imprisonments, and executions of clerics, laity, and entire families followed. Certainly that did not happen only in Albania. The twentieth century is full of moving stories of faithful people, who paid for their dedication to Christ through terrific tortures and executions. However, even in our century, wherever antichristian powers prevail, various persecutions continue against Christians. The constant point of reorientation and comfort of the faithful has been the ceaseless contemplation of Jesus Christ.

The Martyr Par Excellence: Jesus and the Apostles in His Footsteps

From the first steps of his earthly presence, Jesus experienced tribulations. The threats during his childhood due to Herod's mania required him to take refuge in Egypt. From the beginning of his public endeavour, he faced the fierce hostility of the Pharisees and the scribes, who reached the point of spreading the claim that "It is only by Beelzebul, the prince of demons, that this man casts out demons" (Matt 12:24).

Jesus knew that his redeeming work would be realized with the acceptance of martyrdom, the sacrifice of the cross. He did not hide from his own the tragic but also saving aspect of the pain and persecution. On the contrary, he informed them and he called them to follow him, accepting also their own personal cross: "If any man would come after me, let him deny himself and take up his cross and follow me" (Matt 16:24). Jesus, when persecuted, placed his trust in his Father, who sent him and was always with him. As a prerequisite for someone to be one of his genuine disciples, he placed on them the tangible decision of self-sacrifice. The cross became the Christian symbol par excellence; together with the resurrection, it forms the DNA of the church.

After his resurrection, the sacrificial ethos would determine the identity of his apostles. "As the Father has sent me, even so I send you" (John 20:21; cf. 17:18). You will follow in my own footsteps, Christ was telling them, free from all anxiety and fear. Not with your own power, but with that of the Holy Spirit. Not for you to stay in theological reveries and spiritual enjoyment of my gifts, but to be witnesses of my redemptive work throughout the world: "You shall be my witnesses in Jerusalem and in all Judea and Samaria and to the end of the earth" (Acts 1:8).

The word *martyr* (Greek *martus*) has a double meaning in the original Greek text of the New Testament. First, it refers to testimony about a particular fact; second, it involves sealing that testimony with the price of martyrdom. The life of the church for twenty centuries was a constant witness to this double meaning: the announcement of the gospel of Christ and the confirmation of this testimony with an offer of blood.

The apostles constantly followed what the Master "commanded unto them." They experienced the reality of persecution and martyrdom. Their lives moved according to the statement of Paul: "in honour and dishonour, in ill repute and good repute. We are treated as impostors, and yet are true; as unknown, and yet well known; as dying, and behold we live; as punished, and yet not killed; as sorrowful, yet always rejoicing" (2 Cor 6:8–10). As he said elsewhere in the same epistle, the secret of their strength and their resilience comes from God: "We are afflicted in every way, but not crushed; perplexed, but not driven to despair; persecuted, but not forsaken; struck down, but not destroyed" (2 Cor 4:8–9).

In references to the martyrs, which culminate in the book of Revelations, persistence is the divine message: "Be faithful unto death, and I will give you the crown of life" (Rev. 2:10). The entire last book of Holy Scripture celebrates the trials and the glory of the heroes of faith.

The Church is Apostolic and "Martyric"
The Church was founded on the glorious martyrdom of Christ: "And I, when I am lifted up from the earth, will draw all men to myself" (John 12:32). The church as the body of Christ is called in turn to offer to God the martyrdom of blood for the salvation of humankind. In its history, martyrdom acquires a special significance, which is revealed by Jesus himself. This concerns the imitation of Christ by participating in his suffering and in his salvific work (John 15:20). To his disciples he revealed that "unless a grain of wheat falls into the earth and dies, it remains alone; but if it dies, it bears much fruit" (John 12:24).

The Church has adopted a basic guide of prayer: the psalter. The Psalms speak of external pressures, of injustices, of impasses suffered by the just, those dedicated to God: "Deliver me, O Lord, from my enemies! I have fled to thee for refuge!" (Ps 143:9). The cry of anguish and trust that resonates in the Psalter—the exclamations of pain and hope, supplication and anticipation—have not ceased to support Christians over the centuries.

The Church is apostolic not only according to its doctrinal tradition and episcopal succession, but also according to its "martyric" tradition. One cannot follow Christ without taking part, at least partially, in the passion of Christ. "Indeed all who desire to live a godly life in Christ Jesus will be persecuted" (2 Tim 3:12). We may even suffer "dangers from [our] own peoples; … dangers from false brethren" (2 Cor. 11:26). It is certainly not possible for all of us to become martyrs, because martyrdom is one of the special gifts in the church. Nevertheless, everyone ought to follow Christ, ready for any trial.

During the course of the 20 centuries that have passed since Christ's time on earth, the church has endured many trials and has faced persecutions in a variety of forms and intensities. Ultimately, however, it remained resolute. As the incomparable St John Chrysostom, a great figure of the undivided church (354–407), stressed, "The church is of such a magnitude, when attacked it wins, when planned to be surpassed, it is superior, sworn at it becomes brighter, receiving traumas, it does not collapse, it reels but it does not sink, it is plagued but endures a wreck, it ages but it is not defeated, … never old, always flourishing."

Characteristics of the Ethos of a Martyr

Christ clearly warned his disciples about persecutions: "If they persecuted me, they will persecute you also" (John 15:20). "Beware of men; for they will deliver you up to councils, and flog you in their synagogues, and you will be dragged before governors and kings for my sake, to bear testimony before them and the Gentiles" (Matt 10:17–18). He advocated the following behaviours:

- *Integrity and prudence*: "So be wise as serpents and innocent as doves" (Matt 10:16). Maintain inner innocence and purity, but also caution and wisdom towards your persecutors. It is not necessary for you to be superfluously daring. "When they persecute you in one town, flee to the next" (Matt. 10:23).

- *Courage and fearlessness*: "Do not fear those who kill the body" (Matt 10:28). "In the world you have tribulation; but be of good cheer, I have overcome the world" (John 16:33).

- *Resilience and strength*: Certainty for consolation and support which will come at the hour of anxiety from divine grace (Luke 22:43).

- *Patience with accusations and jeering* (Luke 23:9), but resistance to the distortion of the truth by his enemies, the supposedly pious Pharisees and scribes (Matt 12:24–27; 23:13–36).

When driven to martyrdom, the disciple of Christ must be free from anger and hatred for his persecutors. He is called to forgive them and pray for them, imitating his Teacher (Luke 23:54). The heart of the martyr is flooded with love. Without love, martyrdom has no value. St John Chrysostom's emphasis is revealing: "Love itself, not martyrdom, creates a disciple of Christ; martyrdom without love doesn't make a disciple, and neither does it benefit him to endure it."

The core of the believer's resilience is the sense of Christ's constant presence: "Lo, I am with you always, to the close of the age" (Matt 28:20).

The apostle Paul beautifully summarizes how to resist suffering: "As servants of God we commend ourselves in every way: through great endurance, in afflictions, hardships, calamities, beatings, imprisonments, tumults, labours, watching, hunger" (2 Cor. 6:4). And simultaneously with purity, prudence, patience, kindness, with the Holy Spirit, with sincere love, by preaching the truth and with the power of God; with weapons of justice, both offensive and defensive (2 Cor. 6:5-7).

When one is inside the Christian faith, four surprising experiences take place:

- *Reconciliation* with the pain, especially the pain that is connected to martyrdom for the love of Christ. To suffer for Christ is considered a special charisma. "For it has been granted to you that for the sake of Christ you should not only believe in him but also suffer for his sake" (Phil 1:29).

- Existential *communion, koinonia* with Christ, a deeper knowledge and relationship with him. (Phil 3:10). Paul dares to consider that "in my flesh I complete what is lacking in Christ's afflictions for the sake of his body, that is, the church" (Col 1:24).

- *Transformation* of tribulations into factors of spiritual maturity, purification and holiness. In this way, the martyrs are distinguished as free from fear, free from pain, free from death. Eventually, martyrdom in the perspective of Christian faith is transformed into a hymn of love and praise of God. It is characteristic that the memories and celebrations of the martyrs are not an occasion to revive grief, but are lived in the light of the experience of the resurrection of Christ and becomes symbols of victory.

- The culmination of the experience of the martyrs remains *blessedness* and *joy*. With absolute clarity Jesus stressed, "Blessed are those who are persecuted for righteousness' sake, for theirs is the kingdom of heaven. Blessed are you when men revile you and persecute you and utter all kinds of evil against you falsely on my account. Rejoice and be glad, for your reward is great in heaven" (Matt 5:10–12). The first Christians in Thessalonica, imitating the Lord and the apostles, accepted the gospel "in much affliction, with joy inspired by the Holy Spirit" (1 Thess 1:6). Also, the apostle Peter, from his long personal experience, assured the believers, "But rejoice in so far as you share Christ's sufferings. ... If you are reproached for the name of Christ, you are blessed, because the spirit of glory and of God rests upon you" (1 Pet 4:13–14).

The Responsibility of Christians in the Twenty-First Century

To fulfil its mission in the world events of the twenty-first century, the church must maintain intact its sacramental, salvific character, the courage of the martyrs' ethos. It must remain open to the pursuit of humanity, faithfully following the path outlined by Christ and open to experiencing its universal responsibility with cross-resurrectional resilience, peace and joy.

Today Christians live in a complex world, characterized by pluralism and interdependence. In the modern, globalized world we are under an obligation to increase our sensitivity, vigilance and solidarity.

Christians are a majority in some places, a minority elsewhere. In the latter case they are often oppressed in various ways, as is happening in our time in the Middle East, in Africa and in Asia. Christians living in free countries have a huge responsibility. We cannot remain indifferent to the sufferings of our brothers and sisters. We must use our voice to influence rulers. We are obliged to raise our voice by any means available, to protect and actively support our persecuted brothers. The apostle Paul clearly defines our duty: "If one member suffers, all suffer together; if one member is honoured, all rejoice together" (1 Cor 12:26).

Glory to God that many inter-church organizations have been in solidarity with various local churches that have suffered from the storms of persecution. In the new conditions created, those who partake in the Global Christian Forum have to look for new forms of support for persecuted Christians. This consultation certainly offers an opportunity to study the major cases and to search for solutions.

And to be more specific, we should note that the great powers carry general responsibility for the crises in the Middle East, related to their decisions to pursue violent leadership changes, providing weapons, and apathy for the millions of innocent victims. It is now time that all those involved shake off their lethargy and take effective action to stop the hostile conflicts and terrible bloodshed.

A more general problem, which must be constantly worked with is the close relationship between global peace, justice and development. Poverty remains the worst type of oppression. When people are deprived of basic needs for survival, it is not strange for them to turn in other directions and adopt extreme religious beliefs to achieve a just society. In the twenty-first century, we need to cultivate more fully and strengthen the solidarity of all Christians; following up on that which is being accomplished here with insight and discernment: "following Christ together".

An inexhaustible source of the renewal of our spiritual life remains the increase of our love for Christ. That is the secret of the strength and of the endurance of Christians over the course of the centuries.

Let the apostolic experience, as expressed by the apostle Paul, be our personal hymn: "Who shall separate us from the love of Christ? Shall tribulation, or distress, or persecution, or famine, or nakedness, or peril, or sword? ... No, in all these things we are more than conquerors through him who loved us. For I am sure that neither death, nor life ... nor depth, nor anything else in all creation, will be able to separate us from the love of God in Christ Jesus our Lord" (Rom 8:35, 37–39).

Human Rights and Religious Liberty: Perspectives on Discrimination, Persecution and Martyrdom

Dr Thomas Schirrmacher, World Evangelical Alliance

It is not easy to be the speaker coming after a speech by Archbishop Anastasios. Your Beatitude, I thank you very much for putting the Bible and Jesus in the centre of what we are doing here. No evangelical could have done that better. What unites all of us is what God revealed about his Son Jesus Christ in the Holy Scriptures. Whether it is in the Vatican Synod or in a document like *Christian Witness in a Multi-religious World*, what the Bible says about Jesus is what brings us here.

For some of you who wonder why the Archbishop has this honorary title of Beatitude, I tell you it is because he gives such beautiful speeches. I have heard many of them, and I am very glad that his presentation gives us the lead today. His Beatitude and I are long-time friends. I admire the work of his life. He has been a missionary in Africa, starting from scratch; he came to Albania when there was no church, after communism had destroyed all the churches. Anything you find about the Albanian Orthodox Church has been built up by him after 1990. It is an amazing story. And you now know why we wanted to be in Albania.

We have now a presentation in two parts, on the biblical basis for human rights and religious freedom. We have split the topic in two, but it is one presentation. The reason for doing this is that we want to show the cooperation between a speaker coming from Germany, in the West, and one coming from Sri Lanka, in the global South. We also want to show that academic and practical work belong together. Godfrey Yogarajah has been for decades in the middle of the struggle; he has experienced all forms of discrimination and persecution, even martyrdom around him. He has built up a structure in his country that enables the churches to be in solidarity with one another. I am by definition an academic, and the International Institute for Religious Freedom stands for providing governments and media with facts. You can see this in my paper, which I am not going to read because it would take too long. *[Note: The full paper is provided following this transcript of Dr Schirrmacher's written text.]* What Godfrey does is to travel from country to country, visiting the churches, bringing them together, helping and teaching them how to present themselves, how to defend themselves, how to have solidarity. It is an immensely important work. We are delivering this presentation in two parts not as an either-or, but because the two approaches really belong together. You will see that the Germans still believe in the spoken word, without much technical help, while our Asian friends are far ahead of us when it comes to technology. Godfrey will use a PowerPoint; I have to ask my son what that is. So take that also as an example of the complementarity between us, which is true for all that we do.

I am the chair of the international council of the International Society for Human Rights, and our secretary is a Muslim. So for me the topic of where human rights come from is with me day and night. I would rather work with people who are in favour of human rights and do not know where they come from than with people who have a lot of academic ideas about where things come from but are not in favour of human rights. There is no question that in terms of practice, human rights are a model base on which we can work together internationally. But I can tell you, having been involved in debates at the UN with leaders of other religions, that the world at large has no clue as to where human rights come from. All they know is that if you put them into practice, the world will be a little better than if you do not practice them. But if you go in depth at the UN and ask why it is so important where human rights come from, you always end up with Christian terminology like human dignity. This is not to offend any other religion, not to be proud, not to say "Lord, I thank you that I am not like the others." That is not our spirit. But it is true that human rights are rooted in Christian ideas. We are glad when others accept this, even atheists for whom this is not relevant. We have to know why and have confidence in ourselves. We have to know the difference between, say, the Muslim and the Christian approach to this.

Take, for example, human dignity. We all know it goes back to the beginning of the Bible. Human dignity comes from creation. It does not come from being a Christian. You do not have human dignity because you belong to us Christians, but because you were born, because God created you, because God wanted you. We Christians do not have the right to say that another person is not a Christian so he or she deserves less. We have to treat all people as created by God in all dignity, with all the rights and all the duties that stem from this. Love your neighbour as yourself, yes, even love your enemy. Do not say, this enemy is not a believer.

That is the difference I found in talking with my Muslim secretary, and with many other people, at the UN. To understand that it is God who creates people, who gives them dignity, and not us giving dignity to anybody is a different mind-set. That includes Genesis 3, let us not forget. Very early on, those humans with all their dignity get into sin. That was before any of us was around, which means that we Christians are as much affected by sin that leads to violation of human rights as anybody else. Some people think that the world would be better if we had a US president who was evangelical. Well, we had one. George W. Bush, who was an alcoholic, had a genuine conversion. The family knew Billy Graham very well. Did the world get better? I do not intend to get into politics, so let me simply say that being an evangelical does not mean you know best when to go to war. We Christians believe that we all suffer from sin and that when we get into power, we are as open to corruption or misuse of power as anybody else. We saw this in Egypt when President Morsi came to power. He was a devout Muslim, and people thought that everything would become better. We Christians believe that everybody, even a Christian believer, who comes into power can get into the same problems as anybody else. Even the Holy Father, Pope Francis, tells everybody he meets that probably no one is more at risk of misusing power or making mistakes than he is, and that he needs the prayers of millions of people. He told me so several times. This is part of Christianity; we do not say, "I am a Christian so everything is fine." To understand that this is true for everybody has to do a lot with human rights. We cannot distinguish us as the good part of the world from the others who are the bad part.

A biblical passage that has a lot to do with human rights is Romans 13, which speaks about the relation of the state to us as Christians. Every possible form of relationship between state and church has existed in history. We have tried everything. In the Bible we have Revelation 13 in which the anti-Christian state tries to kill the church, and in history we have examples where the state protects Christians from persecution. But at the centre of it all, Romans 13 is very clear: if Christians do evil things, God has ordained the state to punish us. Politically, that means clearly that we do not rule the world and cannot do whatever we want. When we do evil things, when we violate human rights, the state is there to prevent us from doing so. This gives you a very different perspective on human rights than if you think you rule the world and the others have to follow.

The three most important points, when it comes to the biblical basis for human rights, are as follows. First, human rights come from the DNA of our faith because they belong to everybody who has been created. Second, the problem of sin in our life is a problem that belongs to everybody, not only to non-Christians. And third, Christians sin and do evil things which must be punished by the state. We are not always the ones who rule the state or those who criticize the state; it goes both ways.

Following is the written text that Dr Schirrmacher prepared for the consultation and that he summarized in his spoken message.

The Biblical Basis for Human Rights

Man as Creation and Image of God

On December 10, 1948, many states signed the General Declaration of Human Rights passed by the General Assembly of the United Nations. The declaration states that all human beings possess the same dignity (Article 1) and forbids all discrimination due to race, colour, sex, language, religion or political conviction (Article 2). Because all men have the right to life and liberty (Article 3), both slavery (Article 4) and torture (Article 5) are prohibited. All are equal before the law and may be condemned only according to established law, only after being heard in a court of law (Articles 7–11). All are free to emigrate and to choose their place of residence (Article 13), and to request asylum in other countries (Article 14). Every human being is free to choose his spouse, and the family, as the "natural and basic unit in society", must be protected by the state and by society (Articles 16 and 26). The Declaration also demands the right of private property (Article 17); the right to liberty of conscience and religion, which includes the individual's right to change his faith (Article 18); the right of opinion and information (Article 19); the right to congregate and to form associations (Article 20); and the right to vote (Article 21). Everyone has the right to security in social matters (Articles 22, 25 and 28), to labour with just remuneration (Article 23) and to education (Article 26).

Closely related to the idea of human rights is the claim that all people have the same right to be treated as persons, whatever race, religion, sex, political persuasion or social or economic status they may be or have. What is the basis of human equality, if not the fact that all were equally created by God? Thus, a Christian argument for human rights must begin with the biblical account of Creation, "Let us make man in our image, after our likeness: and let them have dominion over the fish of the sea, and over the fowl of the air, and over the cattle, and over all the earth, and over every creeping thing that creepeth upon the earth. So God created man in his own image, in the image of God created he him; male and female created he them" (Gen 1:26–27). The fact that man was created in the image of God plays a major role in the relationships of human beings to each other. Genesis 9:6, for example, requires murder to be punished, for it injures the image of God: "Whoso sheddeth man's blood, by man shall his blood be shed: for in the image of God made he man."

Creation exists for the glory of God and has its meaning from God. This fact holds all the more for the 'crown of creation'. Mankind was created according to the divine order of creation to fulfil the purpose given him by God. God made him ruler over the earth, but also gave him the responsibility for the preservation of the earthly creation. The psalmist writes, "Thou madest him to have dominion over the works of thy hands; thou hast put all things under his feet: All sheep and oxen, yea, and the beasts of the field" (Ps 8:6–7).

For this reason, human rights include only those privileges which God has given man, and no other rights which mankind may choose or claim for himself.

Christians may not, therefore, automatically identify the human rights catalogues formulated by Western countries with those in the Bible. Scripture prescribes the right to an orderly court procedure according to clearly stated laws, to the hearing of witnesses, to judges who have not been bribed and to legal defence. Such legal proceedings cannot, however, be automatically identified with Western jurisdictions. Supposing they could be—with which system? The German system, the British, the French, the American? We all know that these systems are quite different! There is plenty of room for a variety of legal systems, which differ due to the cultural and historical traditions of their people yet still guarantee human rights.

The Christian Roots of Human Rights

No one disputes the fact that human rights, given to protect the individual, are derived from Christian thought. The General Declaration of Human Rights of the United Nations, of December 10, 1948, clearly demonstrates its Christian roots. The bans on slavery and torture, the principle of equality before the law, and the right to rest and recreation—as seen in the Sabbath or Sunday rest—come from Christian traditions. It is not by chance that the governments which confirm these rights and anchor them in their constitutions are mostly in Christian countries. Even Karl Marx acknowledged this, for he rejected human rights as a product of Christianity (for example, see Marx and Engels, *Works*, Vol. 1).

No state and no legal system can survive without a minimum of common and necessarily metaphysically based values. A legal system assumes a value system, for law is derived from moral standards which exist prior to and outside itself.

The guarantee of human dignity assumes that man is more than that which he perceives about himself. He cannot be comprehended by the means and methods of natural science. He is metaphysically open. The modern state, with its legal system, depends on requirements that it cannot itself guarantee.

Enlightenment or Forgiveness and Repentance?

According to the philosophies of the Enlightenment in the eighteenth century, which attempted to establish human rights without God and against the church, all good, including human rights, could be derived from nature and from reason. Rousseau's identification of reason and nature is peculiar to Enlightenment thought. The attempt to base human rights on nature has failed, however, for no one can agree on the meaning of nature or on how its laws can be discovered.

Wolfgang Schild, a professor of penal law, writes, "The Enlightenment cannot and must not be the last word, our last word. Its rationality and functionality must be taken to its limits, for social life with a dignity worthy of man is otherwise impossible. Even and particularly penal law cannot limit itself to rational means in order to achieve peace and order at any price: it requires the recognition of the human dignity even of the felon as its founding principle and its limit."

The thought that human beings could be improved by education, and that human ills could be solved by intellectual enlightenment, is a basic problem of Greek philosophy, of humanism and of the Enlightenment. The humanist ideal of education owes its existence to the idea that morals could be raised through education, for it assumes that the individual does wrong only because he is ignorant or because he thinks wrongly, not because his will is evil or because he is incapable of doing good on his own strength. These philosophies try to reduce the ethical and responsible aspect of thought, words and deeds to the question of knowledge, which holds a man responsible only when he knows what he is doing.

Yet we are surprised to learn that doctors smoke as much as lay people do, that people maintain unhealthy lifestyles, and that women continually become pregnant in spite of a flood of information about birth control. We all know from our own lives that knowing the right answer, even being convinced of it, in no way guarantees that we will live accordingly. A politician who vehemently defends monogamy as the foundation of society in Parliament does not necessarily insist on marital fidelity in his private life and is not immune to adultery or divorce.

The Bible teaches that human sin affects not only our thoughts but also our whole being, and that above all, our wills, which are opposed to God, lead us to act and think falsely, so that more thought and consideration are in themselves insufficient. We must clear up our old, sin-encumbered past. Christians believe that God Himself died in man's place when Christ died on the cross for our lack of love and our egotism. When we acknowledge that we cannot save ourselves by our own strength and our own reason, but rely on Christ's fulfilment of our penalty, we can overcome our evil will by faith in Jesus and renew our will and our mind according to God's will (Romans 1:20–25; 12:1–3). True renewal occurs when the power of God works in our inner selves, not through educational campaigns, but by God's love and forgiveness.

Human Rights Precede the State

Human dignity and human rights are part of man's being as God's creation. Thus, the state does not create human rights, it merely formulates and protects them. Since the right to life belongs to the very essence of the human being, man does not receive this right from the government, and no government has the right to decide that its citizens have no more right to live or that they can be executed at the ruler's whim. Nor does the state confer the right to have a family, for the state does not own the family; it merely acknowledges the duty implied in the order of creation to protect marriage and the family.

There are, therefore, rights which existed prior to the state, and there are rights above the state, rights derived both from human nature and from the various types of human society. The government must respect these rights and accept the limitations implied by these natural, divinely given rights of the individual, the family, the employee (or the employer!) and other human social groups.

Since human rights are rooted in a moral code prescribed to the state, this code equally forbids a false appeal to human rights, because it also defends the human dignity of others. No one has the right to express his own personality through murder or arson, for example.

Human rights assume a state with limited powers and a law valid for all mankind, a law that limits the powers of government. Were this not so, man would indeed receive his rights from the state. The individual would then have only the rights and the claims to protection that his government assured. This is the socialist view, which leaves no place for criticism or correction of a state that has declared itself to be God.

The Meaning of Romans 13

The most important scripture about the role of the state is Romans 13, written by the apostle Paul, who brought Christianity to Europe and Asia in the first century AD:

> *Let every soul be subject unto the higher powers. For there is no power but of God: the powers that be are ordained of God. Whosoever therefore resisteth the power, resisteth the ordinance of God: and they that resist shall receive to themselves damnation. For rulers are not a terror to good works, but to the evil. Wilt thou then not be afraid of the power? do that which is good, and thou shalt have praise of the same: For he is the minister of God to thee for good. But if thou do that which is evil, be afraid; for he beareth not the sword in vain: for he is the minister of God, a revenger to execute wrath upon him that doeth evil. Wherefore ye must needs be subject, not only for wrath, but also for conscience sake. For this cause pay ye tribute also: for they are God's ministers, attending continually upon this very thing. Render therefore to all their dues: tribute to whom tribute is due; custom to whom custom; fear to whom fear; honour to whom honour. (Romans 13:1–7)*

This text makes it clear that no one who opposes the state on principle can appeal to God's authorization. On the contrary: he is opposing God's law and is rightly liable to legal proceedings (Rom. 13:2). Since the state has the duty to stem and to punish evil, Christians must do good if they wish to avoid conflict. If a Christian does wrong, he is justly punished by the state. For the government, as God's minister, has the duty of vengeance (13:4). As a result, the Christian pays his taxes and gives government officials proper respect (13:6-7).

But the question is, who defines what is good or evil? Did Paul leave this up to the state? Can the state declare anything good and demand it from its citizens? No. When Paul spoke of goodness, he defined it according to God's will, and he defined evil as that which was condemned by God's law. "Righteousness exalteth a nation: but sin is a reproach to any people" (Prov 14:34).

The Bible thus gives us clear limitations and directions for taxes, military service and the police. John the Baptist, for example, told the tax inspectors and the police (at that time, a single body served both as police and as military), "Exact no more than that which is appointed you" and "Do violence to no man, neither accuse any falsely; and be content with your wages" (Luke 3:12-14).

From Paul's statements, we can derive two essential thoughts:

(1) *The government can judge only what people do, not what they think.* It is responsible for defining good or evil deeds, or controlling what people do. It is not the state's duty to control all sin, but only those sins whose activity can be observed and which damage public order, which the state has the responsibility to maintain and to protect.

(2) *The state may not distinguish between Christians and other people*, i.e. between believers of different faiths, as long as they pursue their beliefs in a peaceful manner. Since God forbids partiality in legal matters, Christians must be punished just as severely as unbelievers when they break the law. The state cannot distinguish between Christians and members of other religious groups, for it may judge only on the basis of deeds.

Human rights are protective; they serve not so much to define the privileges of the individual as to limit the powers of the state and of other institutions that deal with the lives of individuals. For this reason, Paul limits the state's duties to specific aspects of life, rather than giving it the right to regulate and control all of man's thought and life.

The state is not to be identified with society, as socialist governments have done ever since the French Revolution. In such states, all aspects of society including the family and the church are subject to the government. Society is more than the state. The state does not have authority over all parts of society.

On the Separation of Church and State

Just as the state may not dominate a church or a religion, it may not itself be subject to any church or religion. The separation of church and state does not contradict the Christian faith but arises naturally out of it, for the Bible makes it the state's duty to enable people to live in peace, whatever they believe. It is the responsibility of the church and of religion to point to eternity, to provide moral stability and to encourage man's relationship to God.

The historian Eugen Ewig therefore speaks of the Old Testament doctrine of two powers. Eduard Eichmann, also an historian, wrote with regard to the Old Testament division of powers between priest and king, "Along with the sacred Scripture, Old Testament views have become common property of the Christian West."

Jesus confirmed this separation in the words, "Render to Caesar the things that are Caesar's, and to God the things that are God's" (Mark 12:17). Because this rule comes from God, who is above the emperor, the religious institutions of God on earth, or the organized people of God, are not above the emperor. The first priority is obedience to God, who determines and limits what belongs to Caesar. Caesar has no authority to determine or limit what belongs to God. This does not, however, mean that the ruler is dependent on the church, for God has given the ruler responsibility for all the people in his realm, not only for the members of one religious group.

The separation of church and state does not mean that their duties never overlap, or that neither institution needs the other. On the contrary, the church may advise the government and teach it God's law, as Jehoiada taught Jehoash. "And Jehoash did that which was right in the sight of the Lord all his days wherein Jehoiada the priest instructed him" (2 Kings 12:2). It is sad that the modern church has given up this critical office and prefers to howl with the pack.

The separation of church and state does not become a war against Christianity until the state forgets its obligation to God's law and begins to persecute the faith.

The Biblical Basis for Religious Freedom
Dr Godfrey Yogarajah

Religious freedom

Article 1 of the Universal Declaration of Human Rights (UDHR) states, "All human beings are born free and equal in dignity and rights." The UDHR recognizes that human beings are endowed with reason and conscience and that they should act towards one another in a spirit of brotherhood.

Article 18 of the UDHR states, "Everyone has the right to freedom of thought, conscience and religion; this right includes freedom to change his religion or belief, and freedom, either alone or in community with others and in public or private, to manifest his religion or belief in teaching, practice, worship and observance." Thomas Jefferson, commenting on the right to religious freedom, famously stated that it is "the most inalienable and sacred of all human rights."

Creator God

As seen clearly in Scripture, religious freedom is rooted in human dignity and freedom. We see this demonstrated in the character of God and also in the creation of man in the image of God (Gen 1:26–27). Therefore, since every human being is created in the image of God, he possesses inalienable and innate dignity, worth and respect that no one can rightly take away on any pretext. This is echoed beautifully in Psalms 8:4–8: "What is mankind that you are mindful of them, human beings that you care for them? You have made them a little lower than the angels and crowned them with glory and honour. You made them rulers over the works of your hands; you put everything under their feet: all flocks and herds, and the animals of the wild, the birds in the sky," and the fish in the sea, all that swim the paths of the seas.

This foundation and irreversibility of human rights and dignity are an inherent part of humanity. Human rights cannot be taken away or be manipulated by anyone—neither individuals nor the state. These rights are rendered to all persons simply because they are human beings. As such, these rights cannot be given nor taken by any actor. Rather, they are to be enjoyed by all human beings.

Where religious freedom is restricted, there is a dehumanization of human dignity and a distortion of the image of God in man. However, more severely, it represents an insult to the Creator and an assault on his creation that pronounces human beings as both free and equal. Moreover, human beings were created with free will and equipped with the freedom to choose. Therefore, it is also possible to trace religious freedom to the biblical principle that man was created with a free will.

The fall
Events in the garden of Eden, in Genesis 2, further demonstrate the Creator's willingness to allow humankind the freedom to choose. In Genesis 2:16–17, Adam and Eve were granted the choice to eat from any tree except the tree of the knowledge of good and evil. We see here that humanity was allowed the choice to either follow their Creator or not follow him. Similarly, Cain killed his brother Abel because of a religious act and was condemned by God. Similarly, today, in the name of religion, people all across the globe are being killed, tortured and imprisoned for what they choose to believe.

Salvation
In God's plan of salvation—beginning with Noah's invitation to the society of his time to be saved from judgment and continuing through God's sending his only son to redeem mankind in the New Testament—we see a marked absence of compulsion in God's redemptive work. Although God actively seeks to draw men and women back to himself, there is no violation of humanity's freedom to choose between God and their sinful nature.

Similarly, Jesus also extended freedom of religion to those with whom he came in contact. In Matthew 19:16–23, after a brief conversation with Jesus, a rich young ruler chooses to walk away from following Christ—and Christ lets him go. Jesus does not compel belief or obedience. Likewise, we see that faith is commanded in Scripture but never coerced.

The Church

Scripture also makes it clear that God's freedom of choice rests not only with individuals but with his bride, the church, as well. In Revelation 3:14–22, Jesus rebukes the church in Laodicea for its spiritual failings. In verse 16, he declares this church's people to be lukewarm. However Jesus does not compel them to change. Rather, he gives them an opportunity to repent: "Behold, I stand at the door and knock; if anyone hears my voice and opens the door, then I will come in" (Rev 3:20). We see them choosing either to accept or to reject him, a choice that decides their own fate.

Justice

Justice as an attribute of God is a strong theme in the Old Testament. Deuteronomy 10:18 states, "He defends the cause of the fatherless and the widow and loves the foreigner residing among you, giving them food and clothing." In Jeremiah 7:6, God cautions the Israelites "not to oppress the foreigner, the fatherless or the widow, not to shed innocent blood in this place, and not to follow other gods to their own harm." The alien and the foreigner represent a different way of life and faith to the Jews. However, God cautions the Israelites not to oppress them nor shed innocent blood, but to respect them and their differences and to care for them. Scripture goes beyond the principles of justice and freedom, equality and charity.

Love

In Jesus Christ we see the dearest words and deeds of love. In Matthew 22:39, Jesus is asked by an expert in the law, "Which is the greatest commandment in the Law?" Jesus replies, "Love the Lord your God with all your heart and with all your soul and with all your mind" and, notably, "Love your neighbour as yourself."

In Matthew 7:13 and Luke 6:31, Jesus echoes the law of Moses and the teaching of the prophets when he states, "Do unto others as you would have them do unto you." An extension of this Golden Rule therefore, to the realm of religious freedom would mean that, if we desire that our freedom of religion be respected and treated with respect, worth and dignity, we should in turn extend the same courtesy to others. In his life and ministry, Jesus demonstrated this important virtue of love for humanity in both word and deed, to the point of death, even death on a cross. God through Christ sacrificed himself for all humanity, granting everyone equal access to salvation.

Jesus Christ reveals that the essence of the Old Testament law is the commandment, "Love the Lord your God with all your heart and with all your soul and with all your mind." This is the first and greatest commandment. The second is "Love your neighbour as yourself." These two commandments sum up the relational core of Christianity. In Matthew 5:44, Jesus commands his disciples, "Love your enemies and pray for those who persecute you." As such, we see that the principle of love is to be extended even to those who are hostile and set on causing you harm. This commandment also includes the well-known principle of "do no harm". Therefore, the biblical answer to any possible victimization is love.

The Bible is also rich in its emphasis on the divine purpose of human well-being. Three words, in particular, seem to summarize its teachings: dignity, equality and responsibility.

John Stott puts it beautifully:

> *Here then is a Christian perspective on human rights. First we affirm human dignity: because human beings are created in God's image to know him, to serve one another and be stewards of the earth, therefore they must be respected. Secondly, we affirm human equality because human beings have all been made in the same image by the same creator, therefore we must not be obsequious to some and scornful to others, but behave without partiality to all. Thirdly, we affirm human responsibility because God has laid it upon us to love and serve our neighbours; therefore we*

must fight for their rights, while being ready to renounce our own in order to do so.

Responsibility, therefore, is at the heart of religious liberty and freedom. A Christian, hence, is free to take greater interest in his or her duty to protect the dignity and liberty of others than in his or her own rights.

Religious freedom as the first freedom

Religious freedom is believed to be the most important of all other freedoms. In fact, religious freedom is considered to be the cornerstone of human rights; the foundation on which all rights hinge. Based on this understanding, the Americans refer to religious freedom as the *first freedom*. However, since it is the cornerstone of all other rights, the violation of religious freedom also results in the violation of other freedoms such as the freedom of thought, freedom of conscience, freedom of speech and the freedom of association.

Conclusion

A universal principle of utmost value, religious freedom lies at the heart of a just and free society. Moreover, religious freedom is the source and synthesis of all human rights. This truth has also been embodied in many Christian statements by different ecumenical bodies.

The declaration on religious freedom issued by the Vatican, *Dignitatis Humanae*, argues, "The right to religious freedom is based on the very dignity of the human person ... not in the subjective disposition of the individual but in his very nature."

Church father Tertullian in the second century stated, "It is a human law and a natural right that one should worship whatever he intends, the religious practice of one person neither harms nor helps another. It is no part of religion to coerce religious practice, for it is by free choice, not coercion, that we should be led to religion."

In the 2010 *Cape Town Commitment*, evangelical Christians of the Lausanne movement declared, "Let us strive for the good of religious freedom for all people. This requires advocacy before governments on behalf of Christians and people of other faith who are persecuted."

The World Council of Churches, in its Commission of the Churches on International Affairs study's report *Freedom of Religion and the Rights of Religious Minorities*, states, "Where the right to religious freedom is denied, human development is also impaired. The church promoting and defending religious freedom is an important part of its values and ethos of upholding human dignity and the human rights of every individual."

Comments from the Floor

Joseph Bagoberi, Catholic bishop from northern Nigeria: I am representing the president of the Christian Association of Nigeria, Pastor Ayo Oritsejafo. The Christian Association of Nigeria is a conglomerate of the five basic expressions of Christianity in the country, and we come together to form one single strong voice in projecting the interest of Christianity at the national level.

I have listened to the address by His Beatitude today, and then the two other addresses on human rights and religious liberty. I think that these presentations have brought us to a very critical moment of this conference, in looking at our response collectively as the church to the kind of dangers, sufferings and persecutions that the church is encountering. In these three keynote addresses and in the sessions and panel discussions yesterday, I have seen one cross-cutting trend. Yes, the picture that has been painted is very grimy with regard to the type of sufferings that the church is going through worldwide today, particularly in the Middle East, Africa, Asia and a few other places. The response I have heard all through yesterday is that we shall be prayerful. The question I want to ask is this: in the light of all that we have been hearing, what I am hearing is that the Christian response to this evil of persecution is one of acquiescence—submission, tolerating, accepting suffering and making ourselves heroes in the face of suffering. I have been hearing that we should pray fervently, look for ways of dialogue and forgive. In this way, we are eulogizing our suffering. I want to plead with this Forum that we should not adopt a reductionist approach to this evil. Let us look at the entire content of the gospel, and how it is telling us to respond. All I am hearing is a reductionist view, and I think nobody has said anything about the place of or the right to self-defence. This is what I expected in the paper on religious liberty, and that point has not come out very clearly. I want to see that this point comes out as part of the Christian response.

Tony Peck, Baptist World Alliance: I want to thank all the speakers today. I want to particularly ask the last two speakers about what happens when religious freedom and other human rights clash, which is happening increasingly in Europe when religious freedom clashes with other people's interpretation of the right to expression, or when certain groups who want justice for themselves and religious groups find themselves drawn in. It is just not as straightforward now to see religious freedom as the cornerstone of human rights in the world. I just want to know if they had any comments as to whether we need to redefine what we mean by human rights, and what happens if we have this clash with religious freedom.

Hermen Shastri, Council of Churches of Malaysia: I want to thank the speakers for the points they have made. But I wanted to raise a point with regard to the use of the term sin. I think we must also acknowledge that the Bible has been used to persecute others. In fact, this dynamic appears within the Bible, where the people of God, the covenant people of God, have failed in their duty and have persecuted others. And so I think there must also be a special reference to the hermeneutic of peacebuilding and of religious freedom, from the Christian perspective emanating from the Bible. I think that today when we just talk about religious freedom, we are always talking about our own religious freedom; we are always sometimes even accusing the other side. But we need to recognize that in the Bible there are also enough references to show that there must be respect for the place of others. And if we have that respect, it also puts upon us a certain responsibility as to how we relate to people of other faiths.

Olav Fykse Tveit, General Secretary, World Council of Churches: I want to thank the three excellent speakers we heard today, who are giving us a common platform on which we really can stand firmly, both as Christians and as citizens of each country and of the world, and which we can share also as a platform for our common actions. And in this sense I would like to refer to the voice from Nigeria, which I think is important in guiding our reflections on what is the relevant and the Christian response to the tribulations, the injustices, the conflicts we see. I will refer here to the last paragraphs of His Beatitude's reflections, hoping that this discussion leads us to new efforts for justice and peace, for reconciliation, for peacebuilding, bringing us beyond this situation of conflicts that are also now becoming more and more religiously driven. I think when we begin to discuss the proposed consultation message, it is very important that we also reflect a lot on what we have heard today.

Ahaman Egizbaev, General Secretary, Evangelical Alliance of Kazakhstan: We are doing good work here; thank you for these presentations. My question is how to make it heard by world leaders who are in the majority in different countries. The question is whether these leaders will protect the rights and freedoms of minorities in their countries—whether government leaders will hear the voice of the churches.

Kristin Molander, Ecumenical Officer of the Church of Sweden: I also thank you very much for interesting and good speeches. I just need to add the perspective of the 50% of the population who are women, with regard to the interpretation of following Christ and religious freedom from a female perspective. I would also stress the fact that there are women fleeing right now, giving birth to children as martyrs, giving life and dying. We have heard quite a bit of this kind of martyrdom these days.

Augustino Aguilera, President of the Evangelical Alliance of Bolivia: I have two brief questions. First, new statements on human rights are introducing a new concept of rights, based not only on the human condition but also on human preferences, such as sexual and reproductive rights. How do we as churches take on the defence of human rights in the midst of this new situation? Second, for many years we in Latin America have had to deal with the privileged position of the Catholic Church, which has often resulted in persecution and discrimination toward evangelical churches. That makes it somewhat difficult for us to work together now. What would be the position or the recommendation of this Forum moving forward?

Riad Jarjour (Syria), General Secretary of the Arab Group for Muslim-Christian Dialogue: I was so pleased with the three excellent presentations this morning. I felt so bad yesterday hearing the religious persecution stories. This morning my village was attacked again, for the third time, and people have to defend themselves so that they can stay alive. What I have been hearing that we have to accept what we have. Where can we find a way to protect our rights, the human rights that we have been hearing about today? How can we enable our people to have and to keep these rights, to stay alive as God has given them their dignity? It is not important simply that we fight Daesh or ISIS; it is important that we eradicate the mentality of Daesh and enable peacebuilding. What are the practical steps today to preserve our rights, our dignity and our equality? That is what I have not heard up to now in this conference.

Ali Kalkandelen, Alliance of Evangelical Churches in Turkey: I just want to know a couple things about human rights, freedom of religion, the supremacy of Christ and evangelization. How do we approach together the supremacy of Jesus Christ, Jesus Christ being the only way and the message that we need to take to the world, and then share the good news of Jesus Christ while relating it to what we believe about human rights and freedom of religion?

Responses from the Speakers

Thomas Schirrmacher: Let me just speak on behalf of the World Evangelical Alliance. The WEA has a clear policy to defend the religious freedom of all, of all religions, and we do it. I know the same from the Catholic Church. Point number two is to repent. We will have this in the consultation message, so when the message comes up in a few minutes, you will find the paragraph that we have persecuted ourselves and others. Number three, regarding whether we suffer or defend ourselves, let us not get into the trap of either-or. Paul was stoned and did not do anything; in the next city, they wanted to torture him and he said, "I am a Roman citizen. I want to go to court." In the same Paul, you find situations where he was willing to suffer and others in which he went to court to protect himself. Both belong together. The WEA with the Religious Liberty Commission has a network, Advocates International, of more than one thousand lawyers who are willing to step in for anybody in such a situation. That is one side. The other is that we have people who do not want to be defended, and then we have to respect this fully, believing that the Holy Spirit has directed them on this way. Both belong together. Just to give you an example, we just had a meeting of more than 150 parliamentarians from all over the world who are defending religious freedom and Christians. We are trying to get members of Parliament to build a network worldwide to defend this principle. So a lot is going on in this regard. We are totally in line with the concern that we need both approaches. We just visited the Prime Minister of Nepal to convince him that religious freedom is necessary. Nigeria is very much on our agenda; we are talking to Muslim leaders to convince them to help in stopping all that is going on.

Godfrey Yogarajah: As far as religious freedom is concerned, our principle is religious freedom for all, not only for Christians. In my own country, where I work, we have been fighting for religious freedom not only for Christians but for the Muslim community as well, because the Muslim community also faces discrimination. We work very closely together with the secretariat for Muslims, even training them in how to document, how to do advocacy and how to lobby in the government. So we believe, and I think I mentioned that in my presentation, that religious freedom is for all, not only for Christians.

Archbishop Anastasios: Everybody in every country usually wants religious freedom, and all countries are very optimistic in claiming that they have religious freedom. This is another item about which we must be very careful. For instance, in countries like Saudi Arabia they say that they have religious freedom, and in Turkey they say that they have religious freedom, but there is a lot of discrimination in all these countries. We must be careful to see in a more discerning way what is the actual implementation of these rights.

In the last part of my presentation I insisted on solidarity, on the fact that our conference motto is about following Christ together. I cannot resist here by myself; I need others nearby to raise their voices as well. We Christians now live in a globalized neighbourhood and we must see our responsibility not to be silent when we can speak, or when we can vote for our rulers. We also have the potential to help others. Different people in different situations at the same time may choose either to accept the situation or to try to defend themselves. Where people want to defend themselves, we must defend them in solidarity in a more concrete and organized way.

I have another fear too. In the previous century, we had this organized proletariat on the basis of atheistic theory. Today, in the twenty-first century, we have another great danger that a proletariat could use an atomic bomb over religion. This is for me the most dangerous threat. When there is injustice, then of course we have the creation of these types of groups, and then the responsibility of Christians to ensure justice and development becomes extremely important.

(The moderator asked for a comment on Augustino Aguilera's concern about Catholic persecution of evangelicals in Latin America.)

Thomas Schirrmacher: It really has to do with the DNA of our conference. Please distinguish between history—what has been the case previously—and the present. The Pope officially has apologized for a lot of those things. I know my Catholic friends very well. If there are instances of persecution today, if you can document that this is being done by a local priest, our experience has always been that the Catholic leadership will help us to sort this out. So if you are talking about history, that is one thing; if you are talking about present situations, all I know is that the Catholic Church means it when they say that they don't want to use those methods; give us the evidence and we will talk about it and sort it out. But don't just let it out in public, because that goes against the fabric of our conference. We have a clear statement from the Catholic Church that they don't want what has happened in history to ever happen again, and from all we know, they are working diligently to make this true. The Pope just told Monaco that the Catholic Church no longer wants to be the state religion of Monaco.

That is funny because in Monaco there are only Catholics, yet they say that in principle they don't want it in the Constitution that you have to be a Catholic to live in the country. They really mean it, so let's work on this together.

Left to right:
Ms Zahra Vieneuve
and Most Rev
Joseph Bagobiri.

Session Six –
Voices from Churches in Solidarity

Moderator:

Dr Teresa Francesca Rossi, Associate Director, Centro Pro Unione, Rome

Reflections and Research on Language Use:

Dr Christof Sauer, World Evangelical Alliance

Panel Members:

Rev Fr Duarte Da Cunha (Catholic, Portugal)

Bishop Ivan Abrahams (Methodist, South Africa)

Bishop Isaac Barakat (Orthodox, Syria/Germany)

Rev Tony Peck (Baptist, United Kingdom)

Reflections and Research on Language Use

Dr Christof Sauer, Co-Director of the International Institute for Religious Freedom, World Evangelical Alliance

The issue

Christians of various traditions and different theological persuasions use diverging language when interpreting the realities we are discussing at this consultation. We might use the same terms, but at times we fill them with different meanings. Or we use different terms and often don't consider the terms used by others to be as helpful. Some of us use a highly differentiating or soft-spoken language. The concern in doing so is to avoid engendering further hostilities or harming inter-religious dialogue or cooperation. Such language routinely is met with accusations: "You are downplaying the intensity and the scope of the tragedy!" Others use very straightforward terms. They in turn face a different set of accusations: "You are exaggerating, you do not differentiate enough, your language is too emotionally loaded!"

These are just some typical examples. This means we have a problem. There is a lack of understanding of the language used by others. There are disagreements about what language is appropriate. This contributes to the lack of unity among Christians in their response to persecution.

The planning group for this consultation discovered this challenge early on. Therefore, reflections on language use are on our agenda today. The planning group has commissioned the International Institute for Religious Freedom to undertake a research project on such language use.

The research

What do we want to achieve through these reflections and this research? We want to learn from the churches that are directly affected how they speak about these things. And we want to better understand what language the various GCF member bodies use in their responses to discrimination, persecution or martyrdom elsewhere. This includes churches and their affiliated agencies or para-church organizations.

Therefore, this project is documenting the different concepts and terms used regarding discrimination, persecution and martyrdom in various contexts.

The anticipated outcome of this research project is a comparative glossary, initially mainly in English. It will describe the main concepts and terms related to the realities of discrimination, persecution and martyrdom. It will include terms and concepts that churches and agencies consider very helpful, helpful, less helpful and unhelpful. The glossary will show how these terms are differently understood as well as why, and in which contexts they are used or avoided. It will include comments on advantages and disadvantages of the various terms as perceived by the different groups.

The method chosen to achieve this outcome, is a survey questionnaire. You have received this prior to the consultation, and a copy was handed out to you today.

This survey form consists of three parts. First, it requests your assessment of 12 commonly used terms; second, it asks for further terms and your assessment of these; and third, it requests policies and guidelines on language use or statements that can be analysed for the terminology used. If you think that this is a useful project, you are invited to complete the questionnaire today.

Sample results: persecution

To take one example from the feedback received so far from this survey, let us focus on the term *persecution*. This term is viewed positively by the majority, whereas other terms such as *the persecuted church* or *persecuted countries* are considered unhelpful to varying degrees. We have to distinguish different layers in the use of the term.

Persecution in general means pursuing someone with hostile intent and causing some degree of harm. This could also apply to political persecution. More specifically, there is religious persecution, in which a major characterizing factor needs to be either the religious identity of those being persecuted or the religious convictions of the persecutors. Religious persecution of Christians, then, is a subset of the overall phenomenon, one in which the identity of Christians is the major defining factor.

But even when we distinguish those layers, the term persecution is used in different ways in Christian circles. Some use it very broadly as a generic term covering a broad spectrum of hostility and harm, including harassment, discrimination and violence. One example is the definition used by the World Watch List, where persecution is understood as "any hostility experienced as a result of one's identification with Christ. This can include hostile attitudes, words and actions towards Christians."

There are calls for caution when using the term in this way: "Unless used in an intentionally generic 'all-encompassing' sense, the term 'persecution' is so wide as to usually require some other qualifying statement to indicate the nature or intensity of the maltreatment."

Others use the term persecution more narrowly, in terms of certain defining factors, such as the following or any combination of them:

- The degree of harm caused—namely, only for violence to persons or property, or even only cases of death;
- The order of magnitude—namely, only when it equals that in certain past epochs, mostly in early church history, that are considered normative;
- The frequency—namely, only for systematic persecution;
- Certain perpetrators—namely, only for governments and their associated entities;
- Regarding its victims—namely, groups only and not individuals.

The danger here is a reductionist use of the term, so that it refers to less than what it does actually cover. The term *Christian persecution* is often used colloquially by some native English speakers, while non-native speakers of English and academics object that it does not specify whether this means that Christians are persecuting others or being persecuted. They therefore encourage speaking more precisely of "persecution of Christians" instead.

This is just one example. Looking at the results of the survey so far, it is surprising how little terminology is regarded as very helpful. One prominent feature in the comments is the need for clarification or definition of terms.

Four calls to action

(1) Please do complete the questionnaire today on paper if you have not done so yet and deposit it at the table designated for that purpose. Alternatively, you can complete it electronically. The links to the questionnaire in English, French and Spanish are found at the beginning of the paper questionnaire that you received today. (Please note that this is a different project from the Voices and Data Research Project about which we heard yesterday.)

(2) Discuss language use in your discussion group, using the key terms provided in the questionnaire.

(3) Please also reflect on what further outcomes you expect from this research about language use.

- Should this project continue after the consultation? If so, a mandate would be needed.
- Would you consider it helpful to receive a glossary on the different terms in use?
- And do you think that we need a best practice statement on language use?

(4) If you want to engage more deeply with the topic or have questions, you are invited to a side meeting tonight at the hotel.

Above: *Pantocrator mosaic, dome of the Resurrection of Christ Orthodox Cathedral, Tirana, Albania (Photo: Kim Cain).*

Below: *Cardinal Kurt Koch, President of the Pontifical Council for Promoting Christian Unity (Photo: Eero Antturi).*

Left: *Bishop Efraim Tendero, Secretary General, World Evangelical Alliance (Photo: Eero Antturi).*

Below: *Rev Dr Olav Fykse Tveit, General Secretary, World Council of Churches (Photo: Eero Antturi).*

Left: Rev Dr David Wells, Vice Chairman, Pentecostal World Fellowship (Photo: Eero Antturi).

Right: H.B. Archbishop Anastasios, Orthodox Autocephalous Church of Albania (Photo: Eero Antturi).

Above: Rev Akil Pano, Evangelical Alliance of Albania (Photo: Eero Antturi).

Below: Bishop George Frendo, o.p., Catholic Archdiocese of Tiranë-Durrës (Photo: Peter Kenny).

Left: Prof Dr Andrea Riccardi, Community of Sant'Egidio, delivers the keynote speech (Photo: Eero Antturi).

Below: The consultation took on a spirit of confession and regret as well as concern and hope. Here, a moment of confession during the opening service of morning prayers (Photo: Eero Antturi).

Above: *Huibert van Beek, former GCF Secretary, co-editor of this publication (Photo: Kim Cain).*
Below: *Mrs Connie Kivuti, General Secretary, Evangelical Alliance of Kenya (Photo: Peter Kenny).*

Above: *Planning meeting with Albanian church leaders, Tirana, March 2015: Larry Miller, GCF Secretary (foreground from behind), then Archbishop Anastasios (Orthodox Autocephalous Church of Albania), Bishop George Frendo (Catholic Church, Tirana), Bishop Andon Merdani (Orthodox Autocephalous Church of Albania), and Rev Akil Panko (Evangelical Alliance Albania) (Photo: Kim Cain).*

Below: *World Evangelical Alliance members working together at the planning consultation in March 2015. Prof Dr Thomas Schirrmacher (left) and Prof Dr Christof Sauer (Photo: Kim Cain).*

Above: Centre: Archpriest Mikhail Goundiaev (Moscow Patriarchate – Russian Orthodox Church) was instrumental in suggesting the topic as a common challenge for churches, and the theme for the consultation. Left, Rev Fr Dmitry Safonov (Moscow Patriarchate – Russian Orthodox Church) (Photo: Kim Cain).

Below: A panel session during the consultation: one of eight panel and plenary sessions in three days (Photo: Eero Antturi).

Left: *Prof Dr Teresa Francesca Rossi, Associate Director, Centro Pro Unione, Italy (Photo: Eero Antturi).*

Below: *Left to right: Rev Karna Bahadur Tamang (National Churches Fellowship of Nepal), Rev Nicta Lubaale (Organisation of African Instituted Churches, Uganda), and Bishop Ivan Abrahams (World Methodist Council, South Africa) (Photo: Peter Kenny).*

Above: *Left to right: Rev Margareta Carlenius (Church of Sweden) and Rev Kristin Molander (Church of Sweden), during worship (Photo: Peter Kenny).*

Below: *Left to right: Rev Dr Olav Fykse Tveit (Gen Sec, WCC) and Bishop Efraim Tendero (Sec Gen, WEA) taking notes during panel session (Photo: Peter Kenny).*

Above: Ms Joy Lee, GCF Event Coordinator, was instrumental in the consultation's careful planning and smooth flow (Photo: Kim Cain).

Left: Rev Nordine Benzid, General Secretary, Association of Protestant Churches of Algeria (Photo: Eero Antturi).

Above: *A Communist era mural dominates the entrance of the National Museum, Tirana. The museum includes a section dedicated to those of all faiths who were persecuted during the time of Albania's aggressive atheistic policies. The Albanian experience of religious oppression was an important backdrop for the global consultation (Photo: Kim Cain).*

Below: *Morning prayers at St. Paul's Catholic Cathedral, Tirana (Photo: Peter Kenny).*

Above: Archbishop Stanislav Hočevar, Pontifical Council for Promoting Christian Unity, Solvenia (Photo: Peter Kenny).

Left: Ms Yamini Ravindran, National Christian Evangelical Alliance of Sri Lanka (Photo: Eero Antturi).

Above: *Archbishop Basilos Georges Casmoussa, Syrian Catholic Patriarchate, Iraq (Photo: Eero Antturi).*

Below: *H.E. Metr Prof Dr Gennadios of Sassima, Ecumenical Patriarchate; Vice-moderator of the World Council of Churches Central Committee, Turkey (Photo: Peter Kenny).*

Above: *The consultation was a unique ecumenical experience for young people drawn from Evangelical, Orthodox and Catholic communities in Tirana, as volunteer stewards for the conference. Here, meeting gathering organisers (Photo: Kim Cain).*

Below: *Stewards in the unique GCF T-shirts; happy to meet and help (Photo: Eero Antturi).*

Above: *A lasting memory of a special global gathering: Archbishop Anastasios (left) and Larry Miller join in intercessions for the suffering church during the closing prayer service (Photo: Kim Cain).*

Below: *Resurrection of Christ Orthodox Cathedral, Tirana (and its connected Cultural Centre), provided an inspirational and safe place for the participants as they met, shared and prayed together (Photo: Kim Cain).*

Rev Fr Duarte Da Cunha, Secretary General, Council of European Bishops' Conferences

Dear friends, following Christ is not for us an option among several others. We don't follow Christ to implement any ideology or political system. We believe that Jesus Christ is God made man, who came and still comes to meet us. He calls us and gives us life in abundance. "Anyone who believes in the Son has eternal life" (John 3:36).

This awareness that in Christ we have a new life which we are called to share gives us courage to be, in this world, a sign of contradiction. We are full of gratitude for the loyalty of so many brothers who testify to the world and to us, in these difficult times, that faith unites us to Christ with a love stronger than death (cf. Song 8:6). We can thus understand the meaning of the words of the church fathers who said that the blood of martyrs is the seed of faith. They give their life with a love that is effective. Their lives are not wasted, they don't disappear, they bear fruit—some already visible, other fruit known only to God and that the world will see when God considers that it is the right time.

However, despite all the good that God can draw even from evil, we cannot watch what happens with indifference. In fact, the love that unites all children of God is such that we can even say that we are members of one body. Now when a member suffers, the whole body is in pain. It is necessary to treat or cure the wound and comfort those who suffer. A solidary church, in fact, is first of all a sensitive, moved, attentive and concerned church, which is strongly bound to those who suffer. But all this is true only when it is translated into action, when solidarity is expressed not only in a communion of feelings but also in terms of practical assistance. This love that unites us as brothers and sisters in our faith in Christ and that sends us to everyone all over the world is a love that brings joy to life, but it is also an uncomfortable love because it compels us to action.

Pope Francis has frequently warned us about the importance of not being indifferent, but he also continually challenges us to do something concrete. Political actions are needed, but also immediate actions of solidarity to protect people in danger, to help those who have lost everything and live in refugee camps and to welcome those who had to flee to protect their own family.

Churches in Europe try to be solidary, but they are not NGOs. The church is a family that is present everywhere. Her help is therefore not limited to what is done to welcome those knocking at our doors, or to the financial support given to support those who live in the hardest places of war or persecution. She is there and is here, and she is there in the same way as she is here; it is always the same family. This is also what makes Christians very realistic and aware. Meetings between pastors and Christians from different places, like this one we are having, enable all to become more attentive to what is going on. By getting to know each other better, we feel more bound to each other and are able to understand better what is happening. At the Synod of Catholic Bishops held in Rome in October, there were many delegates and bishops from countries where currently there is persecution. The time we spent with them allowed us to find out a lot about what is going on and what should be done.

It is true, however, that Christian communities are called to help in an efficient way, and that is why Christian organizations have been essential instruments of this solidarity. I especially want to mention all the Caritas offices where people, moved by faith, seek to be close to those who suffer the most or arrange ways to help those coming to Europe while fleeing persecution.

Even in Europe, these are not easy times for Christians. Maybe there is no violent and organized persecution, but being a Christian today in the Western world is often cause for discrimination, mockery and even intolerance. However, since religious freedom is considered a human right, governments and even the European Union tend not to be indifferent towards religious persecution. Hence we can observe this paradox: there are signs of intolerance against Christians in Europe, and some are trying to impose a sort of radical secularization, yet at the same time Europeans feel the need to protect people whose fundamental rights are violated.

In June 2013, the European Union issued some directives on religious freedom, in which it took up the commitment to promote and defend this right in its foreign policy. Authorities know that something has been done, but it does not seem that what has been done is sufficient. Often, what the EU does regarding the persecution of Christians shows the marks of a real fear of commitment. The European Union advocates for religious freedom, but rather in terms of individual rights, and it finds it difficult to recognize the role of religious communities, particularly Christians. Also, the Council of Europe has made an effort to join forces and lobby to ensure religious freedom, but all this will be almost ineffective if Europe as a whole does not assume an active commitment to peace and does not recognize the importance of religion in human life.

There is one thing that we need and ask for: names and stories. In times like ours, where crowds often appear as numbers, it is important to remember that the new martyrs are real people, with a face, a name and a story. For this reason, we must create and strengthen networks of Christians who will share the stories of those who are persecuted and called to a special witness. Faith, which is quite asleep in the Western world, wakes up when real people testify to their faith. It is a reciprocal movement. No one who has a helping attitude remains in a standing position, and no one who suffers is only in need of help—all of us have needs and all of us have something to offer.

Persecuted churches always ask us to keep alive in our communities a special place for them in our prayers. They know that their strength comes from God. And through prayer we feel better that we are in communion with each other. Through prayer we remember our brothers and are mindful that God does not abandon us. Through prayer we feel called to reach out to our brothers because God sends us, and even more so because God commands us to do something. Prayer is a force that changes the world, and this is why it is also a political event. Thanks to prayer, we feel humble and are aware of how little we can do, but we also feel strong because we remember that God is present as Saviour and that no suffering is wasted in the work of redemption. Praying and promoting moments of prayer have been crucial not only as we beg for peace from God, but also to help us keep in mind our brothers who suffer, as well as to make visible to the world that we are really concerned for and united to each other.

Let me make one last observation that seems to me essential in the context of this meeting. We need to be more united among ourselves and to recognize the importance of what Pope Francis calls the ecumenism of blood. The testimony of some helps the faith of others, but tensions among Christians weaken the credibility of our faith and have often been used to justify attacks on Christians. We do not always agree on everything, but on one thing we can and must agree: our faith in Jesus Christ teaches us that only love is effective, and that those who open their hearts to the Holy Spirit receive a new capacity to embrace all men and women who suffer.

Bishop Ivan Abrahams, General Secretary, World Methodist Council, USA/South Africa

I speak to you not just as a passive observer of injustice, discrimination and persecution but as one whose life has been shaped on the anvil of the South African liberation struggle. As you see, I have the blood of both the settler community and the indigenous people of my continent coursing through my veins, and in many ways this has helped me to be a bridge-builder, reconciler and peace-maker for the cause of Christ, not only in South Africa but also further afield. In the African worldview, there is no dualism or dichotomy between the secular and sacred. Jesus is Lord of all creation. I can honestly say that my involvement in the struggle for justice is all because of my understanding of anthropology, but even more importantly because of my understanding of Christology. Who is Jesus? He provides the metaphors, the cultural touch-stones and the prisms through which I view the world. And I believe passionately that only the crucified and risen Jesus can bring about true transformation and healing in our lives, in the church and in this world which God so loves.

Discrimination, persecution and martyrdom cannot be separated. They are defined in the same context of hate, jealousy, oppression and dominance. The voices that we have heard from the churches enduring persecution and suffering must be heard, and we urgently need to respond to our sisters and brothers. We cannot ignore their calls for solidarity and accompaniment.

We know that throughout history, individuals have experienced discrimination and prejudice on the grounds of political persuasion, economics, religion, race, colour, ethnicity, sexual orientation, health and background. We just need to look through the pages of Scripture to see how the Old Testament prophets were at pains to address the problems of foreigners, the poor, women and children. And yet why do people today still feel that they are aliens in the household of God? We are very slow to admit that churches sometimes discriminate against each other along denominational lines; some consider themselves superior and others inferior. Instead of celebrating our differences, we often engage in prejudice and discrimination and, in extreme cases, in persecution.

It is because of discrimination within the very womb of the church that liberation theologies—Latin American theology, Black theology in North America, African Theology, Asian theology, feminist Theology and womanist theology—were all born. I can lament this development in the South African context, as I have seen many of my friends who were priests and prophets in the South African struggle but who have now become politicians, muting the voice of the church.

The Bible is full of examples of persecution. We only have to look at Ahab who, influenced by the queen mother Jezebel, persecuted Yahweh's prophets (1 Kings 17–19 and 21). Amos, Jeremiah and other prophets were also persecuted. In the New Testament, we see John the Baptist beheaded for speaking the truth (Matt 14:3–12). Jesus himself suffered crucifixion on the cross.

We can go throughout church history, but I am not going to bore you with that. We know the persecution in the first century. We know of Polycarp's persecution. We have seen the forerunners of the Reformation, such as Jan Huss and others, being persecuted. Pope Francis argued in 2014 that more Christians are under siege for their faith today than during the time of the early church.

We have heard about the Christian persecution by Muslims, but I am not going to look at that.

I want to look very briefly at the internal persecution within the church, something that we are very reluctant to speak about.

According to Marshal, Gilbert and Shea in their seminal work *Persecuted: The Global Assault on Christianity* (2013), it is estimated that throughout Christian history, across all traditions of Christianity, and in every part of the world, some 70 million Christians have been murdered for their faith. They further argue that many Christians killed as alleged "heretics" or "schismatics" down through the ages should perhaps correctly be included in the demographic enumeration of martyrs. According to the Christian History Institute, Christians tortured and killed countless of their own during the Inquisitions of the twelfth through the fourteenth centuries. That phenomenon continued in the sixteenth and seventeenth centuries during the Reformation.

What does it mean to be in solidarity today with persecuted churches?

I think that the essence of the message that we have looked at earlier today is a good start. We will follow in the tradition of the Barmen Declaration and of the message to the people of South Africa in the 1960s when the church felt that it was under persecution. We will follow in the tradition of the World Council of Churches at its Eighth Assembly (1998), which wrote the pastoral letter entitled *From solidarity to accountability: Letter from the Decade Festival of the Churches in Solidarity with Women*.

I see echoes of the Barmen Declaration and the messages of the people of South Africa and of the WCC in what we have produced. We need to translate our declarations into action. I look forward to our discourse.

Bishop Isaac Barakat, Bishop for Germany and Central Europe, Greek Orthodox Patriarchate of Antioch

(Bishop Barakat spoke in Arabic, with translation by Dr Georges Tamer. In introducing Bishop Barakat, the moderator noted his experience of pastoral work with refugees both in Damascus and in Germany. Bishop Barakat distributed an outline of his message in advance, as reprinted below.)

(1) **Meaning From Christian point of view**
- Churches as Body of Christ;
- Redefining the values of religion;
- Muslim's blood equal to the Christian's.

(2) **Receiving**
- What do you expect us to receive?
- You can receive
  - Homeless and hopeless childhood;
  - Highly educated young people without any future;
  - New blood in old body;
  - Huge Eastern heritage carried by churches (social values) which is rare in this area.

(3) **Working**
- Rebuilding souls focusing on human beings as children of the holy God our Father;
- Encouraging our people to love the high mutual values which hallowed human beings;
- Spreading a spiritual level of culture instead of the dehumanizing of man (which means a globalization of love instead of a globalization of war).

I want to speak in Arabic because I want to share with you the voice of our church in Syria.

I want to clarify a point regarding the persecution of Christians in Syria. There is no relationship between the current war in Syria and the persecution of Christians. The war in Syria is an Islamic war, between Sunnites and Alawites/Shiites. It developed into an international war after the intervention of Russia and other countries. Christians are now paying the penalty for the wrong translation of a passage in a communique issued by the Russian Orthodox Church. The term was falsely translated as "holy war", which is not good for Christians.

Islam in Syria, in the Levant, is a moderate Islam. It is different from Islam as practised in other parts of the world—in particular, the form existing in Saudi Arabia and Turkey. This moderate Islam is one of the main targets of the war in Syria, which started about five years ago. We have seen, as Middle East Christians as well as Christians around the world, that our duty is to promote exchange and dialogue with this kind of moderate Islam in Syria. It is our duty to prevent this moderate Islam from evolving into jihadist Islam, which could happen through statements issued by consultations like this one.

I will now move on to addressing the questions sent to me.

What does it mean to stand as churches in solidarity with suffering and persecuted churches?

First, the church is the body of Christ, as we have heard in many presentations. We are therefore obliged to support each other, but the particularity of each church also has to be respected. Christians have to respect all values in their home countries as well as in the diaspora. We should remember that the blood of Muslims killed in the Middle East by Daesh is equal in value to the blood of Christians who are also victims of violence.

We practise love for our neighbour, the love of the person who is next to us, in such a way that charitable support is distributed to both Christians and Muslims—indeed, perhaps more to Muslims than to Christians.

What do we receive from suffering and persecuted churches?

Europe can benefit from highly educated young people moving to Europe. There will be new blood in an old body. But we need to consider the demographic changes that will also take place.

What are the next steps in walking together as the suffering church?

The most important thing to consider is to rebuild Syria, and especially to rebuild the souls destroyed by the war. We ask for equality so that our people can live in dignity.

Rev Tony Peck, General Secretary, European Baptist Federation, also representing the World Baptist Alliance

It is perhaps worthwhile for me to preface my remarks by saying that Baptists were born into religious persecution in seventeenth-century England. Indeed, the majority of Baptists around the world have known discrimination and/or persecution at some point in their history. But at the same time, again in the early seventeenth century, Baptists were the first in England to argue for religious freedom for all, not just themselves, and they included other faiths in that definition.

This is our heritage, and today along with other minority churches we still find ourselves persecuted and discriminated against in some places and in the region that I serve, especially in the Middle East and Central Asia. So we join you in seeking to stand in solidarity with our suffering brothers and sisters in Christ.

What does it mean to stand as churches in solidarity with suffering and persecuted churches?

There are times when all we can do is pray for situations that it would be difficult to visit physically. Examples for us today would include the churches of the so-called breakaway republics in eastern Ukraine and also in Crimea. There, Protestant groups and individuals such as Baptists have sometimes been violently attacked. This would also include the small congregations of Syria and parts of Iraq, and some indigenous churches in central Asia. For these churches to know that they are part of a fellowship of prayer that also raises awareness in our churches elsewhere is very important, and we believe in the power of such prayer.

But there is also the gift of presence, to go and be with people and listen and try to understand what is happening and what God may be saying in this situation. I think of a journey I made earlier this year to eastern Ukraine, almost as far as the disputed border, on which I met pastors and civic leaders from both sides of the border.

Then there is protest. A few years ago in Azerbaijan, we had two Baptist pastors of unregistered Baptist churches in prison. They were released because we visited the country to protest to the authorities and more significantly were also able to mobilize influential support from around the world.

Fourth, there is active partnership, or ways in which we can engender a sense that these individuals or groups of churches are not alone in what they are facing. They have behind them in our case the 100 million–strong community of the Baptist World Alliance. This is very important when dealing with government authorities in places where our churches are few and suffering repression.

What do we receive from suffering and persecuted churches?

In many of these churches, we see a fidelity to the gospel in the face of overwhelming pressure and persecution, a standing firm for the faith when it might be so easy to give up. We know from the era of Soviet communism that a quality of faith emerges from these situations that takes Christian discipleship and taking up the cross very seriously indeed, and we should learn from it and be inspired by it.

Also, a particular theology often emerges from situations of discrimination and persecution, a theology forged on the anvil of suffering. Baptists in Israel and Palestine are part of a Palestinian evangelical movement that, along with other churches, has positioned itself between the violence of Islamic terrorism and the state-sponsored violence inflicted on Palestinians by the government of Israel. In other words, a theology has emerged that embraces radical reconciliation and peace-making at its heart.

What are the next steps in walking together as the suffering church?

We should develop networking and good communication with other churches in solidarity, but also with NGOs and inter-governmental organizations such as OSCE [the Organization for Solidarity and

Co-operation in Europe] and the UN Human Rights Office. Our experience is that making progress and making a difference in situations of persecution and discrimination often require the contributions of several agencies.

Some situations of discrimination are a direct result of majority state churches influencing governments to discriminate against minority churches by law. We should find places and safe spaces to talk about this openly together as majority and minority churches.

In a similar vein, we should encourage churches in situations of conflict and diminishing numbers, such as in the Middle East, to come together and speak together in unity. Sadly, the tensions between the traditional churches and the evangelicals in the Middle East often prevents this, and our effectiveness as Christ's body in the region is much diminished as a result.

Then we need to listen to what the leaders of suffering churches are actually telling us. For example, there is a two-fold plea from our Baptist leaders under pressure in the Middle East. One is "Please support us to help us stay in the Middle East and don't make it easy for us to leave." And the other is "Please stop talking about the Christian community as a beleaguered minority. We want to see ourselves as part of the silent *majority*: people of all faiths—Christians, Muslims and Jews—who want to live together in peace in the Middle East."

A final comment: solidarity with the suffering and persecuted church throughout the world has at its heart the New Testament concept of *koinonia*—the deepest possible communion in Christ and with each other.

Rev Dr David Wells, General Superintendent, Pentecostal Assemblies of Canada, and member of the Pentecostal World Fellowship's Executive Committee

At this stage in a Pentecostal service, we would get people to dance and stand and sing a rousing chorus. Some of you need it! But I will honour the request and carry on. I want to speak primarily as a denominational leader from Canada. I am privileged to be General Superintendent of the Pentecostal Church in Canada. We are very involved with the Evangelical Fellowship, and in dialogue with the Canadian Council of Churches. November is a very special month for us, because we do specifically zero in nationally on calling our people to pray and to act relative to the persecuted church around the world. Not all of you may know that churches do take special times for a call to prayer and action specifically for suffering churches. I want you to be aware of what we are right in the middle of doing now.

We have titled the campaign this year, in cooperation with other groups, "For the silenced". Information about it can be found at #forthesilenced and at www.poc.org. We draw our materials from many partner ministries. I want to acknowledge this and speak positively, as a denominational leader, of those partner ministries that are actively engaged with the suffering and persecuted church. We draw from Voice of the Martyrs, Christian Freedom International, the International Day of Prayer in Canada for the Persecuted Church, International Christian Concern, Open Doors, and the World Evangelical Alliance. One challenge that we face is that not all their data match up, so we try to contribute to these discussions about terms and numbers.

A principal focus of the work is prayer. We call our people to pray and highlight the need. In our part of the world, we have sought to identify 50 nations of prime concern and then pray specifically for their context. If your nation is missing, I apologize, but it may mean that your country is not viewed as being under as much pressure as some other nations. Today is 3 November, so we are praying particularly for Syria and Myanmar. I invite you to pause for a moment to pray with the international church for Syria and Myanmar. *(Dr Wells paused to pray at this point.)*

The international day of prayer reserved by many churches across the world to remember the persecuted church is this coming Sunday, 8 November. All across Canada, Pakistan and India will be remembered in prayer on 8 November. There is this sense that no one is standing alone, but also of the supernatural ability of God to hear our prayers and to operate in ways that go above and beyond what humans can possibly achieve.

"For the silenced" also has a dimension related to it about action as well as prayer. We add to our prayers a strong response relative to education and awareness. You can find this on our blog. We have a very active blog, drawn from these multiple organizations and the stories they share.

We are highly aware that as we have responded in our own way to the needs in the Middle East, especially from Syria and Iraq and the frontiers with Turkey, Lebanon and Jordan and working directly with our partners on the ground there, we have a lack of awareness in our own circles. Sometimes I am horrified to discover through Facebook messages the attitudes of some of our own people relative to what they understand about that part of the world. I begin to see even hatred and attitudes that I find despicable. I am troubled by the lack of awareness of Canadian Christians relative to the historic Christian communities in these Middle Eastern nations. I repent of that to you, my friends, today. We need to learn and to listen. We all need to learn a lot more, and we all need to listen. Be assured that there are Christian leaders around the world saying that we need to get educated. We work hard on this, but it does break our hearts. I repent to my friends from those nations who may have suffered from our ignorance.

We are one of those groups who are directly responding. We provide immediate care on the ground, food and shelter on the borders of Turkey and Lebanon. We are involved in sponsorship. I hear the cry for Christians to remain within their nations, but others have already fled due to fear of death to Amman and other such places. And so we have worked with the Canadian immigration minister to make it as quick and convenient as possible for people to come to Canada. We are willing to receive first of all those of the household of faith, but we are also willing to receive other refugees, including Muslims, to receive the love of Christ through our churches. We remain very engaged in that kind of response. We have worked alongside our government's ambassador for religious freedoms, Andrew Bennett, a Ukrainian Catholic. He has proved to be a stellar man, raising his voice on behalf of those suffering from persecution and loss of liberty. He has worked with us on various issues. At times we do see our cooperation bringing fruit; at other times it does not appear to bring fruit. But we remain faithful in raising our voice for those who are in prison, wherever they may be. These comments are intended to give you a practical idea of how some of our churches and particularly our church in Canada attempt to be a voice for our church around the world.

Comments from the Floor

Rev Munir Kakish, chairman of the Council of Evangelical Churches in the Holy Land and a long-time pastor: I appreciate what we have heard today, as someone from a church suffering persecution and discrimination. I see people here from different groups: Orthodox, Catholic, Armenian, Evangelical. Our situation in the Middle East as Evangelicals is that we really face discrimination by traditional churches. Can there be help so that we are not persecuted by our Christian brothers? I wish there could be collaboration. ISIS doesn't make distinctions between denominations, but knows that if you are a Christian, you are "done".

Fr Andrzej Choromanski (from Poland, representing the Pontifical Council for Promoting Christian Unity): I would like to stress what the Holy Father says very often: that we are living at this time in a unity of suffering, unity of blood, unity of martyrdom. The persecutors don't ask if you are an Orthodox, Protestant, Evangelical, Pentecostal or Catholic. I have heard many speakers here and testimonies telling how churches are collaborating among themselves in the regions where there is persecution. The next panel will refer to the work of agencies, and I know these agencies work across church borders, fostering collaboration and growing unity through shared suffering. If there are examples of what you [i.e. the previous speaker, Rev Kakish] say, we need to know what you are referring to.

Response by Rev Kakish: In Palestine, Jordan and Israel, it is difficult for us to do things like issuing birth certificates. We are trying to have recognition for activities like issuing marriage certificates and registering church properties. We are opposed by the traditional churches—Orthodox, Catholic, Anglican and Lutheran—on such things when we approach the authorities in Jordan, Palestine or Israel.

Rev Kori Elramla Kuku, Sudan Council of Churches: I want to express appreciation for all the speakers. But the voice of Sudan must be heard, and an opportunity has not been provided to do so. It is important that the voice of Sudan is also heard. Will you give me some time now to speak? *(The moderator invited Rev Kori to speak for two minutes.)*

What is the current situation in Sudan, and how is the life of the churches there? When Sudan was united before the separation between Sudan and South Sudan, Christians were very strong and united and there was no problem. However, when in 2011 South Sudan separated, one week before the separation the President said that now that South Sudan is separating, Sudan was going to apply Sharia law 100 percent, there will be no toleration of any other religion, and only the Arabic language would be used. After the separation, there was great pressure on the churches. Many churches were destroyed on the pretext that they were located in a business area or one designated for investment. When we asked government ministers to give us plots for new churches, they refused, saying that there were enough left behind by the departing South Sudanese and we needed to use these, but that is not the case. Some churches were confiscated (such as the Sudan Interior Church and the Sudan Presbyterian Church) and many Christian-based English institutes were closed down. Church leaders have been called in many times by security agencies and questioned regarding their sources of finance, who are their overseas partners etc. They were even called in during worship on Sunday to present themselves to security and held there all day. Our partners and missionaries were expelled from Sudan, and visitors have not been given visas.

The churches are facing difficult situations. All this relates to Khartoum. In the Nuba Mountains where the majority of Christians live, there is war and the government is bombing civilians. People are suffering. There is no education, no good water there. People outside do not know what is going on in Sudan. The displaced people who come to live in Khartoum or in the northern cities find it difficult to cope; it is difficult to get jobs because they do not have education, and to get jobs you have to be a Muslim. Even in the schools, the presentation of Christianity not allowed. Please stand beside us and pray for us.

Bishop Opoko, Methodist Church, Nigeria: I am happy about what happened at this moment, because there is a practical solidarity in what we have shown to our brother from Sudan. By this simple action, we have encouraged him. He can return to his context and say that he has been heard. How long can we continue to listen to voices or watch videos, social media, CNN and major TV stations and see Christians beheaded and massacred, even pregnant women, in the name of religion, and we only speak about it but do not do anything about it? I hope that at our gathering here we will move beyond words; we must also put action into what we are doing. I am pleased that the Global Christian Forum wanted to come to Nigeria to see the situation for themselves. When persecution is coming from a state as in the case of Sudan or Eritrea, can there not be sanctions?

Morning prayers, Resurrection of Christ Orthodox Cathedral.

Session Seven –

Panel: Voices from Agencies in Solidarity

Moderator:

His Eminence Metropolitan Dr Gennadios of Sassima, Ecumenical Patriarchate of Constantinople

Panel members:

Dr Thomas Freiherr Heine-Geldern (Catholic, Austria)

Archbishop Michael Jackson (Anglican, Ireland)

Rev Thomas Kemper (Methodist, USA)

Dr Ronald Boyd-Macmillan (Evangelical, UK)

Ms Yamini Ravindran (Evangelical, Sri Lanka)

Rev Rauli Lehtonen (Pentecostal, Sweden)

Dr Thomas Freiherr Heine-Geldern, Aid to the Church in Need

With joy and respect, I am here to present to you the nature and the task of the Catholic organization Aid to the Church in Need. As our name indicates, we are especially founded to act in solidarity with the suffering churches all over the world.

We are now a papal foundation with our seat in Rome, chaired by Mauro Cardinal Piacenza and managed by our Executive President Johannes Freiherr von Heereman and his team with its headquarters in Königstein, Germany. We maintain offices in over 20 countries, where we mainly collect the resources to finance over 5,700 projects in over 145 countries.

The origin of our work goes back nearly 70 years to when Father Werenfried van Straten wrote his famous article, "No Room in the Shelter". There he described the misery of the refugees in Europe after World War II. He started an incredible program to help those people, namely millions of Germans being expelled from their homes in Central and Eastern Europe. You have to try to fully understand what that means: a Dutch priest collects gifts and donations in countries which were just liberated from the atrocities of the Nazi regime to help German refugees. This was really an act of Christian solidarity and reconciliation by which he overcame the existing atmosphere of hate and violence. He quickly managed to inspire thousands of people and to create the common understanding that our Christian foundation is the only hope for Europe's future.

The main mission of Aid to the Church in Need remains unchanged since its beginning and consists in helping suffering and persecuted Christians worldwide. Or, as Father Werenfried formulated it, "I have seen it as my mandate as a priest to restore love in the church and the world. This love clearly requires a personal engagement with the hungry, the naked and the prisoners as mentioned by our Lord Jesus when he describes the Last Judgment and where he himself is hidden. This love asks us to see Christ in the most humble persons, to console them and to exclude nobody, not even our enemies."

From the start, Aid to the Church in Need was built on three pillars: prayer, information and action. Therefore, we always declare that we have a large community of our benefactors, including all the people who benefit from our projects as they pray for each other.

We see it as our permanent duty to inform the public and decision makers in political, business and public life clearly and transparently about the situation of our suffering and persecuted brothers and sisters, especially when they are unable to defend themselves or to be heard. We see our scope of action as providing pastoral, spiritual and material support to Christian communities in need and giving financial and humanitarian help in life-threatening environments.

As I said in the beginning, we are a papal foundation and indeed several popes have given us effective help to develop our work. Pius XII focused us on the refugees in Europe, John XXIII gave us direction to go to Latin America and later to Africa and Asia, while John Paul II asked us to establish a sustainable relationship with the Russian Orthodox Church and to support the re-establishing of ecclesiastical structures after the fall of the wall in Eastern Europe. Benedict XVI called us to care for the persecuted Christians in the Middle East.

How can we ensure that we are financing the right projects, allocating the right resources to good initiatives, and ensure that the funds will land where they are needed most? Well, over the years we have accumulated the necessary and proper know-how to evaluate carefully every project application. Within our organization, we rely on professional project management and on country-specific experts. These experts know well the situation of our partners in the various countries, and they visit these countries and the bigger projects regularly. We can build our decision making on our own judgement as well as on the requests and support of the local bishops and the recommendations of the nuncio. The main criteria for our help are always the social and pastoral needs and the aspect of sustainability. To support bigger projects, we seek enhanced cooperation with other support organizations.

Allow me to describe some of our major projects that show how we fulfil our mission:

- The situation of persecuted Christians in north Iraq: after the conquest of Mosul and the Nineveh Plains, a lot of Christians wanted to leave the country as they considered that there would be no future for them and their children especially as no schooling was available for them. Aid to the Church in Need was able to provide eight prefabricated school buildings for a total of 15,000 children in the area of Erbil and Dohouk. I had the chance to attend the inauguration of the first school last December and was very impressed that the buildings are used in three shifts during the week and over the weekend for preparation classes for first communion, confirmation and marriage. I will always remember the joyful laughter of the children from local and displaced families. Additionally, we are providing massive humanitarian help to Syria and Iraq, where we have received urgent requests from the bishops, who also ensure fair distribution of the goods.

- The Bible Project: Some 36 years ago, we started to publish a Bible specially edited for children. Since then, we have distributed worldwide over 52 million copies in 178 languages. Keep in mind that this Bible will often remain the one and only book that these recipients will ever have. So by means of the gospel they are learning to write and to read.

- We have supported over 1,500 construction sites, mainly for churches and chapels. Nearly all of the many seminaries constructed in Eastern Europe and Africa have received assistance from Aid to the Church in Need.

- We have Farms of Hope, where drug addicts are given the chance to reorganize their lives through hard work and living according to the gospel.

- The famous "swimming churches" located on boats along the Volga and Don Rivers brought priests back to areas of

Russia after decades of absence. I visited Siberia last spring and was deeply impressed by the heroic engagement of Catholic priests and sisters operating—completely on their own—orphanages, schools and shelters, often in good cooperation with the Orthodox Church.

We fulfil our mandate to provide information in several ways:

- The *Mirror*, a newsletter published eight times a year for our friends and benefactors;
- Maintaining several websites regarding the situation of suffering and persecuted Christians;
- Publishing regularly our report on religious freedom;
- Maintaining a large archive of photos and videos;
- Running and supporting several TV and radio studios and stations;
- Maintaining an office in Brussels to permanently inform the different agencies and offices of the European Union.

All these activities require sustainable and generous funding. This is possible as over 600,000 benefactors in more than 20 countries are making regular donations to Aid to the Church in Need and contribute toward helping our brothers and sisters to survive as faithful Christians under difficult circumstances. The total volume of donations has exceeded 100 million euros per year and has grown consistently over recent years, despite—or maybe even due to—wars and crises. This evidence of dedication and love proves the saying of our founder: "Humans are much better than we are prepared to think."

Very often our benefactors who help to support people in need are poor themselves, and we have a vast collection of letters describing this fact in a very touching way. Here are a few excerpts:

- "I pray daily for your work; please accept $15 from a poor widow and pray for me. My leg has to be amputated and I will need a lot of strength for the rest of my way."

- "I am only 14 but I am sending you some money I earned by babysitting."

- A young man wrote, "Reading the *Mirror* opened my eyes to the needs of others. Instead of buying a new CD player, I am sending you the money for the education of poor priests and young Christians in need."

When you hear these messages, you can certainly understand that we see Aid to the Church in Need not merely as a fundraising and project management organization. Rather, Aid to the Church in Need is a community that unifies benefactors and suffering Christians through prayers, charity, mercy and material support. With the Lord's help, in the future we will remain true to our motto: "Ask not what we could do but what we have to do."

The Most Rev Michael Jackson, Archbishop, Church of Ireland

Thank you very much indeed for your welcome and your invitation. I'm here, I suppose, in a couple of capacities. At one stage, we had hoped that the new General Secretary of the Anglican Communion office, Archbishop Josiah Atkins Idowu-Fearon, who may be known to some of you, might be here. But unfortunately he is not able to be here. So I am in a sense representing the Anglican Communion office and also work that is done by one of its networks. We in the Anglican Communion tend to work in terms of networks, because our understanding of who we are as a church requires that we be in relationship with other churches and other ecclesial bodies and also in increasingly strong connection with people of other world faiths. We have, I think, 37 provinces across the world, and in every context Anglicans are a minority. So in a sense we start at the bottom of the pile, and that's a very useful place to start.

Some years back, the creation of NIFCON, the Network for Inter Faith Concerns, was requested by the bishops of the Anglican Communion meeting at Lambeth. Their anxiety was that they lived among people of world faiths other than Christianity. They also engaged with people who had different religious, theological and sociological presuppositions. And they wanted resources and solidarity in their engagement. So a number of us, including three who are here in this room, produced a book entitled *Generous Love*, which had to do with principles of inter-faith engagement from an Anglican perspective. It featured three pairs of components: presence and engagement, sending and abiding, and embassy and hospitality. The simplicity of these pairs is probably clear to see. To take presence and engagement, it's virtually impossible to engage if you are not present, and if you are present it's much better if you can try to engage. Sending and abiding brings us very much into the understanding of the church of God as it overlaps with and is inspired by the person of Jesus Christ, particularly through the gospel of John. And third, as for embassy and hospitality, people in their discipleship have God's authority to represent in a very strong way God's presence in their place, and very often hospitality is a way of opening up understanding and sustaining relationships. So that is the background to what we try to do and who we are.

At present, we are in the process of writing a theological resource entitled *Out of the Depths*. The resonance in the Psalms will be, I think, clear to everybody. It is a theological resource to facilitate solidarity and understanding across and between people who suffer and are persecuted for their faith.

One of the things that I think has come through very clearly from the first two days of this conference is the whole question of the need to underwrite religious freedom and also to recognize that at particular times—some of them sporadic, some of them sustained—Christians have been involved in active persecution. Therefore, in a very real sense, any engagement with this area requires both honesty and compassion, and a recognition, if I may use a phrase that is common in Northern Ireland where I come from, that if you want to be part of the solution, you have to admit that you are already part of the problem. That, I think, is one of the considerations that we have brought to bear on this situation.

I would like to share something of this work in progress. We'd also like to continue our engagement with this particular forum as we develop this work towards a meeting of the Anglican Consultative Council to be held in 2016.

Why did we initiate this work in 2015? One reason, in fact, was this conference. Another reason is the fiftieth anniversary of *Dignitatis Humanae*. And the third is the recognition of our solidarity with those who experienced and suffer from the Armenian genocide. Because, yet again, if I go back to my expression of what the Anglican Communion is, it is a series of relationships. And one of the very important relationships for us is with the family of Oriental Orthodox Christians, as well as other Orthodox, Catholics and Reformed. Those relationships help to give us our identity as an ecclesial body in relationship.

This document, *Out of the Depths*, obviously includes an introduction, and also obviously a section on prayer. And that highlights something which again was brought to the fore yesterday and today. The pivotal role of the prayer that Jesus taught his disciples expresses witness. Again this morning, we heard very forcefully about *witness* being the primary expression, interpretation or translation of the word *martyr*. So some of the things that have come through to us in relation to the Lord's Prayer are belonging, presence, witness and proclamation. As we all know, we have received the text of the Lord's Prayer, in different forms, in Matthew and Luke. There would seem also to be an allusion to the content of the Lord's Prayer in Gethsemane, as expressed in Mark's Gospel. So that brings us again to the heart of something that was articulated in this conference: the crucifixion entails both death and glory along with the resurrection.

One of the other things we are very concerned about is an appropriate use of language. I said earlier that we are very concerned to realize that the primary understanding of martyrdom is that of witness. But in our own way, we have begun to identify a number of words on a kind of sliding scale that describe how human beings make themselves irrelevant to other human beings by choice, by association and by a number of factors. An early manifestation of this might be harassment. The next manifestation might be subjugation. The next might be persecution. Others might be martyrdom, annihilation and obliteration. Yesterday we heard of the great fear and anxiety over the possible obliteration of Christian presence and witness where Christianity has been present not just for centuries but for millennia.

Another continuing and important principle is, very simply, that human beings are made in God's image and likeness, and loving God and loving your neighbour must be primary concerns and primary motivating forces in the way in which we respond, live and react to people of all faith and of no expressed faith.

There are three principles of theological interpretation within the Anglican tradition: Scripture, tradition and reason. You might think that Scripture is the simplest. But I am sure that, from your own traditions, you are aware that Scripture is far from simple. It's very labyrinthine, very complex. My interpretation may be just as good as yours but yours is just as good as mine. And so the debate continues about the implication and the application of Scripture. But for Anglicans, Scripture lies at the heart and at the root of any subsequent theology that we do.

The understanding of tradition and of reason, understandably, I think, changes as the world changes around us. The sort of pivot on which we are working in relation to *Out of the Depths* would be the following: tradition is an expression of the mind that the Christian shares as a believing member of the Church, while reason is the mind that a Christian shares as a participant in a particular culture. Therefore, it brings in the perspective of those of other world faiths. And so Scripture, tradition and reason, which were brought into Anglican theological thinking through Richard Hooker in the seventeenth century, and were reconsidered in the eighteenth and nineteenth centuries and again in the twentieth century, still are very much the tools of interpretation that we bring to bear.

Now under that umbrella of reason, there is, as I say, a recognition of the perspectives of other world faiths. And in that section of our book, what we're doing is exploring the persecution of and by a range of world faiths. But we're also conscious that the context in which we live requires some appreciation and understanding of at least the following: phenomenology, sociology, history, politics and economics. Things don't simply happen in a theological or an ecclesiastical bubble. There's a whole range of things that are happening around people and within them. And that actually helps to make up the complex human beings that they are in relationship with others.

Another thing that we've tried to do within the section on tradition as a response to martyrdom and persecution is to explore feminist theology, Black and Dalit theology and liberation theology, because we feel that these developments within the theological method are themselves also important.

Finally, one of the things that we have had no option but to explore is the Holocaust, because that again brings us into a dilemma of the understanding of faith and politics, of geography, of nationality, of personality and the depersonalizing of people who stand within a particular ethnicity and a particular world faith. We are of the conviction that this is very much part of who we are, as Judeo-Christians as well as Jesus-focused Christians.

So I hope that in some way that's helpful. We've talked with a number of the organizers of this gathering and we would hope to continue to work with you as we move towards bringing together a final version of this document. But it is designed to be a theological resource for Anglicans in their relationship with people of other Christian traditions and also people of other world faiths. There will of course be a study guide along with it.

Rev Thomas Kemper, General Secretary, General Board of Global Ministries, United Methodist Church, USA

(Rev Kemper could not be present due to his wife's illness, and his message was read by Dr Üllas Tankler, European Secretary of the General Board of Global Ministries, United Methodist Church. Dr Tankler began with some remarks of his own.)

I have a message from Rev Kemper, but before I read it, I will give you a brief introduction to my own background. I come from Estonia. This means that I grew up when Estonia was part of the Soviet Union. My parents and their generation suffered seriously in many different ways, and also through martyrdom. I personally have experienced only what I would call mild discrimination. But I have experienced something that I feel we have not touched upon yet in this conference. So I really ask you to pay attention. What I have experienced, and what my generation has experienced in that system, is a form of discrimination that I would call discrimination of one ideology. It means that I was not physically persecuted as a Christian during the Soviet system, but the Soviet ideology brainwashed my generation, people like myself and others around me. We grew up in a society of one ideology and one information source only, because all other information was blocked. You might say, "Well, this is not possible today because we live in the age of Internet and social media. You cannot have just one ideology." But I believe that there is at least something that we should pay attention to, and be aware of, because even in the age of social media and the Internet, when the information in one region, country or society comes only from the governing regime, and this information is so loud, this may affect the way people think. This is something that I believe we should pay attention to.

(Dr Tankler then went on to read the message from Rev Kemper.)

In Solidarity with Christians who Suffer

The General Board of Global Ministries is the worldwide mission and humanitarian relief agency of the United Methodist Church. One of our goals is to promote justice, peace and freedom, including religious freedom. As an agency, we relate to units of our own church and to partner denominations and various organizations in more than 125 countries. We have an international board of directors. This plethora of relationships represents both opportunity and challenge when it comes to walking with those who experience religious persecution. We are aware of many instances of oppression and can often be in open solidarity with those who suffer; at other times, our solidarity must be less visible because what we say or do could jeopardize communities or colleagues. There are areas of Central Asia and the East Indies where we dare not publicly say we have personnel or openly provide spiritual or material sustenance to oppressed indigenous Christians. We have been asked by Christian leaders to forego criticism of human rights violations in their countries for fear of bringing down the wrath of tyrants on their congregations. Such ambiguities accompany the fact of our global nature.

Our global scope also gives us a broad base for multicultural learning, including ways of witness and worship but also how diverse religious communities respond to restrictions and oppression. And our sharing of experiences is, as we say of our missionaries, from everywhere to everywhere; the whole is challenged and enriched. Our walk with those who suffer teaches us humility, patience and hope.

I am hoping that this event will help us to link into a network for consideration of how we publicly speak out for religious freedom in ways that are fair, responsible and inter-cultural. I recall an occasion in which words were counterproductive. We were in dialogue with a high Asian official about legal status for our church in his country. Just then, one of our colleague United Methodist agencies issued a statement protesting religious liberty violations in that country. It did not make for productive negotiations. We also welcome and learn from inter-faith relations. Even now, we have welcomed in a certain place a Muslim leader to serve as peacemaker-negotiator between contending United Methodist factions in that area.

Our church has a long and deep commitment to religious freedom. Such a stance was built into our founding by John Wesley who himself, along with his early eighteenth-century British Methodist societies, was subjected to mob violence. Our contemporary *Book of Discipline*, our manual of doctrine and jurisprudence, endorses the "right of every religious group to exercise its faith free from legal, political, or economic restrictions." Such a right reflects the Enlightenment affirmation of the dignity of persons enshrined in the Universal Declaration of Human Rights. The directors of Global Ministries have recently identified an even more biblical basis of support for religious freedom, a rationale founded on the love ethic of the New Testament as set forth by Jesus and explored by Saint Paul in his letters. We hope that our 2016 legislating General Conference will embrace our statement on "Religious Freedom: Grounded in Love," which asserts both vertical and horizontal dimensions of religious freedom. The vertical recognizes divine endowment and the horizontal posits loving concern for the rights of all brothers and sisters. The implication of what I am saying is that when I support the rights of Christians or protest oppression of followers of Jesus Christ, I do so in the context of advocacy for broad religious freedom—of application of the Golden Rule to religious relationships.

Solidarity and Humility

Let me now focus on our effort to be in solidarity in two very different situations in which Christians are disadvantaged. One is Pakistan, where Christians are oppressed by both Islamic culture and law. The other is Israel and Palestine, where legal restrictions are likely less troublesome than being a minority within a minority; Christians hold minority status within a predominantly Palestinian Muslim culture and are also Arabs within the political, economic and violent struggle that marks the Israeli-Palestinian conflict. I will not attempt to describe these situations in detail; the broad parameters are public knowledge. My aim is to share what Global Ministries is doing to show solidarity with these suffering Christian communities.

Our concern for the Christian minority in Pakistan emerges from more than a century of relationships, first with a mission presence and since 1970 with the Church of Pakistan, a union of Anglican, Lutheran, Methodist and Scottish Presbyterian denominations and the major Protestant church in the country. Our walk with this community includes:

- Visitations, consultations and regular staff contacts; articles on the situation.
- Public statements questioning the fairness of the blasphemy law and its arbitrary application to Christians and sometimes also to Muslims, which has been increasingly frequent over the last decade.

- The burning of Protestant and Roman Catholic churches in 2009; the assassination in March 2011 of Shahbaz Bhatti, Pakistani minister of minority affairs and the most prominent Christian in the government; the arrest of 11-year-old Rimsha Masih for allegedly burning a Koran in August 2012; the bombing of All Saints Church in Peshawar in September 2013, resulting in some 90 deaths; and the deaths of more than 145 students and teachers in the bombing of a public school in Peshawar in December 2014.

- Financial backing for a World Council of Churches hearing on "The Misuse of the Blasphemy Law and the Plight of Religious Minorities in Pakistan" in September 2012 in Geneva.

- Support for Church of Pakistan personnel, including a current scholarship for Insar Gohar, a staff member of the Peshawar Diocese, to study at Claremont School of Theology in California. He and his wife Uzma lost two children and other relatives in the bombing of All Saints Church, and they have been deeply involved in promoting religious liberty and positive inter-faith relations in their home area of northern Pakistan.

- A grant toward a Church of Pakistan project to improve security in church-run schools in Pakistan, as required by the government.

- Humanitarian assistance following natural disasters, notably floods; such assistance is provided without religious distinction, but national or local partners of the United Methodist Committee on Relief often include the Church of Pakistan or other Christian associations, giving Christians an opportunity to participate in general community rebuilding.

The United Methodist Church has no congregations in Israel or Palestine and seeks to establish none. We do have missionaries—for more than 30 years—serving with mission partners; we have a long history of work with Palestinian refugees, and a keen awareness that all

Christians share in the responsibility to work for peace, justice and freedom in the Holy Land. The United Methodist Church and our agency have a firm policy of support for the creation and peaceful existence of Israel; we also have a strong and increasing concern for the welfare of the Palestinians, Arabs among whom a small minority are Christians. Palestinian Christians form a dwindling minority in the Holy Land, down to fewer than 200,000 persons, having been reduced by economic, social and political realities. We have not always taken seriously the adverse realities affecting this minority. We have too often looked away, often in the name of laudable support for Israel, as decades of military occupation resulted in self-selected and forced emigration and exile of the Christians. Palestinians, including Christians, are today caught between militant Arab political expressions and the policies of Israel, notably the illegal Jewish settlements in the West Bank, occupied for almost half a century, and the building of a wall of separation during the last decade.

To express concern for Palestinians, even to give attention to what is happening to our Palestinian brothers and sisters in faith, has not been an easy or even popular decision. I have visited Palestine twice in the past two years and met many very hard-pressed Christians who experience constant fear and sporadic persecution. Our agency's walk with Palestinian Christians includes:

- General Conference endorsement of the United Nations' appeal for Israeli withdrawal from the occupied territories.

- Collaboration with the British Methodist Church and the World Methodist Council in organizing a Jerusalem liaison office with a mandate, among other roles, to offer full briefings on Holy Land realities and Christian Palestinians to pilgrims.

- Work with the Middle East Council of Churches to promote peace and also to respond to the continuing needs of refugees, Christian and Muslim. We have worked for years with the council's Department of Services to Palestinian Refugees.

- Providing personnel to key Christian institutions, such as Bethlehem Bible College, where one of our missionaries has been a dean and professor for many years.

- Advocacy for implementation of denominational resolutions supporting the boycott of products made by Israeli companies operating in occupied Palestinian territories.

Peace and justice will not come to the Holy Land until all the contending groups recognize the existence and the humanity of the others. Two liberation movements must make peace with one another. I say this as a German horrified by the historical treatment of Jews and a staunch supporter of Israel, and as a world citizen who recognizes the injustices being done to Palestinians. It is often difficult to hear the voice of the Palestinian Christian minority as it has repeatedly recognized Israel while rejecting the occupation and also condemning violence on both sides of the conflict. Only when Israelis and Palestinians acknowledge the humanity of the other will all the religious communities, including followers of Jesus, find peace, justice and freedom in the Holy Land.

I conclude with the opening sentences, a quotation from Galatians, from Global Ministries' proposed statement on "Religious Freedom: Grounded in Love":

> *For you were called to freedom, brothers and sisters; only do not use your freedom as an opportunity for self-indulgence, but through love become slaves to one another. For the whole law is summed up in a single commandment, "You shall love your neighbour as yourself." If, however, you bite and devour one another, take care that you are not consumed by one another. (Gal 5:13–15)*

Through God's grace, we will continue to walk and learn from those who suffer, loving as neighbours in the name of Jesus Christ.

Dr Ronald Boyd-Macmillan, Chief Strategy Officer, Open Doors International

What does it mean to stand in solidarity with suffering and persecuted countries and churches?

In our interaction with persecuted Christians, the greatest fear we find they have is that they are suffering alone; that they have been forgotten; that the rest of the body of Christ does not know of their plight. And this is a sad fact. Once I infiltrated an Islamic extremist cell. We were asked what we would do about Christians, and we were being urged to do terrible things to them. I remember asking, "Why is this the case?" And they answered: "Because the Christians are a people alone. No one stands up for them. You can do what you like to them." They said, "We are different, we are a brotherhood." I wanted to shout back, "But we are a body"—a much more intimate and powerful metaphor.

Now, of course, this is partly a libel, but the phrase haunted me: "the people alone". It did strike me how the Christian churches were perceived as exhibiting a lack of solidarity with the persecuted, at least from an outsider's perspective.

So what does solidarity look like, more positively? Persecuted Christians in our experience—and our organization celebrates sixty years of existence this year—do not want something from me, *they want me!* Solidarity must begin—if we can manage it—as a face-to-face encouragement of the persecuted by ourselves. That is why in Open Doors we feel that our primary ministry is simply presence: to be present physically, praying with them, listening to them, fellowshipping with them, without an agenda. Our founder Brother Andrew's challenge always was "Go, and be with them. If God is with you, the doors will never be closed. They may close behind you and you may not get back out, but that's not the point. The point is to be with them. No persecuted Christian should suffer alone."

And from that friendship, from that presence, methods of how we can strengthen persecuted Christians will emerge. Do they need Scriptures? Do they need investment in micro-loans? Do they need teaching or training? Do they need advocacy for a better deal? But everything grows out of that initial fellowship of presence. And one of the most important lessons we have learned is that we are not there to fix it. "Persecution is an honour you have to deserve", the great Wang Ming Dao said to me when I visited him in Shanghai. When persecution takes a spiritual form, it cannot be removed, nor should it. When persecution, though, takes a legal form, it can be removed, and it should. And the persecuted—if we make friends of them—will show us the difference.

What do we receive from suffering and persecuted churches?

Listen to this wonderful verse, Isaiah 45:3: "And I will give you the treasures of darkness—secret riches. I will do this so that you may know that I am the Lord, the God of Israel, the one who calls you by name." I love that phrase, the *treasures of darkness*. We all hit hard times, and persecution is one of the most acute forms of suffering. But the persecuted have a treasure to share—most profoundly about how God shows his faith in the midst of the void of human suffering and darkness.

I remember giving a Bible to a persecuted Christian in Slovakia. He was a farmer who had pastored a church for twenty years with a few pages of a Bible from Paul's letters to Timothy. He sniffed it, licked it, marvelling at the leather binding, and then he fixed me with a stare and said, "Have you read the whole book?" Yes, I have. He said then, "Well, then, what's God really like?" What do you mean? "I mean, how dangerous is he?"

What a question, and it turned into a life quest for me. And it came from a persecuted Christian. I think their greatest gift to me personally has been showing me how dangerous God is, that Christ has enemies, that the world is a battleground and not a playground, and that very often God is a lot less safe than the preachers in the churches I go to make him out to be. Treasures of darkness.

I know there is no typical persecuted Christian. It's important not to idolize them, or to assume that they are all united or have overcome the problems of Western churches. No, their great gift to the body is their insistence that only a very personal encounter with the divine-human Jesus will get you through the dark. That's the treasure. If you know God as force, that's not enough. If you serve God out of duty, that's not enough. If you have a God who is stern and demanding, that's not enough to get through the darkness and see the Face that never goes away. The treasure of the persecuted is showing us (not explaining) how to find the face of God that never goes away in the midst of human suffering. That helps me to read my newspaper with hope. My newspaper basically is telling me that darkness has the last word. And I need a story to tell me that actually Christ has the last word, and his face is full of sympathy and power for those who suffer … as he did.

What are the next steps in walking together as a suffering church?

I don't want to give the usual list: not forgetting them, being with them, developing that inter-dependence especially in prayer, assisting where we can. We do have an emphasis, an absolute insistence that all strategies of intervention must start in a good grounding of the facts. This is why we produce the annual Open Doors World Watch List, the country reports on the top fifty countries where persecution is present. We need to get the facts right. We need to get the story out. We need to get the help in, we need to get the changes made, we need to get the churches united, and we need to get the risen Christ exalted. Of course, this is done in cooperation with the Holy Spirit and with each other, with other organizations. It cannot be done alone. The whole project is by definition inter-denominational and ecumenical.

Let me suggest two very practical ways of walking together. One is what I call the conflict walk. "We may not sit on the same thorn, but we do sit on the same branch", a Chinese pastor said to me. He meant that in a broad sense everyone is persecuted; the difference is one of degree. He was going to the spiritual heart of the suffering church: following Christ should bring trouble. Christ has enemies, and when we identify with him, his enemies become our enemies. All cultures worship whatever is not Christ, and so in living out the life of Christ, we accept conflict, indeed welcome it as a badge of effectiveness. William Sloane Coffin used to say, "Jesus said to love your enemies; he didn't say 'Don't make any.' " Walking together means accepting that if Jesus asks us to love him, it involves confronting evil, including religious evil. That means confronting Western governments that try to blank out religion as a factor and ignore the persecuted as victims. That is the walk of conflict.

There's another way of walking together; I call it the walk of joy. The ancient tradition of Easter laughter, *risus paschalis*, needs urgently to be revived. You remember the service that goes back to patristic times, where an entire service is dedicated at Easter to celebrating how God brings good out of evil. The ultimate illustration is the devil thinking he was killing God, only to discover that he has assisted the act of atonement for everyone. Tricked. And so the people of God celebrate—and remember—that even when evil does its worst, God can still bring good out of it. What better illustration of Easter laughter can we have in the world today than many of the stories of the persecuted church? I'm going to Johannesburg next Easter to lead an Easter laughter service. We will start with the devil and the cross, but we will come up to date by telling the stories of the persecuted. Like the intervention of the Ayatollah Khomeini in Iran, when he got so angry about the size of the house churches and on television harangued the whole population, "Don't go to the house churches, the Trojan horses for the CIA." And most of the population looked at each other and said, "What's a house church? If he doesn't like it, we might like it." And so there was a great spike in the numbers. Easter laughter.

What a faith boost it is … it illustrates that amazing paradox at the heart of all we do here: that joy and suffering are twins, thanks to the plan of God. This is not a trivial project. No one is more dangerous in this world than the person who takes himself too seriously, who cannot laugh at himself, who thinks he is God. They are the persecutors. And no one is more encouraged than the person who fears that evil is going to have the last say, but sees in jubilant faith that it's just another living stone in the palace that God is always building.

Ms Yamini Ravindran, Head of Legal and Advocacy, Religious Liberty Commission, National Christian Evangelical Alliance of Sri Lanka

I would like to thank you all for the opportunity to present on this panel. My comments will largely centre on answers to the three specific questions concerning agencies working in solidarity with the suffering church.

What does it mean to stand in solidarity with the suffering or persecuted church?

Standing in solidarity with the suffering church has not been an easy task for the NCEASL as an organization, or for me in my personal experience. It is only when you work along with the persecuted church that you realize how difficult and challenging the task before you really is. Along with the strength, endurance and faith of the suffering church, you also see the brokenness and the imperfections and the lack of awareness of the persecuted church in certain areas. To truly stand in solidarity, therefore, would be to stand with the suffering church amidst its brokenness as well.

Also, standing in solidarity is not merely to convey it in words or to say that we will pray for them, which is very essential, but to show it in action. While preparing for this, I began to question, from the perspective of the suffering church, what it really considers as standing in solidarity with them. What is really valuable for them? Often, as agencies, missionaries and organizations that work with the suffering church, we are so busy implementing activities and projects. Do we really take the time to spend time with the suffering church? Do we actually listen to the suffering church? I think that alone shows them that we are standing in solidarity with them.

I would like to share a story. A pastor in Meegoda, Sri Lanka faced violent mob attacks and an arson attack because of his Christian activities. Moreover, a court case was also filed against him, questioning the legality of his church. Due to fears of being attacked further, the congregation began to gradually stop attending worship services, and there came a point when no one was attending the church. Ironically, after he lost his entire congregation, the pastor won the case and received an order from the court that he had the right to continue. That is not an order you receive often in Sri Lanka. I called this pastor to tell him the good news and he said, "As much as I should be happy, I am not, because I no longer have a congregation." That was such a sad story. Now, a lot of people may criticize this pastor, as agencies do sometimes. Maybe he did not provide a solid enough foundation for his congregation; maybe that is why they completely left the church. But to truly stand in solidarity with the suffering church would also be to stand alongside such churches as well, to encourage them, to help them to revive their ministries and maybe even learn from past mistakes. It would mean that we stand with them through their mistakes, through their pressure, darkness and depression.

Also, standing in solidarity would mean:

- Responding to their practical needs;
- Praying for them;
- Encouraging them and being close to them;
- Equipping them to stand up for their rights;
- Being a voice and a strength to them, sometimes at the expense of your own strength, safety and security;

and on a deeper level:

- Continuing the work that we are doing as agencies, in spite of sometimes not seeing changes around us, and most importantly, to make their voices stronger, so that they would be heard;
- Working hard to ensure that you are not discouraged and not disengaged emotionally and spiritually from your work;
- Reflecting deeply that we are all part of God's family and that when one suffers, we all suffer;
- Remembering that persecuted Christians, too, are human with weaknesses and imperfections;

- Thanking God for the opportunity to serve his suffering saints;
- Helping them, depending on God to help us;
- Hoping and trusting in God and his sovereignty.

What do we receive from suffering or persecuted churches?

Here I would like to quote Dr Boyd-MacMillan, from his article "What Do We Learn from the Persecuted?" in his book *Sorrow and Blood*. He talks about three things: how the persecuted church can be a faith boost for us, a faith model, and also a faith warning.

A faith model leading to a faith boost: How can you still believe in God after you have seen your very husband shot in front of your eyes? Sister Lalani and sister Shiromi are two women who witnessed their husbands being shot dead. But they did not leave the situation; they both continue to stay in the very areas where their husbands were martyred because of their evangelization. Today they have flourishing ministries that touch the lives of so many people. So we learn from them.

We receive faith warnings from the suffering church: Even as we work with the suffering church, we need to ask ourselves, are we really walking the walk with Christ? Why are we not in those situations? Are we merely living a very comfortable life, dodging persecution or dodging suffering? This is something we need to learn and receive from them.

We learn not to romanticize suffering: It is also important that we learn from the darkest hour of the church. We tend to romanticize persecution by saying that it is always good and makes the church grow. But in some instances, when you actually go through persecution, you realize that it is not good all the time. In some instances there is no growth. Also, often persecution can be a lonesome experience for those who have to face it. We learn therefore from the suffering church not to romanticize persecution, but to accept the reality of it.

We receive our calling from the suffering church: Our calling comes from God, but most of us are here today at this conference because we serve the suffering church, work with them, and receive our calling and our ministry from them.

What are next steps in walking together with the suffering church?

As agencies, missionaries and people who work with the suffering church, we often tend to make the suffering church dependent on our ministry and work. So we need to keep three things in mind.

First, we need to empower the suffering church in our work with them, empowering them to be independent and not to depend on our work, our ministry. Empower them also to make independent decisions. For instance, in the present Middle East refugee crisis, as agencies we have such strong opinions; some of us think they need to be there, some of us think they need to flee. But we need to help them to decide for themselves whether to flee, endure or fight back.

Second, we need to equip them to formulate biblical theologies on persecution, religious freedom and human rights. Most of us have done this, but we need to make sure that these theologies actually reach the rural communities. Often in Asia, a lot of pastors cannot be helped because they don't believe in religious freedom, human rights and legal interventions, and that is very sad. We need to prepare them, train them and disciple them to face and overcome persecution.

Third, we need to enlighten them on best practices of evangelism, and to distinguish between suffering for righteousness' sake and suffering because of ignorance. We also need to educate the church on the importance of being part of the society and the community.

One final point I would like to leave is that we should not, as agencies that work with the suffering church, romanticize suffering. When we come from communities or places where we don't really go through suffering, we often tend to think that persecution and suffering only bring revival and growth. In the example of Pastor Prianka from Sri Lanka, there was no revival, no growth. He was lonely and depressed. So, even as we work with them, we need to realize that there are practical realities that come along with suffering and persecution. We need to work along with them in that path.

Rev Rauli Lehtonen, Chairman, Regional Council of Eurasia, Swedish Pentecostal Movement

Dear brothers and sisters, very often I am thinking about what it really means to stand in solidarity with the persecuted church. And I would like to ask you also the same question: what does it mean for you personally?

If I were to summarize my opinion in three sentences, I would emphasize first the needs of the saints and that we need to contribute towards them. We need to bless those who persecute, rejoice with those who rejoice and weep with those who are weeping (Rom 12:13–15). To make this possible and fulfil these challenges, I think we need to join our persecuted brothers and sisters. We need to visit them (Matt 25), to encourage them, to walk beside them in the midst of their dangers and threats and show their persecutors that we love them! We love our brothers and sisters, but may I ask you, have we really done that? Have we shown the persecutors that we are loving the suffering church? Have we shown them that we stand beside those who are ready to pay the price for their belief?

During the Soviet period, over 500 churches in Scandinavia were involved in a prayer and sister church program in which churches in Sweden, Norway and Finland adopted sister churches in the Soviet Union, from Russia, Ukraine, Belarus, the Baltic states and Central Asia. They built up close relations through regular visits and joint projects. Many Scandinavian churches became a voice for the persecuted with appeals, demonstrations and different kinds of activities to support and defend the suffering ones. During the 1970s and 1980s, almost one thousand Christians were put in prisons and labour camps in the Soviet Union, and we knew the names and backgrounds of most of those Christians who were suffering because of their belief in Jesus Christ. They came from Orthodox, Catholic and Protestant churches. And Christians from different denominations and churches supported and helped those persecuted ones together. What if this could happen again? What if this conference could be a starting point to develop networks and efforts? What if we worked hand in hand to try to do something in walking beside the suffering church?

Today, the churches in the Scandinavian countries are still supporting and building relations with the different countries in Central Asia and the Caucasus area. They are supporting church planters, but also training lawyers and advocates and organizing training seminars about the religious laws of the different Central Asian countries, so that the pastors and leaders can get information about their rights and their possibilities for serving in the society. The IBRA Christian radio and television organization in Sweden, together with some other religious organizations, has started a Christian television channel called Canal Hayat in the Turkmen language, Azeri, Turkish and Uzbek, where we are trying to emphasize the need for Christian values and also to bring up questions about religious freedom and human rights, so that the audience can get more knowledge about their human rights.

If we go back to the 1970s and 1980s, there was also a time when Light for the Peoples did research on where those persecuted Christians and those pastors who were put in jail came from, from which regions and republics of the Soviet Union. We were able to find out that only a handful of them were from cities and churches that had regular visitors from abroad and organized sister church relations. This testified to the importance of close relations between local churches in the West and those in the East, because when the authorities knew about those relations, the space for activities and freedom increased quite a lot in those regions where that kind of relationship had been established. It is of great value even today that we are ready to pay a price for supporting the Christians who are suffering; we need to visit them when they are hungry and to take care of them when they are naked and sick. We must not forget our brothers and sisters who have been put in prison.

What do we receive from the suffering and persecuted church?

During the most intensive years of the sister church programs, many Christians from the suffering churches and countries came to Scandinavia and visited their sister churches there. Their example and their readiness to offer everything to follow Jesus Christ in their lives, and to spread the kingdom of God, changed the viewpoint of many Christians in Scandinavia. The younger generation was deeply touched when they met with those individuals who were ready to suffer.

Some of those young people became Bible smugglers to closed countries, and others were ready to make risky trips to deliver support to the suffering church. Others were staying at the barricades, defending and lifting up the needs of the suffering people, and they became a voice for them and an example. I think that the readiness to pay the price, to go all the way to the end, changed much of the thinking in those churches that had sister church relations with Scandinavia. And I think that we still need to learn this lesson from the suffering church.

What are the next steps in walking together with the suffering church?

I think that there is a need for Christians from the "free world" to organize regular efforts to walk beside those who are ready to pay the price. We need to start prayer programs, prayer campaigns, and maybe sister church relations and programs between churches in the east and west, and north and south, on a local level. The enthusiasm and desire of the suffering churches can offer something for us, and it can be a decisive example that could save the secularized churches in the western part of the world, when they see that there are people ready to pay a price and become an example for us who many times have lost the vision and the belief of a future with Jesus.

If churches from the west and north could risk and offer themselves to assist and "walk alongside", I think that the suffering churches facing the most demanding persecutions could become victorious, and we could feel that we are brothers and sisters in Jesus Christ. I think that could even have the result that some of the persecutors could find the way to the living God.

Comments from the Floor

Feije Duim, ICCO—Kerk in Actie [Church in Action], the Netherlands: It is not forbidden to make enemies, and it is certainly not forbidden to make friends. This is an issue that I want to put on the table, and I want to ask the panel what they think about it. At the height of the jihad in the Moluccas in Indonesia in 1999, we formed a strong group of Muslims and Christians to discuss what was happening in their society, and we worked for religious freedom. Among my Muslim friends in Indonesia from that time, there are still some who are very strong defenders of freedom of faith for Christians. These are friends we need. We need to reach out. We have a Muslim group, the Asian Muslim Network for Human Rights, that is taking up the issue of Pakistani Christian refugees in Thailand. They are doing the job to help our brothers and sisters who have fled from Pakistan to Thailand and got stuck there. When I hear my Syrian brothers and sisters discuss the situation, they say, "We do not want to be isolated from the others in our society. We want to be part of society. We want to claim our role as Christians in society." For that, we need allies among Muslims also. My question is: how is that need reflected in this forum?

Julia Bicknell from London, part of the forum's communication team and also from the World Watch Monitor news agency: Our last panellist was encouraging churches in the West to connect and be friends with other churches around the world. I am wondering if in the light of all the accusations like "You are linked with foreigners", "Where do you get your money from?" and "You are agents of the CIA", the climate has changed now, and whether we need to hear from our brothers and sisters around the world as to whether actually we might be causing them more harm than good by doing this kind of cross-cultural cooperation. This is a real concern for me.

Andre Karamaga, general secretary of the All Africa Conference of Churches, Nairobi, Kenya: My dilemma has been expressed by my brother from the Netherlands. When we have this tension and suffering, "official Islam" comes to us to say "It is not Islam, it is not us." We had that in the Central African Republic when the imam was living in the compound of the Archbishop, and in Kenya when we had discussions with the official leaders of Islam. They were with us in condemning the situation. Of course, we would have loved it if they had made it clearer, but I am dealing with the dilemma of how we approach this situation without undermining this timid but real collaboration.

Brian Stiller, Global Ambassador with the World Evangelical Alliance: I come from Canada. This is in line with some of the conversation we just heard. Given that the Global Christian Forum is emerging as a composite of major Christian communions in dialogue on major issues, and given that so much of the issue of persecution and martyrdom lies within the Islamic world, and in the interfacing of Christians in those countries that are majority-Islamic, might there be a thought within the Global Christian Forum to consider creating another setting in which major Islamic people might be brought into the conversation? We may as well talk about it specifically and invite them officially. I don't know of any other forum that might work as well as the Global Christian Forum. It is just a suggestion.

Prof Georges Tamer, Friedrich-Alexander University, Germany: As the issue of persecuting Christians in Muslim-majority countries has been raised a couple of times now and was in the air yesterday and today, I would like to say a few words about it. I am speaking in my capacity as an Orthodox Christian from the Patriarchate of Antioch and as a professor of Islamic studies at the University of Lübeck in Germany.

I will mention first of all the basic attitude of the Quran towards non-Muslims, including Christians. Then I will say a few words about historical practice and will make a couple of suggestions about the need today.

In the Quran, Christians are considered "people of the book", and people of the book are not objects of persecution according to the Quran. Actual practice throughout history has had its ups and downs: periods of freedom and tolerance for Christians, relative freedom in the medieval period and in the Ottoman period, and of course periods of persecution. This is not unusual if we compare the history of the Muslim societies with the history of Christian societies, in the medieval period and later on. So the historical practice shows that Muslim societies are able to live in freedom with Christians and to allow them to live under a certain legal system, the dhimmi system, enjoying some rights and not being persecuted at all.

Now, what is needed today? We should not forget that in recent times the Muslim-majority societies are struggling with themselves, as a result of the period of colonialism. Islamic societies are seeking their own identity, trying to develop answers to the challenges of modernity. And in such turbulent times, we have to expect such phenomena as persecution to occur in some countries and regions of the world. The best way to deal with these challenges is to build bridges and talk to Muslims, especially to moderate Muslims, trying to understand why they persecute us in certain contexts. Persecution must be understood in its context, in relation to geopolitical, economic and cultural factors.

Morning prayers, St. Paul's Catholic Cathedral.

Session Nine –

Visions of Walking Together as the Suffering Church: Next Steps

Moderator:

Mrs Esme R. Bowers, Evangelical Alliance, South Africa

Panel:

Archbishop Felix Machado (Catholic, India)

His Eminence Archbishop Mor Dionysus Jean Kawak (Orthodox, Syria)

Rev Dr Panti Filibus Musa (Protestant, Nigeria)

Dr Brian Stiller (Evangelical, Canada)

Rev Rodhe Gonzalez Zorilla (Pentecostal, Cuba)

His Grace Bishop Angaelos (Orthodox, United Kingdom)

Archbishop Felix Machado, Catholic Church, India

In practically every part of the world, Christians have become victims of unprovoked violence. While some are direct targets of this violence, others are indirect victims of subtle anti-Christian hatred. By and large, following the teaching of Jesus in the gospels, Christianity champions the cause of mutual respect and interreligious dialogue, yet there are about 100 million persecuted Christians throughout the world. According to the World Evangelical Alliance, the problem has worsened dramatically since the turn of the millennium, and about 200 million Christians are now under threat.

It is no time to seek refuge in fear and trembling. To resort to panic is unbecoming of us Christians. I suggest the following three steps:

(1) Following some principles that should be observed by every Christian believer in bearing witness to Christ's commission for evangelisation (Matt 28:19–20). We have the first-ever document endorsed by a majority of Christians throughout the world, namely *Christian Witness in a Multi-Religious World: Recommendations for Conduct* (co-authored in 2011 by the World Council of Churches, Pontifical Council for Interreligious Dialogue, and World Evangelical Alliance).

(2) All Christians should together uphold religious freedom for all. Religious Freedom constitutes the very heart of human rights. Its inviolability is such that individuals must be recognized as having the right to change their religion, if their conscience so demands.

(3) Mutual respect for the dignity of every human person. Religious plurality is to be accepted and efforts should be made to promote "all positive and constructive interreligious relations with individuals and communities of other religions which are directed at mutual understanding and enrichment". Pope St John Paul warned, "Either we learn to walk together in peace and harmony, or we drift apart and ruin ourselves and others; [we are] to be aware of the common origin and common destiny of humankind. Let us see in it

an anticipation of what God would like the developing history of humanity to be: a fraternal journey in which we accompany one another toward the transcendent goal which he sets for us."

Dignity of the human person is "a transcendent value, always recognized as such by those who sincerely search for the truth". Failure to respect this dignity leads to the various and often tragic forms of discrimination, exploitation, social unrest and national and international conflicts with which we are unfortunately so familiar in these times.

Without the element of freedom, any definition of religion risks being dangerously restricted and weak. Respect for human dignity finds one of its expressions in religious freedom. And "religious freedom, if it means the right freely to choose one's beliefs about the meaning and purpose of life, is a fundamental freedom, arguably the most important human right of all." Religious freedom is not only about our ability to practise religion in the private sphere, but also about whether we can make our contribution to the common good of all people in society. Without religious freedom properly understood, people of all religions suffer because they are deprived of the essential contributions that religious believers, especially Christians, are making in the fields of education, health care, feeding the hungry, and giving voice to the voiceless in society.

Sadly, religious freedom in many parts of the world is in great peril. Unless believers of each religion, whether in the majority or minority population group, defend religious freedom robustly, no religion will escape the great plight that all religious believers face around the world. In India, assassinations, burning of sacred places, torching of religious institutions, etc. take place because systematic denials of basic human rights are found in the acts of persecution, especially of Christians.

The Hindu nationalist ideology that has arisen over the past century in India (*Hindutva*) begins with a conception that India is a Hindu nation, in which Hinduism is a default way of life for Indians. This model entails a distinction between conversions *away* from Hinduism, which are seen as a threat to the national integrity of India and a key contributor to the alleged decline of Hinduism, and conversions *to* Hinduism, which are described by the term *ghar vapsi*, meaning a "homecoming" to where one belongs, or a "reconversion" to one's original religion. Thus, the issue of religious freedom has become extremely complex in India in recent years. Several states in India have passed anti-conversion bills, which ironically are formally known as Freedom of Religion Acts!

Instrumentalization of religion by politicians is at the root of the grave concern for religious freedom in India. More precisely, it is a nationalist movement appealing to religious sentiment. It is a violent reaction sparked by fears of "Indian secularism".

While Christians and their institutions are attacked systematically by the proponents of Hindu nationalist ideologies, there is a subtle, but strongly growing movement among neo-intellectuals who, influenced by the West, are spreading secularist ideas. The tide of secularism in post-modern society has marginalized religion; consequently, freedom of religion is restricted if not altogether prohibited. Secularism conceives that the world in which we live may be understood entirely on its own terms; there is no need to refer to any other point beyond history, society or the state in order to understand the meaning and value of these entities. Eternal truth is relativized, particularly through recourse to historical investigation, falling into the error of nihilism which ultimately ends up in a sort of totalitarianism of the ideological world. It is a complete absolutization of the act of reason, giving rise to atheism. All those who follow God and religion are ridiculed and are labelled as blind in their belief.

Unfortunately, it cannot be denied that along with the mushrooming of various Christian groups throughout the country, an aggressive propaganda, denigration and vilification of neighbours' religions, operating often in competition one against the other to gather as many adherents as possible—winning followers by inducement, attracting members by allurements, or working in complete isolation—has displayed to the world a sad picture of a still more divided body of Christ. The preaching of the gospel is placed in jeopardy because this division of the body of Christ plays into the hands of those who look for opportunities to destroy any trace of the gospel of Jesus Christ. This kind of situation also disrupts efforts to promote peace and harmony.

I wish to submit that the spirit of the Catholic Church's teaching on religious freedom should become the norm, at least for every Christian of every denomination. In unequivocal terms, the Church distinguishes the double meaning of freedom from coercion: that no one is to be forced to act contrary to his or her convictions, and that no one is to be restrained from acting in accordance with one's own convictions.

Dignitatis Humanae warns followers of all religions, in no uncertain terms: "In spreading religious faith and in introducing religious practices, everyone ought at all times to refrain from any manner of action which might seem to carry a hint of coercion or of a kind of persuasion that would be dishonourable or unworthy, especially when dealing with poor or uneducated people. Such a manner of action would have to be considered an abuse of one's own right and a violation of the right of others." The Second Vatican Council does not speak merely of religious individuals. Freedom of religion is a right of the individual human person as well as that of every religious community. Religious communities should "not be prevented from publicly teaching and bearing witness to their beliefs by the spoken or written word" (*Dignitatis Humanae*, 4).

The core of all religions teaches promotion of interreligious harmony; there is in every religion a golden rule that favours freedom of religion. Religion, by its very nature, cannot be but an instrument of peace. Subjectivism, a mistaken notion of freedom that exalts the isolated individual in an absolute way, is to be questioned. Ethical relativism, the fallout of subjectivism, brings with it the implication that everything is negotiable and open to bargaining—even the first of the fundamental rights, the right to life.

Once the fact of religious plurality is accepted, the path of dialogue becomes obligatory. In this dialogue, openness to others is not separated from fidelity to Christ. Being open to dialogue means being absolutely consistent with one's own religious tradition. The Catholic Church has made interreligious dialogue an obligatory path for its followers: "Interreligious dialogue is part of the evangelising mission of the Church. ... Dialogue is fundamental for the Church. ... All Christians are called to dialogue. ... Dialogue finds its place within the Church's salvific mission." However, it must be said that the path of dialogue is never an easy one. It is important for believers to have an open mind and a welcoming spirit. This means that two extremes should be avoided: on one hand, a certain ingenuousness that accepts everything without further questioning, and on the other hand, a hypercritical attitude that leads to suspicion. Being open-minded does not imply being without personal convictions. On the contrary, rootedness in one's own convictions will allow for greater openness, for it takes away the fear of losing one's identity. Whereas, on one hand, openness without rootedness almost always ends in relativism, on the other hand, rootedness without openness leads to fundamentalism.

His Eminence Archbishop Jean Kawak, Syriac Orthodox Patriarchate of Antioch and All the East

I would like to apologize first of all that His Holiness Patriarch Mor Ignatius Aphrem II was not able to attend this meeting because he had to go back to Syria due to the recent attacks and attempts by ISIS to invade two Christian villages near Homs. This week, once again, the town of Saddad, which offered some sixty martyrs two years ago, was under threat of being overtaken by ISIS and perhaps being completely destroyed. This would be another tragedy to add to the list of tragedies that the Christians of the Middle East have been going through recently. We believe that the persecutions of Christians in the Middle East are becoming more and more part of our identity. Christians have been expelled from Mosul and the villages of the Nineveh plain. They are facing crisis in Syria and possible death if they attempt to leave Syria, such as drowning in the sea crossing from Turkey to Greece. They have been victims of all sorts of abuse and violence. I agree with all who have spoken before me from the Middle East regarding their description of the conditions of Christians in Iraq and

Syria. It is a bitter reality, full of emigration and uprooting from our ancestral homelands. Christians who have lived in the Orient or the Middle East since the dawn of Christianity are under the threat of disappearing from that area due to the terrorist attacks.

To have a future in that region, we need to work and walk together on many levels. I suggest that the following steps and measures be taken to rescue, if possible, the Christians in question.

First, we are eager to see the churches, especially in the West, supporting us and making our needs a priority. Indeed, we need them to listen to us and answer our needs. The right to decide our fate should be ours, and true help comes in support of what we need, not what others think we need.

Second, we need help from the churches in the West to relay our needs to their governments. Eastern Christians need advocacy from churches in the West to gain credibility and succeed in getting the necessary help we need to survive.

Third, we should monitor the policies that govern reception of immigrants in the West, particularly in Europe. All the churches in the East encourage their faithful to remain in the Middle East and to remain attached to their homelands. We tell our faithful that if one endures a little bit more, one will enjoy the rebuilding of the devastated country. It is difficult, though, to stop people from emigrating. It is impossible to convince them to stay when insecurity and war are the norm. How can you convince a father to keep his family in danger, even when we continuously remind our faithful that the war cannot go on forever and that behind all the destruction there is hope for a better and brighter future? We cannot make them see what seems to be a remote hope and wishful thinking. At the end of the day, we cannot stop anybody from leaving their country. But we are trying our best to keep our youth and our faithful from going abroad.

Here we raise the following question: why does Europe watch immigrants arrive through illegal and life-endangering ways, when they could prevent all this and simplify things by providing those people with support, defence and protection in their homelands, as well as offering humanitarian aid where needed?

If we truly desire to help Eastern Christians to stay in their homelands, we have to review their needs and attempt to help them in a humanitarian way. This can be ensured only when help and relief are channelled through the local churches, which offer help without any discrimination.

Rev Dr Panti Filibus Musa, Bishop, Lutheran Church of Christ in Nigeria

With gratitude for the opportunity to participate in this consultation, I bring greetings on behalf of the Lutheran World Federation, which made it possible for me to come, and the Lutheran Church of Christ in Nigeria, which has many members at the heart of the insurgency in northern Nigeria.

I would like to highlight a few issues as we reflect on our visions of walking together as the suffering church.

1. Personal relationships with our Lord and Saviour Jesus Christ as disciples

While we grapple with how to deal with the challenges of discrimination and persecution, we should never lose sight of our call to discipleship. We affirm our need to be nurtured and nourished by the Word, holy communion and prayer. Our love for Christ brings us to fellowship with brothers and sisters with whom we share a common journey. This then leads to concern for the unity of the church.

2. Call to unity in Christ: a gift and a task

We must never give up working towards realizing visible unity as the body of Christ. Cardinal Koch reminded us that those who persecute the church seem to understand better than we do that the church is one—they do not differentiate. We have seen over the years that Nigerian Muslims demonstrate solidarity in their reactions to the slightest provocation by anyone understood to be a Christian anywhere in the world (e.g. a Danish cartoon). We are also confronted by double messages of celebrating and condemning acts of extremists as not representing Islam.

This reminds us that walking together demands that we work towards realization of Christ's prayer in John 17:21 "that they may be one". This has implications for how we intercede for each other: Dietrich Bonhoeffer wrote in *Life Together*, "I can no longer condemn or hate a brother for whom I pray, no matter how much trouble he causes me. His face, that hitherto may have been strange and intolerable to me, is transformed in intercession into the countenance of a brother for whom Christ died, the face of a forgiven sinner" (p. 96). We pray for the grace of God and the transforming power of the Holy Spirit. Practically, we should take more seriously the week of prayer for Christian unity.

3. Responses that take into account local, regional and global realities

Each context of discrimination, persecution or even martyrdom is different. Hence we need to carefully analyse each context, to understand the *root causes and motivations* of discrimination and persecution and the *forces* (sponsors) behind them. This would inform how the church responds. In Nigeria, the church is not clear as to who is supporting the ongoing atrocities and how very poor young people obtain deadly weapons that would have required a lifetime of earnings to acquire even if they were available in the open market. Besides, we do not have a shared theological understanding of how to deal with the situation. What we have now is voices that sometimes contradict each other, saying either "Be pacific and accept suffering" or "Prepare to defend our right to life and existence." This results in discussions on the right to self-defence and what constitutes self-defence or differentiates it from vengeance (a very uncomfortable subject).

In any case, the church needs to carefully discern what can be done in each given situation. From the ministry of Jesus, we see that no one response fits all situations. In one instance, Jesus Christ slipped through the crowd and continued his ministry elsewhere. In another instance, the same Christ obeyed the Father and journeyed to Jerusalem despite what was to come. Some suggestions:

- Diplomatic and political pressure on governments to take responsibility to protect life and property; diplomatic pressure on governments dealing with regimes that perpetuate suffering;
- National councils and similar bodies to jointly develop theological and Bible study material to educate their members on these very delicate matters;
- More organized and rapid response in terms of material support.

4. Solidarity: when one part suffers, every part suffers (1 Cor 12:26)

We have spoken so much of solidarity, accompaniment, encouragement and material support. We recognize that the church has no monopoly on these concepts. It is therefore incumbent on us to articulate what it means theologically and in practice that "if one part suffers, every part suffers", so as to inform in practical terms our mutual solidarity. We must be concerned for the suffering of our neighbours generally, but also for fellow Christians. The apostle Paul teaches, "As we have opportunity, let us do good to all people, especially to those who belong to the family of believers" (Gal 6:10).

It is a call to the duty of praying together and for each other. Pray for the Holy Spirit to console those in difficult circumstances; to transform us and the world; to enable us to recognize the presence of and witness to God's Kingdom even amidst suffering and tragedy; and empower us to follow the footsteps of Christ in enduring the cross for the joy set before us (Heb 12:2). The church anywhere finds strength in mutually praying for each other: "A Christian fellowship lives and exists by the intercession of its members for one another, or it collapses" (Bonhoeffer, *Life Together*, p. 96). We pray even for the smallest seeds of hope, wherever they are, to flourish and bear fruit. Some practical suggestions are (1) to create room in our individual church calendars to pray for each other, and (2) to adopt special days of prayer within churches or organizations, as occasions for the one church to raise its one voice for the healing and reconciliation of our broken world.

5. *Documenting, reporting, sharing*

This would help us to inform each other and encourage those in similar situations and prepare us for mutual intercession. Local people should tell their stories, as long as doing so does not expose them to greater risks. As Kurt Cardinal Koch reminds us, this ensures that the tears and blood of the persecuted are not lost. Their stories must live on. Memorial services are powerful for remembering victims and bringing healing to survivors. Many members of the Church I represent share how important it was that the church organized special services in memory of those who disappeared or were killed, or whose bodies could not be buried. National church bodies could also take similar steps.

6. *Some pitfalls we should avoid on our journey together as the suffering church*

Seeking martyrdom. While keeping in mind the words of Jesus in John 15:20 that "a servant is not greater than his master; since they have persecuted me, naturally they will persecute you, and if they had listened to me, they would listen to you", it is not our role to seek after martyrdom. That would constitute seeking glory for oneself.

Allowing extremist voices within and outside the church to take over the public space. The gospel message and acts of love must interrupt those acts of hate and making enemies. This is the hard task of loving our enemies and praying for those who persecute us (Matt 5:44). Hateful language must have no place in Christian witness. Peace-building cannot be done without love. Again, Cardinal Koch reminded us that only love can change the hearts of people and then bring sustainable structural changes. God's love in us can change the world. After all, "Our struggle is not against enemies of blood and flesh, but against the rulers, against the authorities, against the cosmic powers of this present darkness, against the spiritual forces of evil in the heavenly places" (Eph 6:12).

Apathy, especially among churches in countries still considered safe. No church should be indifferent when others are facing hostility. Assault on any part of the body of Christ is assault on all. We have a mutual responsibility to stand for each other, for peace and justice for all. This could include refusing to cooperate with repressive governments and with those that perpetuate persecution.

Ignoring the suffering of other religious minorities. We must also take responsibility for the dignity of all persons, regardless of their religious affiliation.

Portraying ourselves only as the victims of discrimination, persecution and martyrdom. History shows that the church has not always been most loving and most caring, even within itself. We have inflicted pain on each other—for example, because of differences of understanding and expressions of the faith. Hence, as someone remarked, we are both persecuted and persecutors. Thus we must always pray, "Lord, have mercy!"

Dr Brian Stiller, Global Ambassador, World Evangelical Alliance, Canada

Thank you, brothers and sisters, and the Global Christian Forum for hosting this. I follow in the line of thinking of my colleagues.

As we move forward in considering our next steps, I want to underscore a reality that often, in my experience, is missed in our discussion of what we are to do. To understand the disturbing reality of Christians being persecuted and martyred for their stand as followers of Jesus, it matters that we begin with the larger picture. As much as various factors shape how neighbours treat Christians, there is a dynamic at work that inflames those factors, inciting persecution and martyrdom. We live in a world set within the larger creational reality, our Universe. Its physical size and contents are sources of continuing fascination. But we also live in a world that is something other than our physical manifestations which we know as matter. The battles that rage between nations are physical, but they arise out of human hatred, mistrust, envy and territorial greed. How can we quantify or measure such human attitudes?

On the wider human canvas is the Christian understanding that such human factors, symptomatic of a disobedient race, have been addressed by God, Creator of life, who in his son Jesus Christ made provision for the human spirit to be changed. Would that all we needed was to quell the hatred, rid ourselves of greed and neutralize that hatred. But there are forces at work, forces that our human construct tends to dismiss or trivialize. And that is the war that rages between good and evil, beneficence and hatred. My home is in Canada, and so I speak a bit from that context, realizing that Canada is not the centre of the world. I suspect that we often are caught within the secularizing trend so as to view these combatants of good and evil as only ideas, human feelings, emotional tirades, but all solely within the human construct.

Christian theology sees these antithetical forces as something that begins and indeed is in battle with what is called in the New Testament the "heavenlies". The apostle Paul pointed out that our struggles cannot be seen as societal or even personal but should be viewed within the wider metaphysical construct, which he says is part of the "heavenly realms":

> *Finally, be strong in the Lord and in his mighty power. Put on the full armour of God, so that you can take your stand against the devil's schemes. For our struggle is not against flesh and blood, but against the rulers, against the authorities, against the powers of this dark world and against the spiritual forces of evil in the heavenly realms. Therefore put on the full armour of God, so that when the day of evil comes, you may be able to stand your ground, and after you have done everything, to stand. Stand firm then, with the belt of truth buckled around your waist, with the breastplate of righteousness in place, and with your feet fitted with the readiness that comes from the gospel of peace. (Eph 6:10–15)*

The evil one despises the provisions of grace and does anything and everything to undo the love that flows from the Father. This is real power, the will of Satan, exacerbating the fallen human spirit, linking its self-interested motives to undo this grand narrative of God, coming in Jesus Christ, who answers that false and self-serving question, "Am I my brother's keeper?" As we search for ways to rid our world of persecution, to soften the blows of the martyr's hammer, we must not pretend that our witness of Christ is just a socially acceptable religious story that brings peace and happiness. Rather, it is a declaration that the Creator of life has taken up opposition against the overwhelming force of evil, and the witness we give of God in Christ is in the power of the Holy Spirit doing battle in the heavenlies, a cosmos that includes within it our world of time and space. Thus our reality of persecution is a manifestation of that wider reality. We return again to the apostle Paul for insight on this. He noted: "For though we live in the world, we do not wage war as the world does. The weapons we fight with are not the weapons of the world. On the contrary, they have divine power to demolish strongholds. We demolish arguments and every pretension that sets itself up against the knowledge of God, and we take captive every thought to make it obedient to Christ" (2 Cor 10:3–5).

St John in the book of Revelation also pushes us forward in faith: "Do not be afraid of what you are about to suffer. I tell you, the devil will put some of you in prison to test you, and you will suffer persecution for ten days. Be faithful, even to the point of death, and I will give you life as your victor's crown" (Rev 2:10).

We cannot make sense of persecution unless we understand that it is within the global and cosmic interface of God, tearing down the walls of separation and hatred—all the while, in the power of the Spirit, bringing healing and life to those who are grieved and resurrection to the fallen human spirit of his own creation.

In terms of specific actions, let us do advocacy, for the safety of people in countries today. Let us encourage governments to be open to receiving immigrants. But with respect to what I have just said, let us also set in place specifically prayers of intercession across our countries, across our communions and across the ministerial territories of our various agencies. We may want to kick-start the World Day of Prayer, which I have found in Canada to be anaemic and tired. It may need a *cause célèbre* for which it could come alive in new and vital ways.

To inspire a sense of urgency in prayer, we should take seriously this factor of "the heavenlies", see it as part of the larger narrative, and build that into our messaging to those facing persecution by alerting them that what they experience is being played out beyond their own circumstances.

Moreover, for our own communities, we should communicate that to engage in deep, intercessory prayer for those within circumstances of persecution and those trapped within its ferocious walls represents a serious engagement with the issue, and that by the mystery of the Spirit we will all become participants in the matter of persecution.

Rev Rodhe Gonzalez Zorilla, Past President, Cuban Council of Churches

I give profound thanks to God and to the leaders of this gathering who have made it possible through their multiple efforts for two representatives of the Cuban churches to share with you their experiences of life as part of the church of Jesus Christ.

Neither can I omit thanking God for this opportunity, because I grew up and journeyed for more than fifty years with a Pentecostal church in Cuba, and because I had no other resources than divine providence, the guidance of the Holy Spirit, and our call to serve God where he puts us. And so also has it been for the Cuban Council of Churches, an institution that will celebrate the 75th anniversary of its founding next year, which was called to unite the Protestant churches and Christian organizations of Cuba in their purpose of service to the people. I have had the opportunity to serve the Cuban churches for more than thirty years, in different areas of work and even as the first female president of that institution.

The challenges for the church in Cuba in the last sixty years have been numerous and huge. We have gone through several stages, which we could classify in periods:

- Enthusiasm, because of the political, social and economic changes in the country and the measures taken for the benefit of the people;
- Confrontation, because of measures taken that affected the churches;
- Marginalization and discrimination, at a later stage, but God in His mercy helped us during that time;
- After that, a period of re-education, dialogue and accompanying the people;
- And lately, strengthening and growth of our churches.

During these years we have often suffered a double discrimination, partly from the structures of government according to which believers could be viewed as the opposition, and partly from brothers and sisters elsewhere in the world who did not understand the steps we were taking to recover our rights as churches and seek solutions to situations of conflict. Believers elsewhere saw us as being too close to the government, because it was our premise to show that as churches we desired the well-being of our people and the consolidation of justice and peace for all men and women.

I recall Paul's words to the Colossians: "I am now rejoicing in my sufferings for your sake, and in my flesh I am completing what is lacking in Christ's afflictions for the sake of his body, that is the church" (1:24).

To suffer has been part of the Christian witness from the very beginning of the Christian church. Indeed, the sacrifice of our Lord has exemplified the history of the church. There would be no point in recounting how many Christian men and women have put their lives at stake at various stages of church history as they gave testimony to their faith. Once again, it is our desire to be witnesses in our country.

As Cuban Christians, we can repeat with the apostle Paul that we rejoice in our sufferings for the sake of the body of Christ. We have suffered together with our people so that the message of God's good news could prevail in Cuba, regardless of the political and economic changes in our country. We have been among the people, not in the structures of power but in humble companionship, discrete where necessary, weeping with those who weep and rejoicing with those who rejoice, stimulating hope and faith.

We are learning with Jesus to dialogue with all who need a word of love, but also with the head priests and the scribes and the Pharisees. We seek to be the church not only within our walls but also in the streets and homes, like the early church—to give what we have from the little we have, bringing about love and good works.

From this journey we can share the following experiences and challenges:

- One of the experiences that has had the most impact on our life as a church, has been the fraternal and caring support received from churches in various parts of the world, through prayer, presence and resources. This companionship began in the seventies and still exists today, under the principle of respect for our identity as a country and as a church, and of our criteria and concepts of what we could agree with.

- The support in those areas that could provide mutual edification also led to a growth in the number of visits from congregations seeking to get to know us from within rather than through the media, who might respond to interests that are very removed from our communities. We can affirm that these exchanges have contributed to the climate of relaxation and rapprochement even between the governments of our countries, and to the steps that are being taken to re-establish relations with the United States. But we can say the same of the fraternal Christian organizations and agencies from different parts of the world that also have accompanied us and helped us, not only in terms of our needs as a church but also as people.

- They helped us also in our need for spiritual formation by sending teachers for our seminaries and Bible schools, opening our horizons to the different realities of our world.

- The challenge that remains with us is to continue to work for the maximum possible extent of justice, in order to eliminate any form of discrimination, and for the unity of our churches.

Based on these experiences, we can propose as next steps the following:

- In James 5:16, we read that "the prayer of a righteous man is powerful and effective." We see as one possible next step, and here we agree with the Lutheran bishop, to have an annual prayer calendar for the suffering churches, so as to convene as many believers as possible on such a particular day, and to inform about the difficulties they experience.

- Another step that has greatly helped us is to learn to listen to one another, respecting our differences, our characteristics and our decisions, through visits with various groups, depending on the availability of human resources. That personal, human exchange has helped us a lot to grow closer, especially to those who suffer discrimination and persecution in other countries.

- To create spaces of capacity building for discriminated and persecuted communities where they are provided with economic and other resources for the development of active initiatives in the face of their difficult situations.

Brothers and sisters, we have conflicts and difficult situations, but as in the vision of the prophet Ezekiel in the valley of the dry and dispersed bones, so in the painful realities we have listened to, the Spirit of God can breathe and bring to life a vigorous church body. Come, Spirit of God, breathe on us and unite, restore and hearten your Church in our world.

His Grace Bishop Angaelos, Coptic Orthodox Church, United Kingdom (by video)

Greetings to you all. It is really with deep regret that I cannot be with you. I am sure that it is going to be a very blessed meeting, a very important meeting. Since I first heard about it from my dear friend Larry Miller, I wanted to be there, and I had it in my diary, but then, with the just recently announced visit of His All Holiness, the Ecumenical Patriarch here in Britain, I need to be here to engage with our Eastern Orthodox brothers and sisters in the churches as well as the wider ecumenical family.

The fact that so many wonderful and dedicated people are gathered in Tirana today, though, is significant. It is significant because as Christians we have a role and a responsibility. We need to speak for those who are still persecuted. Of course, we are gathering predominantly for Christians who are facing brutal, medieval persecution, the likes of which we have only read about in our Synexarion, the book of the Saints, for decades and centuries. But I think we are also gathered to be a voice for those who are persecuted, marginalized and suffering in the world, at many, many levels. We are seeing an unprecedented movement and displacement of people, from Iraq, from Syria, throughout the Middle East and around the world. We are seeing hundreds of thousands arriving over very treacherous journeys onto our shores in Europe. We are seeing displaced communities, from Iraq, Syria and Libya, who really have nowhere to go. And it is our responsibility as light in the world, as God's presence, as the body of Christ, to speak to all of that. This is a journey, but it is an unprecedented journey that needs all of us to be together. As I have been saying recently, there is no single, individual church or community, not even a nation-state, that can face this problem on its own. There is no one who can provide for the needs at a material level, or even at a moral, conceptual level of trying to find a solution.

Our greatest power, our greatest weapon is prayer. And directly after that is our voice, our collective voice as the body of Christ. So we pray for those who are persecuted, those who are marginalized, those who can't experience their faith (Christian or otherwise) with the same freedom that we are experiencing today. And unfortunately, many millions of people are suffering in that condition around the world. Today we look towards being a voice for them.

In our own Coptic Orthodox Church, we suffered the loss of twenty-one very dedicated men in Libya, as did our Ethiopian and Eritrean brothers and sisters only a month later. What we saw at that time was an incredible outpouring of love, of graciousness, of fellowship, of partnership from across the Christian body, expressed to all our churches around the world. That brought us together. What brought us together was the horrific evil, but also the powerful defiance and the resilience of a peaceful, forgiving Christian countenance. What touched people most was the fact that these men faced that destiny so honourably, and that their families, their communities and even their church forgave in such a Christ-like manner. Evil exists. Persecution exists. It is the cross we carry. We can accept it for ourselves, but at the same time, when we see others carrying that cross, we need to try to lighten that load and provide for them. At the moment, there is a need for immediate, humanitarian aid, immediate advocacy. But there is also a need for long-term thinking: where do those communities go, how do they survive, what do they need from us, what can we do?

We come with our five loaves and our two fish. We come as twelve men who followed the carpenter's son. None of that really meant anything in the world, but it could change the world. With the power of God, with the presence of his Holy Spirit in us, with the likeness of Christ, we can, in St Paul's words, "do all things in Christ who strengthens us". That's why we are here. We are here to pray, to think, to advocate, to propose. But above all, we are here to walk this journey with our brothers and sisters who are part of us, indivisibly and indistinguishably, and who need us to be with them today, as much as we need their witness, their strength, their diligence and their example to strengthen us. God bless you all. I pray that this may be a wonderful successful gathering, I look forward to being part of this process as it continues. I assure you of my prayers, as I also ask you to pray for me and for my ministry.

Rev Dr Pirjo-Liisa Penttinen with Missionaries of Charity sisters.

Session Eleven –

Next Steps: Walking Together as the Suffering Church

Moderator:

Rev Nicta Lubaale, General Secretary of the Organisation of African Instituted Churches, Global Christian Forum

Panel of Representatives of the World Church Bodies:

His Eminence Stanislav Hočevar, Pontifical Council for Promoting Christian Unity

Rev Dr David Wells, Pentecostal World Fellowship

Rev Dr Olav Fykse Tveit, World Council of Churches

Bishop Efraim Tendero, World Evangelical Alliance

Respondents:

Archbishop Anton Audo, Chaldean Catholic Patriarchate

Ms Connie Kivuti, Evangelical Alliance of Kenya

Rev Dr Larry Miller, Global Christian Forum

His Eminence Stanislav Hočevar, Member of the Pontifical Council for Promoting Christian Unity

First of all, I thank God and I thank you most warmly for your welcome in such an important meeting. I greet all of you cordially also on behalf of His Eminence Kurt Cardinal Koch, who was able to join us only for the first day. I would like also to extend my most sincere regards in the name of other representatives and structures of the Catholic Church.

It is a great joy to participate in the Global Christian Forum, and I am extremely grateful to the organizers and all participants for the cordial atmosphere at this meeting. We truly appreciate this ecumenical event, thanks to which we experience the mystical body of Christ, even if it is still divided. For that reason, this is an occasion for us to nurture a profounder hope.

We are aware that this event helps us in promoting a renewed unity among us, following the appeal of Pope Francis, and we are delighted that all Christian groups—not only those that have been established for a long time but also the new ones, especially the evangelical and Pentecostal groups—are gathered together on this occasion.

In dealing with discrimination, persecution and martyrdom, we are mindful of the impossibility of examining in depth here all the causes behind such events. We also recognize that we have not talked sufficiently about the kind of discrimination that occurs in Western countries, where we observe that the phenomenon of secularization sometimes appears to be very aggressive. The roots of persecution are extremely complex (just as Islam, for example, is itself complex); politicians also—especially Western politicians—play a key role in promoting the arms market; and so on.

We are pleased to observe that we have not been overly dramatic in this regard. While keeping the values of the gospel in mind, we look to the modern world in a positive way. We know very well what it means to live in this world while following the example of Jesus Christ. For this reason, we are in favour of using "positive" language and avoiding expressions that may foment persecution.

Inspired by the theology of the Second Vatican Council, we believe that some reflection should take place with regard to methods of evangelization. How we should evangelize in today's world? Methodologies are extremely important, as we should incarnate ourselves into today's reality. Along with this, we should cooperate with groups, civil society and international organizations that promote human rights. Where such cooperation exists, it should be strengthened. We should also encourage the pursuit and dissemination of objective information, helping people to be properly informed about discrimination, and always presenting this issue in a broader perspective that encompasses possible solutions to the problems.

Inside our church, there are many structures that support people who are persecuted or discriminated against: the Pontifical Council Cor Unum, the Pontifical Council for Promoting Christian Unity, the Pontifical Council for Interreligious Dialogue, Caritas Internationalis, Aid to the Church in Need, etc. Those organizations always welcome any kind of collaboration, fully aware that networks of solidarity should be further developed. Prayer is always essential and crucial among those who suffer. It is also important to promote and build schools and places where the younger generation can be raised so as to value living together peacefully.

We find this initiative praiseworthy, and we are open to any further step in the future that can help us to grow in unity and solidarity, hoping especially that we can give a strong witness.

Rev Dr David Wells, Executive Committee member, Pentecostal World Fellowship

The Pentecostal World Fellowship (PWF) group first of all met with our evangelical friends for a period of time, to model good unity, but then we met separately to talk about next steps to enhance our ability to walk together with the suffering church.

First of all, our members are very affirming of the Global Christian Forum experience here. It has been a positive experience. We found ourselves dealing with some of our own prejudices and hurts, and we were made aware of our lack of knowledge in so many areas. So we thank all of you as participants and as presenters for adding to our experience in Christ and helping us to draw closer to Him.

We do want to go back to the PWF executive with specific recommendations. Our group met to discuss those, especially how to enhance PWF and other related agencies such as the Assemblies of God World Fellowship. We also discussed how to relate to the broader body of Christ and how to enhance our ability to walk with the suffering church, by providing a platform to equip our people to pray and to speak with one voice. We know this is a priority of our chair, Dr Guneratnam, and we want to pick up on this opportunity and move it along in a practical way that causes the global awareness to move to the regional level, then to the national and local levels. We do want to see local churches strongly engaged, feeling that they are part of one voice globally to address issues in multi-faceted ways, and also to be part of prayer that shakes the "heavenlies", as we heard today. And so we will be talking about enhancing our fellowship as a platform for developing a strong, prayerful, consistent voice, especially at the local level.

We do appreciate the official message that is coming out of this conference. We want to affirm the decision not to mention specific nations that have their own particular contextual situations and may distract us from the main issues. In the same way, we ask the committee to consider that two or three social justice issues are being addressed in the message. We understand that they are in a larger context and do need to be addressed, but we find that it distracts from rather than helps with the central focus of calling the church to engage on behalf of that part of the church that is discriminated against. So we leave that with you; that is the observation of the Pentecostal community.

We do want to call PWF to sponsor events for those living in persecuted regions, to stand with member bodies that already are coming alongside the persecuted church, and to equip them in responding to persecution and discrimination. We will be talking in a more intense manner about making that type of support available to all our members. A friend from Pakistan affirmed the benefit of that assistance for him in his country, and yet nothing has happened up to this point, so we are looking forward to responding in that way.

We do want to go back to the Executive of the PWF with an encouragement regarding the expression of mutual repentance, and to clearly communicate that it was offered in a statement coming out of this conference. We know that we must address our own issues, where we have shown arrogance and pride and at times discrimination and persecution, and we appreciate the other bodies of brothers and sisters in Christ expressing similar sentiments to us as well. I cannot emphasize enough how important this is to the Pentecostal community.

This statement of mutual repentance is a priority, and the big question is how we will address, from this point on, internal discrimination and persecution within the church. We must clarify and communicate the processes to resolve when grievances are identified. We will have big work to do in the Pentecostal world community. I sit with brothers and sisters who are fixated on a certain period of time when, as a minority people, they have felt the pain of being looked down on and at times even worked against systemically by governments and churches, and it is hard for them to envision a new day. Please work with us, in believing God for a new day in the church of Jesus globally.

Let's find the pragmatic processes that will allow us to dialogue and address discrimination and issues that yet remain. We are encouraged by the positive example shared by a brother from Ukraine, where a council has been formed that basically represents the bodies here, and some of their positive experiences of being able to address grievances and to have a shared faith as they address very practical issues like buildings, licencing, official status, etc. We appreciate all the positive examples that already have been offered.

So my brothers and sisters, be assured that the Pentecostal community worldwide will continue to pray for you and with you, and we will continue to work alongside our suffering brothers and sisters so that they know they are not alone.

Rev Dr Olav Fykse Tveit, General Secretary, World Council of Churches

Sisters and brothers, we have come to a very important moment in our journey together in these days. I would like to start by reflecting on what we shared as the World Council of Churches in this meeting by saying that we see this event as a very important stage in our pilgrimage of justice and peace. This is the theme that the 10th Assembly of the WCC gave to the whole fellowship as a lens by which to see everything we plan and do together in our programmes and projects, but also everything we do as a fellowship of churches in an ecumenical movement that is wider than the WCC. We are together on a faith journey, on a pilgrimage led by God, open to being together, and also entering into new landscapes together with this commitment to being pilgrims of justice and peace.

Not that we ourselves know everything about how to bring justice and peace, but we are committed to praying and working for the Kingdom of God to be present and manifested in this world, as life, justice, and peace. This consultation has reminded us of this purpose as well as calling us to be stronger and more focussed on what it means to address the injustices and conflicts that are particularly affecting our Christian sisters and brothers these days. We need to continue and even strengthen our work for human rights and religious freedom, particularly looking at it from the perspective of what is Christian solidarity in the cross of Christ today.

I would like to share my summary of what we see from our common experiences these days by referring back to a biblical quotation that I shared in my opening remarks, from the Beatitudes and the words immediately after the Beatitudes, where Christ says, "You are the light of the world." There are three dimensions of this passage that, I think, have become quite clear to us these days and which I think we should have as our focus when we follow up as the WCC, the WEA, the Roman Catholic Church, Pentecostals, and so on (because I think we should agree that the GCF is not an implementing body). We are here together to talk to and to listen to one another so that we can do better that which we are committed to do, with our constituencies, churches, and fellowships. In these days, as I have listened to you and to what God has challenged us to do and be, I have seen clearly three dimensions of this notion of being the light of the world.

First, we are actually called to be the light of God in this world. We are not called to be our own light. So when we discuss what it means that we are troubled, persecuted, and discriminated against, we must ask ourselves, "Are we really the light of God? Is it the real witness of the Triune God that we bring to the world?" Then there will be real resistance; many will not like it, and we have to be prepared for that. But this has to be the first question before all others: "Are we really the light of God or are we our own light?" That means also that we have to understand that this light from God is also shining upon our own lives as a critical light. What do we need to address in how we work, or in how we are not working? Self-critically, we are helping one another to enlighten our own way of being this light in the world.

This light is also the light of righteousness. It is the light of God's justice and peace. Therefore, it is not primarily there to be a provocation, in the sense that nobody likes it, but it is the light that brings God's light of creation and salvation into this world. So the second dimension that I would like to emphasize is that we need enlightenment—in the broad sense, not in a narrow philosophical sense. We need enlightenment that is deeper and more profound, as well as a biblical theology of the cross and the resurrection. I think that we have touched on this in many ways, and we need to continue this reflection both in our own constituencies and also together. What does it mean to be Christians, marked by the cross, carrying the cross? We need to educate our young people and one another. We need to work theologically on what it means to carry this cross as a sign of God's justice, resistance, and liberation, as well as a sign of solidarity, a willingness to sacrifice in order to be always signs of God's light given through the cross and the resurrection. This leads us as the WCC to again ask how we are doing this in our many kinds of programmes. How do we strengthen our ability to be churches of the cross and the resurrection? It happens through meetings like this one, but it also happens through programmes—not only advocacy programmes, which are very important, but also theological studies and educational programmes. How do we work together on really going deeper into this, and also in strengthening our way in practical terms and in principal perspectives?

My third dimension is very important: we need to be a light for one another. I see the significance of the Global Christian Forum in this regard. Our light and our enlightenment are stronger when we are the light of God together. We have all shared many conversations and listened to many sources of input in these days. It has really helped us to see how the others can strengthen our light, our way of being light. In our conversation this afternoon, we have also shared how we can more strongly be the light together for peoples of other faiths. How can we talk not only about our suffering, in a credible way, but also about theirs, so that they really see us as partners whom they trust and with whom they want to work to address their problems?

This openness to fellowship based on how and why we are the light of the world needs to be strengthened as an ecumenical movement. Another dimension that we also reflected on is how we can consider some issues more strongly than we have done here—for example, how women are more effective in many cases in carrying out their responsibility for the faith community and the family. We should also examine their many sacrifices, particularly related to gender-based violence in general and in the domestic sphere. We must look at how violence works. It never ends. It has an impact in many circles and in many aspects of our daily lives, as families and as local communities. How can women bring new contributions to the issues we have raised here? How can they also, as a substantial part of the world family and the world's churches, bring other perspectives on how we address and prevent violence, and on how to be light in other areas of darkness in the world?

Finally, I see in this meeting an opportunity to use the Global Christian Forum as a real platform to share, to invite one another, to strengthen our light, and to be a clearer light. The GCF should be an instrument to make our light stronger.

Bishop Efraim Tendero, General Secretary, World Evangelical Alliance

On behalf of the World Evangelical Alliance, we would like to express our appreciation to the Global Christian Forum for providing an avenue where we can address this issue of discrimination, persecution, and martyrdom, all with that desire that we would be following Christ together. As we end our several days of deliberation, we would like to suggest these next steps of walking together as a suffering church. We have identified several items in our discussions.

(1) We are glad that repentance of persecuting each other is part of our consultation message. We consider it important to heal memories wherever this has happened. We will encourage our pastors and churches to do this on a local level, and we will discuss among the four bodies participating in this consultation how to facilitate this on a national, regional and global level.

(2) We will do whatever is possible to help and train our people to overcome prejudices against other Christian traditions, and not to confuse past with present realities. Among other things in this regard, we will be sharing with local churches, promoting this issue with top leadership, and replicating the GCF experience at regional and local levels. We want specifically to harness our youth in this training as well as in assisting our older people.

(3) We want to state very clearly that we wish to continue the work started at this consultation. The four bodies need to work together, and our Christian churches worldwide have to work together, on ongoing matters of discrimination, persecution and martyrdom, which includes going beyond the surface to address some of the hard problems among us.

(4) We will start appointing evangelical ambassadors to other Christian communities, with an emphasis on religious freedom, both to improve relations with them, in order to overcome suspicions from history, and to cooperate in reacting

to discrimination and persecution together, particularly in dealing with governments. In some cases, we may need to commission a task force from the different church bodies to address a common area or problem related to discrimination and persecution.

(5) We will ask our Religious Liberty Commission, and especially the International Institute for Religious Freedom, to cooperate even more with non-evangelical Christians and churches and their research and educational organizations, and we would be glad if the other organizations would reciprocate.

Finally, prayer always has to be the first form of solidarity among Christians and churches. Therefore, the WEA will strengthen the International Day of Prayer for the Persecuted Church, which is actually held on the second Sunday of November, and invite as many churches worldwide as possible to take part in it—suffering and non-suffering churches alike. It should be possible for every congregation to reserve one Sunday service a year for suffering sisters and brothers in Christ. Let us be reminded of the experience of the apostle Paul in his conversion, as stated in Acts 9:4–5: "And falling to the ground, he heard a voice saying to him, 'Saul, Saul, why are you persecuting me?' And he said, 'Who are you, Lord?' And he said, 'I am Jesus whom you are persecuting.' "

Respondents

Archbishop Anton Audo, Archbishop of Aleppo, Chaldean Catholic Patriarchate

This gathering of the Global Christian Forum represents for us, the oriental churches of the Middle East, a unique opportunity. As Chaldean bishop of Syria, I consider the Forum to be a concrete ecumenical experience, very important and entirely new for me.

Second, the choice of Albania as venue for the encounter is highly significant for all of us, as it has introduced us to the humbleness and hope of the Christians and the citizens of this country.

As oriental Christians, we are suffering greatly from the war situation which is causing the emigration of Christians from our country. We do not weep for ourselves, but we weep over our country, our churches, our families, and even our Muslim friends who are at each other's throats. We suffer a lot because Christian communities well rooted in the East are disappearing, the Arab world does not care about the situation, and the West also does not care.

We consider our role as living and apostolic churches, capable of living with Muslims, willing to dialogue with them and to pursue with them a future of justice and peace.

A few points have caught my attention in the presentations by the church leaders. The most significant one is the matter of repentance, or our ability to forgive one another. I consider this point very important as a testimony of Christians walking together. I was therefore touched by the concept of pilgrimage of which Rev Fykse Tveit spoke. That concept brings us dynamism, I believe. We are not in a dynamic of coming to an end, or of accusation. Rather, our attitude is one of setting out, of walking together. And as you know, in the tradition of the church, the word synod means moving together and listening to what the Spirit is saying to the church.

Finally, I would like to react also to what the leader of the Pentecostal church said. I understand the suffering and the suspicion that these communities may experience when they arrive in countries like Iraq, where the war is going on, or in Syria or Jordan, countries where Christians have been present since the beginning of Christianity. Sometimes they present themselves as coming to teach us how to be Christian, and that creates a lot of tension and sensitivity. Therefore, both sides have to pay attention. We must be receptive to these calls of the Spirit. And I think that these new churches should respect the reality in which we live and try to avoid making mistakes.

Mrs Connie Kivuti, General Secretary, Evangelical Alliance of Kenya

I want to thank you very much for this opportunity to respond. This is a very opportune time to speak, as we come to the end of this particular consultation.

First, I want to express appreciation for what has happened—the effort that has been made, the people who have taken time to prepare various papers and also to think about what they needed to say at this global event. I think this is something that we need to appreciate.

But it has also been a time when we could vent our frustrations and a lot of issues that many of us have been having. As one of the speakers said, we are really just scratching the surface. We have yet to really to go deep and address some of the issues that have been raised. We talked about repentance, and my issue is that we ought to have started doing it right here at this particular gathering. I mean that we also need to practically repent, rather than just putting out a press statement that says that we need to repent to one another. I think that practically we need to show it.

Prayer is very important, but we need to also be a body that is engaged in much more than just prayer. And addressing our various prejudices must happen not only at this level, but at the apex of everything, and then percolate downward. What would the world say if the Pope, the president of the WEA, and the leaders of the PWF and WCC met together for a meal or a cup of tea? It would send quite a message. I believe that we need to talk not just about how this spirit can move down to the local level, but also about how it can actually start from the top, because perception is everything and we need to send that message of unity.

We also need to unpack our terms. We are talking about solidarity, and we go home saying, "Yes, Christians, we are in solidarity with you," but what does that mean? Remember, we were talking about the perception of language and what various terms mean. We need to discuss that further.

The Global Christian Forum may be not an implementing body, but it is a body that creates accountability, so we need to be held accountable for what we have said and discussed here.

But my challenge is really also to the umbrella bodies that have access even to the UN Security Council and similar places. We know that certain bodies have seats there: the Catholic Church, the WEA, and so on. My question is how you are engaging at that level towards addressing the persecution that is happening and the suffering that Christians are enduring, and whether you are bringing enough effort to bear to actually make a difference. If not, are we trying to be politically correct rather than making sure that we do have an agenda and that we are pursuing that agenda to the fullest? I think we need to be less apologetic, because if non-Christians were suffering as the Christians are, the world would be in an uproar, because of the various engagements that would be taking place. We have had a good shaking here, a good opportunity for awareness, but we need to do much more than that.

To conclude, I want to refer to an anonymous letter, probably from the second century, that has been reproduced in a book called *Christianity through the Ages*. It illustrates the point that we have been trying to emphasize in this consultation. It was written at the height of persecution of the church, and the author highlights not just the paradoxical nature of the Christians but their peculiarity. This is how the letter reads:

> *For Christians are not differentiated from other people by country, language or customs. You see, they do not live in cities of their own, or speak some strange dialect, or have some peculiar lifestyle. They love everyone, but they are persecuted by all. They are*

unknown and condemned, they are put to death and gain life, they are poor and yet make many rich, they are short of everything yet they have plenty of all things, they are dishonoured yet gain glory through dishonour. To put it simply, the soul is to the body as the Christians are to the world.

We are the salt of the earth, and we believe that Christ has given us the direction that we need to respond to persecution. Most of you will remember talking about "what would Jesus do," and really the same question would be asked of us today. If Christ were living in our time, what would he do? How would he address this particular situation that we are going through? I would say that he has given us a way to respond. It is up to us who are here to bring it down and contextualize what we have discussed, so that it can bear fruit within our context and so that we can raise that united voice that we have been speaking about. And then also, let us repent one to another for what we have done to each other and to the world. I believe that in this way, we can experience mutual respect for and also mutual forgiveness of one another.

Rev Dr Larry Miller, Secretary, Global Christian Forum

My first regret about these three days is the relative absence of women in our midst. It is a result of what I would call structural discrimination. We are all structured in such ways that when we came to the nominating process, asking these four bodies in the Forum to nominate participants, this is what the result was. I regret it deeply and I think many others among us do as well.

My biggest satisfaction is that you have used the Forum as a place to meet, which is what we have said is the purpose of the Forum. This is deeply satisfying to me personally and, I think, to all of us who are engaged in the Forum.

My most important affirmation of commitment is that I think all of you have said that you want the Forum to continue as a place for you to meet, and for others to meet, as the widest Christian gathering possible. I like the words that you said, Connie: we are not an implementing body, but there is a kind of accountability here. I would like to apply the concept that we find in 1 Peter 3, where Peter calls us to give an account of the hope that is in us. That is the kind of accountability that can take place in the Forum. It is a place where you as leaders of Christianity are called or can be called to give an account to each other of the hope that is with you, and of what you are doing about that.

Perhaps the most important information about next steps for the Forum, apart from follow-up to this event, has to do with the other major initiative that is just underway, which we are now calling "Call to Mission and Perceptions of Proselytism". And this relates, I think, to the moving words from David Wells which have been picked up by others, on the need for mutual repentance and the healing of memories. Archbishop Audo also mentioned this source of tension between us, dating back decades and maybe even centuries. Mission and proselytism—what is mission in one person's eyes is proselytism to another. These four same bodies are beginning to work together with the Forum as the platform for addressing this issue. And I think a very significant part of it is going to be also a process of healing memories.

Thank you for coming. Thank you for going out together in the days ahead.

Left to right:
Archbishop Dr Joris Vercammen and Rev Dr Hielke Wolters

Over Lunch Session

Tuesday, 3 November

Testimonies

Msgr Basilios Georges Casmoussa,
Catholic Archbishop Emeritus of Mosul, Iraq

H.E. Archbishop Sebouh Sarkissian,
Armenian Prelacy Diocese of Tehran
Holy See of Cilicia, Iran

Testimony of *Msgr Basilios Georges Casmoussa*, Catholic Archbishop Emeritus of Mosul, Iraq

Christians of Iraq ... Last Call?

Have we really arrived at that point? This question chokes me up. It tears me so that I dare not pronounce it. It was inconceivable until July 10, 2014, which was the 52nd anniversary of my ordination as a priest in 1962 in Mosul. This town, considered the cultural and spiritual capital of the Christians of Iraq, was entirely emptied of its Christian population last June, when the city fell under the total control of the so-called "Islamic State". There were still some 25,000 Christians in Mosul under the 2003 American occupation, including approximately 30 churches, four Catholic and Orthodox bishoprics, female and male religious congregations, monasteries, parochial and Christian training centres, Christian printing and publishing houses, orphanages and schools. In short, Christians were recognized for their active presence and their socio-economic potential. The Muslims held them in high esteem.

Everything was swept away in less than 24 hours when Daesh branded all Christian houses with the letter ن (N) and gave an ultimatum to the city's Christians: convert to Islam, pay the *jizya*[1], leave town, or die. They left taking nothing with them, only what they had on them at the time. Even that was taken away from them if it was money or valuable belongings, including their identification documents. The Christians found refuge in the towns and cities of the Nineveh Plains[2]. But as soon as they had settled, Daesh cannons forced them and the host towns' inhabitants to evacuate hastily. Qaraqosh, my hometown, the largest Syriac Catholic concentration in the Middle East and a Christian bastion of the Nineveh Plains, was emptied of its 50,000 inhabitants in a few hours, on the night of August 6–7, 2014. On the morning of August 6, the day of the Transfiguration feast, Daesh bombs killed a young girl and two boys. This raised a general warning.

---

1   [Translator's footnote:] The *jizya* is a tax required of all non-Muslim pubescent men old enough to perform their military duty.
2   [Translator's footnote:] Also known as the Mosul Plains or Sinjar Plain, situated in Nineveh province in Iraq, northeast of Mosul.

The Kurdish Peshmarga, the only armed force defending the city, left. The panic caused by the atrocities that Daesh was perpetrating—rape and selling of women and young girls—on the Sinjar Mountains[3] against the Yezidis[4] led the people of all 13 Christian towns and cities of the Nineveh Plains to leave everything behind and flee in panic to Kurdistan. Ainkawa, a Christian city on the outskirts of Erbil, the capital of Kurdistan, was literally invaded by an exhausted population, in need of everything. Church forecourts and naves, public squares, church halls, side streets, then schools … everything was filled to capacity. A flock at a complete loss. A disaster as never before. The general exodus of a people.[5]

After the very difficult first months, lodging improved. Caravans and sometimes also communal meals were offered by Caritas from Jordan. Church halls or school rooms were converted into cubicles or enclosures for families, though they lacked intimacy. Full apartments or sections of them were rented by the church in Erbil.

The church is expected to furnish everything: lodging, food, healthcare, and even procedures for the liberation of our territories occupied by Daesh, or speeding up emigration authorization processes. The church, while affirming its spiritual mission, does not hide its preferences: humanitarian needs are its priority, then prefabricated school buildings, or houses rented to be turned into classrooms. Culture is a Christian's equity and number-one "weapon" alongside his or her

---

3   [Translator's footnote:] A mountain range on the west side of Tall Afar, near the north of the eponymous town of Sinjar, in Nineveh province in Iraq.
4   [Translator's footnote:] A Kurdish-speaking community of between 100,000 and 600,000 people in Iraq. They are one of the oldest populations of Mesopotamia, from where came their beliefs more than four thousand years ago. Their main place of worship is Lalesh, in the Iraqi Kurdistan, but several thousand Yezidis live in Syria, Turkey, Armenia and Georgia.
5   According to statistics maintained by the Holy Family Centre, the total number of uprooted and migrant Catholic Syriacs from the Mosul diocese would be 26,835 people in Erbil-Ainkawa, 4,662 in Duhok, 1,208 in Suleimanieh, and 1,000 in Kirkuk. There would be around 4,000 people in Lebanon, the same if not more in Jordan, and maybe 2,000 in Turkey. Add to this over 1,000 people who have already arrived in France and in Germany, and you have a total of approximately 45,000 people, excluding those who were already waiting in neighbouring countries or had already reached host countries such as the United States, Sweden, Australia, western Europe, and New Zealand.

faith. Priests, bishops assisted by local committed laypersons, along with NGOs and international Christian humanitarian organizations play the role of the brave good Samaritan ... but for how long?

Outside help is getting increasingly scarce. So we were told by alarmed voices in Jordan. NGOs increasingly hesitate to help Iraqi Christian refugees as such, so as not to be accused of religious sectarianism. Despair and impatience grow among the 100,000 to 120,000 displaced Iraqi Christians. Everywhere the same daunting question: When are we going back home? Can't the church speed up the emigration applications that we submitted to the UN?

Emigration is becoming the emergency exit for an increasingly large number of people. About 2,000 refugee families in Lebanon, the same number if not more in Jordan, 1,000 in Turkey, all in all around 25,000 have explicitly chosen emigration by registering with United Nations offices. That does not count all those who have already arrived in the West. Some sources state that 50,000 files have been or are about to be submitted to the American Congress by prominent Chaldean personalities living within the United States. According to the church's official position, emigration is a human right that falls under freedom and individual and family responsibilities, although the church prefers to retain the land after it has been liberated. We are in the twelfth month of the great exodus and still there is no liberation in sight. People are exasperated.

Daesh or Muslim ex-neighbours control Christians' houses and properties; Christian children and youths are deprived of every level of education; there is general unemployment, lack of income and a state freeze of wages and bank accounts. Daesh targets not only people but also Christian symbols and our cultural and architectural heritage, using dynamite to blow up churches, libraries, manuscripts, sculptures and historic monasteries, desecrating Christian crosses and cemeteries, destroying museums and ancient archaeological sites, or even Muslim heritage ... all to erase the historic memory, our people's pride, the memory of any Christian presence on our land, even though it predates by 630 years any Muslim presence. The liberation is repeatedly postponed. Obama has been speaking for three years and the endless and bloody Sunni-Shiite war goes on, in the face of a certain carelessness or incapacity of the central government. There are so many demoralizing factors for Christians that cause them to lose faith in their land and in the possibility of living side by side with Muslims.

Is this not a social and cultural genocide and an irreversible uprooting of the Christians of Iraq? Genocide is not only the physical massacre of a people; it is also the systematic massacre of their social fabric, culture, historic and collective memory, future, and active presence in the land of their ancestors. Do the Christians of the Nineveh Plains feel abandoned and subject to a social and cultural genocide and an irreversible uprooting? If the Nineveh Plains are emptied of all Christians, the entire Christianity of Iraq, a Christianity dating back to the apostolic era, is threatened with extinction.

Daesh does not come from nowhere. Daesh and every other jihadist Islamist organisation rely on religious and legal texts, some of which were written several centuries after the Koran and never rejected by Islam's official authorities. As a military force, Daesh will not hold out. Sooner or later, it will be vanquished. However, the intensity of the Daesh phenomenon is not only military, nor is it short-lived malevolence carried out by enlightened terrorists—which is why we will have to target its ideological roots and textual references if we wish to truly understand the phenomenon and counter it. Otherwise, a humanitarian disaster and other genocides will occur every so often. Maybe they will be called differently and the methods will be different, but with the same results and the same objectives.

In quick succession, from the beginning of the Islamic expansion in the Middle East up to the emergence of Daesh: from Iraq to Egypt, via Syria, the Holy Land and Turkey, the number of Christians is being whittled away under the pressure of a conquering and unyielding Islam. Before 2003, the number of Christians in Iraq was about a million. Today, they are only in the region of 300,000. Why? Is it because Christians are cowards and deserters? Is it because they are tormented and being forced out of the country? Their trust has run out. They have lost hope for change in their country or in its prevailing frame of mind that continually humiliates them by marginalizing them with the term *dhimmis*⁶ (under protection). Never are they referred to using such terms as parity of rights and equality.

Underlying the legitimating and provocative religious speech, there is a sly manipulation, emanating from Islam's expansionist aims (every Islamic organization advocates the establishment of the Islamic State or of the "Caliphate", the religious and political regime of Islam, using violence if necessary). This is what the Christians of Iraq and of the Middle East fear.

Fifty years ago, 18% of the population of the city of Mosul and 5% of the Iraqi population were Christians. Their cultural, humanitarian and economic activities gave the impression that they represented 20%. They are now 1%. From one million in 2003, we have now dropped to a mere 300,000. What is left of the Christianity of the west and south of Turkey, of Upper Mesopotamia and of the south and centre of present Iraq? Are we turning the last page of our Christian history in this Middle East that is permanently ablaze? Are these not symptoms?!⁷

Is there hope? The world quickly settles into accepting this phenomenon of "emigration". Just like natural disasters, we forget them so quickly. Palestinians have been refugees without a country for 70 years. International conventions take place to debate whether to continue or to stop providing aid. The international conscience doesn't feel guilty as long as it can provide a few tents, caravans, canned goods or pieces of clothing. Are we, Christians of Iraq driven out of our homes and towns, meandering for a year now, doomed to being treated only as an emergency situation or as requiring assistance?

In the face of the tragedy we have been experiencing for 12 months now, what has been the reaction from the central government? Ignorance

---

6 [Translator's footnote:] According to Muslim legislation, the term dhimmi refers to non-Muslims who have signed a treaty of surrender (dhimma) defining their rights and duties, for which they have to pay a tax (jizya).

7 An assessment conducted in March 2010 by the human rights agency Hammurabi found over 1,000 martyrs, including 47 massacres in the Catholic Syriac cathedral of Baghdad, among whom were two priests, in addition to five others killed between 2006 and 2008, 13 priests kidnapped (including myself in 2005) and 45 explosions or destructions of churches or monasteries.

... helplessness, chronic marginalization. At best, kind words during visits from our religious leaders. Always the same tune: You are not the only ones affected by this general violence. Hold on tight!

But to hold on, we need tangible signs of a true solidarity on the part of our government or signs of their understanding of our distress. Our distress is not a financial issue; it is above all an issue of rights, of respect for our identity, of the recognition of our equal citizenship.

Although emigration is a human right and a solution for increasing numbers, unfortunately, we know that it is not the ideal solution. Our cities and our land are our homeland and asset, and this is where we wish to continue to develop our roots. But for emigration not to become indeed the solution, there are basic conditions to guarantee before it is too late.

(1) We ask the international community to support the efforts of the Iraqi and Kurdistan governments toward a complete liberation of the Nineveh Plains from the control of Daesh, and to cut off all supplies in arms and logistical support in favour of armed jihadist organisations, so that our people may return to their towns and villages and rebuild their lives peacefully. Reliable international and local guaranties from Baghdad and Kurdistan are needed to promote renewed living together side by side.

(2) The Iraqi government will have to ensure the rights of families, individuals and institutions, including the church, to obtain compensation for losses incurred, and it will have to rebuild the fractured infrastructure of the territory.

(3) An in-depth reform of public discourse, school programs and media is necessary so as to rid them of anything compromising civil peace and mutual respect for traditions, religions, cultures, ethnicities, languages and history. We must acknowledge each other as peers, not parasites.

(4) We must remove from the constitution and the law all discriminatory articles based on religious, ethnic or racial affiliation, or on gender, and promote the culture of civil

citizenship and the distinction between religion and state in mutual respect and not intending any tutelage or manipulation.

(5) We must carry out and encourage an enlightened, scientific and moderate renewed reading of religious texts, particularly from the Muslim angle, for that is where radicalism lies and where the use of texts can turn them into time bombs. Choose what can serve to bring the faithful closer to God and to their neighbour and not what will, even if done in his name, be harmful to humankind.

In conclusion, if the political regimes of our countries and our Muslim societies decide to apply the aforementioned basic conditions, we can continue to co-exist in these lands. If not, "many Christians will continue to choose exile—the only solution, alas, offered to them today to live serenely". ("*Jusqu'au bout*": Nlle Cité, p.11).

Testimony of **_H.E. Archbishop Sebouh Sarkissian_**, Armenian Prelacy Diocese of Tehran – Holy See of Cilicia, Iran

Good afternoon, dear sisters and brothers in Christ.

It is a unique joy to be here in this gathering. During the last two days, we have discussed matters related to the life of the church all over the world, and especially in specific areas where there is persecution, discrimination and martyrdom.

I am focussing on Iran. I have to point out what happened in Iran just prior to and at the time of the revolution. Prior to the revolution, the authorities were more interested in national and ethnic identities than in religions as such. The Muslim clergy were looking forward to the withdrawal of the Shah. They were very unhappy with the activities of western Christians who came to Iran during the Shah's regime to convert Muslims to Christianity, and they were waiting for an opportunity to take revenge. The opportunity came, fortunately or unfortunately: the revolution happened, and the Shah left the country.

During the first ten years, the people in charge were much worse than the Taliban. They were fanatic and intolerant in their attitude towards Christians, especially those with an evangelical or missionary orientation. During this period, many bad things happened. People were killed, assassinated, persecuted, and put in prison. Those Christians who had not been involved in missionary activities, like the Armenians, did not suffer. But ethnically and on the national level, we were also harmed a bit. They tried to close our schools. They tried to force us to teach Christianity in Farsi. Our people did not accept that. Finally, unfortunately, they imposed on us the requirement to teach religion in Farsi besides the Armenian texts.

This is my sixteenth year in Tehran. Every time I meet with the president or ministers or other responsible persons, I tell them, "You have insulted us and you are still insulting us because you are imposing on us the teaching of your textbooks of religion." I say to them, "Would you like me to prepare a textbook for Islamic religion, to be used in your schools?" They start laughing, but this is the reality.

On the other hand, I should say that when I was asked if there is there discrimination in Iran, I answered, "Show me a single country in the world where there is no discrimination." Everywhere, even in the United States, there is discrimination. But it differs from place to place. In Tehran, and in Iran in general, we are facing some difficulties. We are not living in paradise, but neither are we living in hell. As I keep telling my friends, whenever people talk about Iran, they take off their white glasses and put on black glasses, to see everything as black. Not everything is black; there are good signs in Iran.

Just prior to my arrival in Tirana, one of the fundamentalists published an article on a website, attacking all Christians, archbishops, bishops, pastors and even our members of Parliament, with their pictures. I asked my deputy to tell the security authorities that they should withdraw the text if it was not their own product. They were angry, saying that they did not know about it, and in 24 hours this piece of information, accusing us of patronizing missionary activity, was removed from the website.

We are trying to work wisely with the government and to get what we are asking for peacefully and in mutual understanding. To give an example: two weeks ago it was the Ashura in Iran, the commemoration of the Imam Hussein. For the Shiite Muslims, it is one of the most important ceremonies. We discovered that they had involved our people. A priest with a cross was standing at the table of Imam Hussein. This was an insult, and I immediately handed a letter to the people in charge, saying, "We respect your Imam, but don't force on us something that is yours and not ours." Because sometimes they say, "We accept and respect your Jesus, but you are not respecting our Prophet." I respond very frankly, "My friends, you are not accepting my Jesus, because my Jesus for me is God, God incarnate. He came to save humanity, while for you Jesus is only a prophet, a word from God, and not God as we accept Him, as we follow Him and worship Him."

So yes, there are difficulties. But I believe it is not as the westerners imagine Iran is. Some of my Mennonite friends told me that before coming to Iran they were thinking, "What country are we going to?" But after their visit, they realized that whatever they had heard and were hearing about Iran was completely different from the reality on the ground. I will stop here; maybe you have some questions.

Mansour Borgi: I am from Iran, from an evangelical background. I very much appreciate what the Archbishop said about the situation of the church and the Christians in general in Iran. But I understand that to be the perspective of somebody from a traditional church, an Orthodox church. As he mentioned, from the beginning of the Islamic revolution his church has had a different relationship with the Iranian authorities, whereas many of the evangelicals have suffered greatly under the Islamic state in the last 35 or 36 years. Let me mention a few things, to bring a different perspective: closure of at least 12 churches; closure and confiscation of church properties, from church buildings to schools, hospitals, cemeteries and retreat camps; closure of the Bible Society, and a ban on publication of Bibles and other Christian literature in Farsi; arrest and detention of at least 370 Christians only in the last five years, because of their Christian and evangelistic activities, on the charge of acting against national security; arrest, detention and threatening of church leaders, forcing them to abandon their ministry and leave the country; execution and extrajudicial killing, and assassination as mentioned of some of the Christian leaders, at least seven of them known to the rest of the world; restrictions on church services, on leadership training and theological training; the use of terminology that could be described as hate speech, dehumanizing Christians in general and more specifically a section of the Christian community, describing them as deviant, corrupt, misleading and pests that have to be eliminated, paving the way for further violation of their rights. And finally, threatening the family members of the Christian leaders in exile. That is why, in addition to how they treat the Baha'i and members of other faiths, Iran is among the fifty states with the worst records of human rights violations.

Archbishop Sarkissian: Well, every act has its reason and its background. As I said before, in Iran, especially after the revolution, missionary activity is not allowed. Unfortunately, it is still going on in some areas. The government is watching very closely what is happening. Let me put it another way. We as Christians believe in dialogue, in mutual respect and mutual understanding. If we believe in that, how can we go to a Muslim and say to him in a very impolite way that his religion is false and ours is right, that he should leave his religion and come to us? I as an Orthodox, forgive me for saying this, will not be happy if an evangelical comes to my church and tries to convert one of my believers to his denomination. Throughout our history, my church—the Syrian Orthodox Church, the Coptic Church—we kept our Christian faith according to our tradition that came to us over centuries, from the blood of our forefathers. Yes, they confiscate the schools, the churches maybe. I don't encourage that and I don't say that what they have done is right. But we have to find out the main reasons behind it. That is the most important. Otherwise we can easily blame the government; we can easily say that they have done so and so, that they have persecuted, marginalized and martyred our people. Yes, we have had martyrs also, during the first days of the revolution. A friend of mine who is an ayatollah said to me, "You know, Your Eminence, that during the first period of the revolution we were worse than the Taliban, but later on we realized that we cannot go on with this mentality and this behaviour."

Bishop Joseph Bagobiri: I want to commend the two speakers. They have helped to give a balanced picture of the situation of Christians in Iran. The picture I got listening to His Eminence is not what I have been hearing about the fate of Christians in Iran. I want to ask if you have in Iran a forum where the different expressions of Christianity come together, to stand as a formidable force in the country. I want to recommend the Nigerian model. In Nigeria, we have five different expressions of Christianity: the evangelicals, the Pentecostals, the African-instituted churches (these are churches that were born in Africa), the Christian Council and the Catholics. Initially the Catholic Church did not want to be part of this. But we had to join together so that we can stand together as the Christian body and be able to speak with one voice on issues that affect the church, on politics, on the economy and other issues. I want to recommend this model to Iran. If that model is there, you will not have the kind of situation that you are in. You can come together and encourage one another, and say to those who are going to excesses on certain things to calm down.

Archbishop Sarkissian: Thank you very much for the question. Indeed, from the very beginning of my arrival in Tehran my Catholicos Aram I, who is a pioneer of the ecumenical movement and was for a long time the moderator of the central and executive committees of the World Council of Churches, told me to establish an Iranian Council of Churches. That is something that was not and still is not so easy. But now that, fortunately enough, the situation is improving towards much more tolerance, I talked to the officials saying that I would like to establish an Iranian Council of Churches, and I involved our member of Parliament. I hope that we will succeed in doing so, and if we do, it will be a benefit for all of us in Iran.

Mansour Borgi: Thank you very much Your Eminence. I do join you in that desire and wish that it becomes a reality. At the same time I realize that the Iranian government knows the uniqueness and the opportunity that this unity brings about, and that it has tried to separate Christians. Many years ago, several councils of churches were initiated, but the government strongly opposed them. One example was the day of prayer, which I think was initiated by the Catholic Church in Tehran, at which many church leaders from different denominations were coming together and praying together. Two years ago, after one of these days of prayer, the Iranian government called several of them and threatened them that should stop these prayer meetings. So I hope that with the friendship and influence that you have, this dream can become a reality. I would be very glad if my colleagues from various denominations would be part of this council.

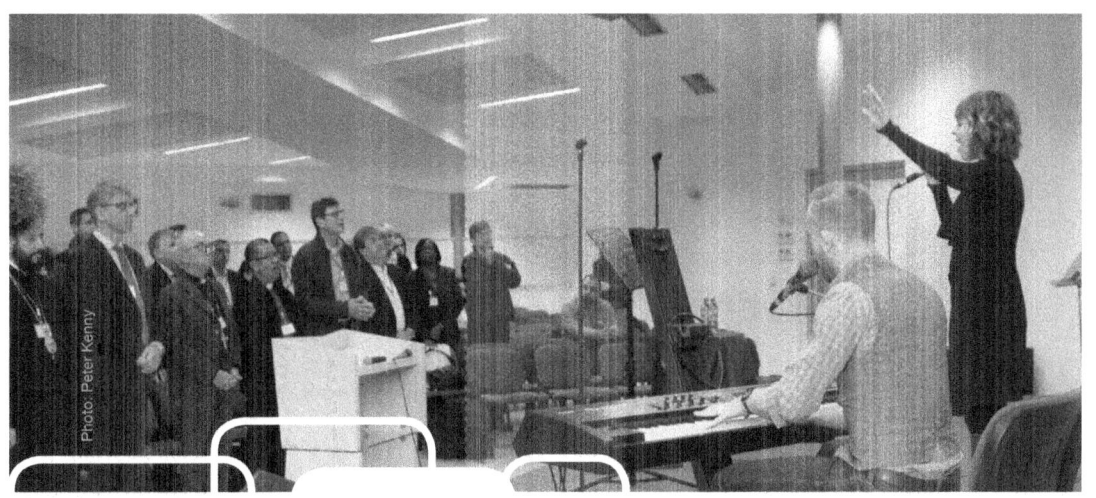

Morning prayers, Albania Christian Centre.

Summary of Small Group Reports

Sessions Four and Eight

Methodology

The participants in the consultation met twice in small groups of about 12 to 15 people. The composition of each group was a reflection of the diversity represented in the gathering. The small group meetings took place on the first and the second day, after the plenary sessions, at the end of the afternoon.

The tasks given to the groups were as follows:

- Learning to know one another: telling personal and ecclesial stories related to the theme;
- Discerning together: responding to the presentations and panels; and
- Considering the draft of the consultation message (at their second meeting).

The groups concluded their meetings with evening prayers.

In their effort to respond to the presentations and panels of the day, the members of the small groups were guided by a common question: What does your voice add to the voices we have heard today?

Reporting

The work of the small groups was not reported back into plenary during the consultation. The groups did not formulate recommendations for consideration by the consultation. The reporters provided summaries of the discussions in their group, which they addressed directly to the Report Committee. Comments and suggestions concerning the draft consultation message were shared with the Message Committee.

Synthesis of the small group discussions

The discussions in the small groups covered a wide range of subjects: personal presentations, sharing of stories, themes and issues. The following synthesis is based on a careful analytical reading of the group reports.

Personal presentations and stories

All the groups engaged in a round of personal presentations and the sharing of stories, but not all reported back on this part of the time that they spent together. Some did, however, communicate particular stories reflecting personal experiences of discrimination or persecution, or difficult situations in several countries. Following are some examples.

"My father was a pastor. He was very passionate about preaching the gospel. He tried to preach in the whole area. From my hometown, 270 km from the city, he went to remote areas to preach the gospel. And one day we heard that our father was kept by the religious [meaning Muslim fanatics, mainly sheikhs]. They tied him to a tree. I was just starting college. When I heard it, I went there with my friends to rescue him. When they learned who we were, they beat us. We made a deal with them that my father would never come back here to preach the gospel. My father, my friends and I were beaten badly. I still have scars. I was persecuted because of my father's preaching of the gospel. He never returned to this village again but preached in neighbouring villages."

"My name is Archbishop Audo. I have been a bishop for 25 years, and for 25 years I have been working in Syria. Now I am witnessing the destruction of everything in Syria. I am from a Chaldean Christian family well rooted in the history of Iraq. Among my ancestors, I have a martyred priest. I often ask myself, 'Will I be martyred or will I be the last Chaldean bishop in Syria?' People ask me, 'Are you going back to Aleppo?' I tell them there is no other place where I should be. My place is Syria and Aleppo, and this is what the Lord has asked me to be. Pray for us."

"My name is Bishop Joseph Bagobiri. I come from the northern part of Nigeria. Northern Nigeria has a population of 80 million people. In terms of land mass, it is the biggest region of Nigeria. It is very pluralistic in terms of Christians and Muslims. Christians are feared because they are the largest minority in the north and are thought to be allies with the west, which wants to exterminate the Muslim north. Between 2002 and 2014, a total number of 47,000 people have been killed in the north; 50% were Christians. The year 2014 was the worst in terms of persecution, as the portion of Christian victims rose from 50% to over 80%. The number of churches destroyed in northern Nigeria is 30,000. Other forms of persecution: refusing land. In my diocese (the northern part of Nigeria, predominantly Christian) we have lost 900 Christians between 2011 and 2014. We have four communities in which mass burials had to be conducted (graves of over 100 people each). In 2011, when we had the presidential elections and Buhari lost, he said the elections were rigged and people started killing left and right. When that happened, there was a conflict between a Muslim and a Christian community close to my house. One night, the Muslim community started shooting sporadically in the Christian village. When I heard that, I had to go and stand between Muslims and Christians. While I was in the middle, gunshots were exchanged. I had to leave. It was devastating."

"I am Titus Vogt. My father is a Lutheran pastor. Sometimes it was not so easy during the communist time in East Germany, but it is nothing compared to what we are hearing in this consultation. One of our students was [among the three Christians recently] killed in Turkey. I am still in close contact with his widow. She speaks a lot about forgiveness."

"I have lived in the time of communism. The communists killed my father before I was born. This was the most important event in my life. My mother used to pray for the murderer of my father. My mother knew the man who killed my father and used to say at home, 'This person is suffering more than us now.' This has shaped my life and vocation. Perhaps for this reason, for this vocation of reconciliation, I was sent to Serbia to serve there and to work on reconciliation."

"I am Bishop Vasiliy Yevchik. I was born and raised in Ukraine. My parents were believers. I experienced a lot of humiliation in school because I was a believer. My grandfather spent five years in prison for preaching the gospel, my uncle two years. My parents paid fines because a Bible was found in the house. My dream as a child was to preach the gospel. In 1991, I went to Russia to preach the gospel. I had a deep desire to speak about Jesus. I started a ministry in Tatarstan

Republic of Russia, where I formed a church. We faced a lot of trouble. Now the church has over one thousand members and we have planted 22 churches. We are part of the United Pentecostal Church in Russia, and I am the vice president. I am in charge of social ministry: drug addition, alcohol, etc."

"I am Archbishop Sebouh Sarkissian. I was born in Syria and served in Kuwait, in Basra, Iraq and then in Aleppo. Now I am primate of the diocese of Tehran. The existence of Christianity in Iran goes back to the first century AD. Iran for Armenians has been and is a homeland, where they have been living for so many centuries. The major flow of Armenians to Iran was the deportation of large numbers of Armenians by Shah Abbas in the beginning of the 17th century. The settlement of the Assyrians, generally known as Nestorians, started from the middle of the fourth century, whereas the Catholics and Evangelicals are the latest arrivals in Iran. Today there are three Armenian dioceses or bishoprics in Iran; there are also dioceses of the Assyrians, Chaldeans and Latin Catholics, and Evangelicals.

"In the beginning of the Islamic revolution, for a while the Christians were in a desperate situation, especially those with missionary inclinations. The traditional churches had no difficulties because they never have had any missionary activity; their main aim was and still is to keep their Christian faith and witness to the Gospel. Once the Iran-Iraq war was over and things were settled down, life was normalized and the Christians as minorities enjoyed their rights in practicing their religious ceremonies and running their schools.

"I have been serving my community in Tehran since 1999. From that time onwards, we have had a department of Christian education and inter-church publication. During the last years, we have published thousands of Holy Bibles, New Testaments and religious books for the people in general and for the youth, children and Sunday School students in particular. Armenians and other Christian communities are indigenous and are rooted in the history of Iran. They have all integrated into the Iranian society, while keeping their Christian and national identity. For the Armenians, the Christian identity is mixed with the ethnic identity. The most challenging phenomenon is how we as Christians can keep firm our faith and Christian identity as citizens of Iran. Fortunately enough, the constitution of the state has in it two articles related to religious minorities. Therefore, the rights of religious minorities are protected. Besides our religious activities we are hoping to establish a council of churches in Iran, to facilitate our cooperation together on one hand and with the state on the other hand. Nowadays, along with many good endeavours, we see an obvious effort by the state in rebuilding trust and enhancing respect towards each other."

"Before 1952, Egypt was a liberal country. But after Nasser, Islamism increased in Egypt through the Muslim Brotherhood and Christians were isolated from the society. After Mubarak and with the revolution in 2011, the Egyptians wanted freedom, social justice and human dignity, but they were without a leader and the Brotherhood took over. It sought to change the identity of Egypt. Christians suffered a lot; many emigrated. The second revolution, in 2013, was a huge manifestation rejecting Morsi and Islamism. The people became more aware of their rights. The president gave permission to build two churches. Now the Christians have 40 to 50 members in Parliament (about 10%). A new law on the rights of the churches will probably be passed. A new council of churches has been established for all the churches in Egypt. The Presbyterian Church—Synod of the Nile is the largest Protestant church in the Middle East. It has 400 local churches and is running 24 schools and two hospitals, which are being used by all groups of society. Over the last three years, the church has been concerned about the increased number of Egyptians emigrating to Europe and North America. We have established seven churches in Europe and 30 in the US. We had five pastors in Iraq until the crisis, but now just one in Basra and two in Kuwait. Every year, we see more refugees attending at church. This is a very big challenge for us."

"In Tajikistan where I come from, there is a disconnect between the first revival of religion, the Russian Orthodox Church, and the new Christian entities. With Russian Orthodoxy, there was such a tight relationship between the church and the national identity that anything that emerges today is seen as a threat. When there is a request for engagement with a Christian tradition, it always begins with the Orthodox Church and anything outside that tradition is seen as a threat. Persecution takes on an insidious tone as long-time government employees are not allowed to progress in their career because of their religion. You must have a degree to hold a position of authority, but getting a degree is not easy for Tajiks. Non-Tajiks are not allowed to hold the position of pastor regardless of their degree. There are laws against home meetings for religious purposes, but in Tajikistan all meetings take place in homes, so all are illegal. If the persecuted are breaking a law, does that justify persecution? This global initiative will help to signal to our government that peaceful coexistence and trust are possible."

"I was born and raised in a Muslim family and converted to Christianity in 1994. My wife and I went to the US to study counselling and complement our degrees in psychology. Back in Turkey, we discovered our calling for church leadership and church planting. In 2012 we started a church in Istanbul and welcomed regularly people who converted to Christianity. Turkey has a secular constitution, although the government admits to being Muslim. The number of Christians remains small, less than 1% of the 80 million people in Turkey. There is still a lot to do and Christians can openly share the good news. Our team uses mass media in television, publishing houses and radio 24/7. Many cities do not have a single convert. There is no organized persecution led by the government but conversion is seen as a big threat. Our hope is to become one of the fastest-growing churches in Turkey!"

"I am Jerry Pillay, from South Africa. My parents were Hindu but I went to Sunday school unimpeded by my parents and eventually converted. My family followed suit when my father was recovering after surgery and could not eat. He told God that if God would allow him to eat at least a few bites, he would believe. Two plates of food later he was a believer and he still is.

"The South African constitution guarantees religious freedom and despite the difficulties of apartheid, it brought people together to unite against a cause. People who suffer persecution unite. Most people in South Africa know how to work together. For example, I have a relationship with a Muslim community where we share a great deal. Yet people who convert from being Muslim to Christian are often victimized, which results in some faiths advising the faithful that 'you don't have to share your faith publicly.'"

"I am from Ukraine, I am a Pentecostal. Under communist rule, the people in my town were not allowed to declare their faith and were forced to worship underground. Now, in their current situation, the faithful from all denominations are able to worship freely and organize meetings together. Officials from the town attended prayer services and the mayor, after attending church for the first time, asked to be invited to church again. The message we can give to our Christian brothers and sisters who are suffering is: *have courage and stay strong*."

"I am a Pentecostal from Cuba. The Cuban people since 1959 faced many struggles and suffered a lot. Christians were not able to worship in public. Despite all the pressure, the believers held on to their faith and managed to meet secretly and worship together. After the Pope's visit, there are encouraging signs that a dialogue between Cuba and the USA is opening. Now the Christians are able to worship publicly, with some restrictions. Building new churches is not yet possible. We appreciate the help we are receiving from American and Canadian churches. I encourage you to keep praying for Cuba."

"In Kazakhstan, conversion to Christianity means bearing the suffering of being ostracized by family and community. Besides that, there is also open discrimination in terms of job opportunities. Because of the cost of converting, many converts revert back to their previous faith. For Christians, remaining true to the faith is a daily experience. Russians living in Kazakhstan are more easily accepted than Kazakhs who have converted. Out of a population of 17 million Kazahks, about 15,000 are Christians. The Kazakh Evangelical Church, which began in 1993 is very young and struggling."

Reactions to voices from suffering churches

In several groups, the pain of listening to the stories of discrimination and persecution was mentioned. For some, the information shared was disturbing, but many said that it was good to be aware of what is going on the world, especially in places where Christians are suffering:

> *When one is part of a church that represents the religious majority in the country and has the privileges of academic training, it is difficult and sometimes overwhelming to hear and understand stories of persecution, but it is also moving and inspiring. Listening to these stories helps to understand that to lose a position of privilege is not the equivalent of being persecuted.*

It was also noted that pain should not be idealized. One group reported that the stories of the panellists resonated with the experiences of the group members in their respective contexts. It was also observed that the experience of discrimination and persecution depends on the role of the churches in a particular society. On the other hand, much information was entirely new for some of the listeners. One said, "I see now how little I know about the situation of Christians in other countries." In another group, a participant from a suffering church felt that only negative aspects were shared and that the positive side of courageous witness to the faith was missing: "It is also good to share that the church suffers, but still exists in a wonderful way." The importance of telling stories in the media was underscored. It was observed that persecution happens mostly in the Middle East and South Asia, where the church is not the same as in the western part of the world.

Another reaction highlighted by several groups was that all Christians must be prepared for persecution. Challenges and suffering are everywhere, especially in countries where Christians are part of the majority. All suffer, though in different ways: "If you are not suffering you might not really be a good Christian, and if you are, you are probably not fighting." Taking this reflection a step further, in one group it was stated that we are all persecuted and at the same time, we are all persecutors. The same sentiment was expressed in another comment speaking of mixed feelings: "There is the pain of listening to our brothers and sisters who are suffering, but we need to take into account that some of those who persecute Christians today are motivated by fear caused by several centuries of persecution and discrimination perpetrated by colonizing countries known as 'Christian.' " The role of the churches was also highlighted in this regard, in particular with respect to colonialism. It was acknowledged that how Christian mission is carried out in majority-Muslim countries can lead to hostile reactions. And in some countries where Christian churches are the majority, there has been persecution of Muslims and mosques have been burned. Fear of losing privileges can lead us to persecute others: "When we are the minority we want dialogue and tolerance, but when we are the majority we can become persecutors and discriminate against others."

Listening to voices of suffering prompted theological and ecclesiological reflections. One of the comments was that Christianity is still Eurocentric. The churches in the West have not paid adequate attention to the voices from contexts to which they once brought the gospel. Another remark suggested that the issue of persecution offers the opportunity to reflect on the identity of the church. The witness to the gospel includes bearing the burden of persecution. In the context of Islam, which does not tolerate conversion from the faith, there is a great cost to bear in being Christian. Converts often find themselves ostracized from family and community. "We have to be prepared to suffer persecution, but we do not have to simply accept it", one participant said.

Suffering may strengthen the faith of Christians and sometimes make the church grow. What makes this possible? Why is it that in other situations, persecution causes extinction of the church instead of growth? In the history of Christianity, some churches have been exterminated because of persecution, such as the seven churches of the book of Revelation, or churches in China and Japan after missionary efforts in past centuries. The theology of martyrdom helps churches to live between hope and hopelessness. "The stories of persecution are strong reminders for us to be the church. We need to walk alongside those who are facing extermination today."

The importance of church unity in relation to persecution was also highlighted. In some places, Christian churches are divided when facing persecution because of personal interests or the benefits that some of them get from the government, while the government persecutes other churches in the same context. This causes fragmentation and lack of unity. It is necessary to build good and practical relationships with neighbouring churches, and with other communities as well: "The body of Christ has to be strong together." In one group, the example of Albania was cited where the local churches all suffered and were able to work together in building peace and harmony.

The question of how to define persecution in the global context was also part of the discussions. Several comments affirmed that the situation today is a result of globalization, and that persecution is a global problem with local geo-political factors. It therefore needs to be contextualized, historically, socially, culturally and economically. Sometimes persecution is an issue of power, rather than being related to a clash between religions. There can be various reasons such as political interests, sociological differences, colonial background, untouchability, personal advantages, etc. Religion may not matter much, but it can be used to harass Christians.

The situation in Pakistan was given as an illustration. Legal discrimination, as in Pakistan with the law on blasphemy, allows for virtual impunity and results in de facto persecution, where shades of legality allow for a person to be vindicated for a perceived (or real) transgression, but then be killed by a mob, which suffers no consequences. Mob rule in countries like Indonesia has seen numerous churches burned in places where Christians are a minority, e.g. Aceh, without the authorities taking appropriate action. In these situations, the judiciary has a particular role to play in protecting religious freedom. It was reported that the Supreme Court of Pakistan wants to review judgements of blasphemy, and that the Parliament has called for a revision of the law because of its abuse in several cases. In Sri Lanka, the judiciary has yet to set a precedent in countering the anti-conversion law. One participant suggested speaking specifically of persecution when life and property are at stake. Another said, "We do not have to exaggerate or dramatize persecution."

Walking with the persecuted church

A common response to the voices from suffering churches was that discovering the cost paid by persecuted Christians enables those who have not experienced persecution to identify more meaningfully with the suffering church. The language of "we" and "they", as in "How can we help them?" was discouraged; we are all one body, so together we are the persecuted church. Rather, the key word is *responsibility*. What is my personal responsibility in this situation, and what is the responsibility of my church? To remain silent and do nothing is not an option.

Several groups noted that many churches tend to delegate their response to persecution to specialized agencies and experts. This has meant that in some cases the suffering church feels alone. It was also noted that visits paid to Christians facing persecution are influenced by one's understanding of what a church is. Is it a local congregation, or is it the hierarchy? Whereas some participants requested more visits from international Christian organizations to persecuted churches, others felt that the actions taken by agencies are good but not sufficient. To respond to the level of suffering that churches are experiencing today, the active participation of the whole body of Christ is required. It is the church's calling to bring hope to those who are afflicted. Advocacy and solidarity with those who suffer torment and persecution are integral to building relationships between churches. There was agreement that the way of walking with suffering churches should not be decided from outside, but by these churches themselves. One group stated that the fundamental question to be considered is whether walking with the persecuted church can be harmful to that church. The norm should be that the persecuted church decides the level of relationship with a sister church.

Multiple groups discussed the need for political action. Churches in the West should press their governments, not only to care for persecuted Christians and refugees, but also to act in ways that can bring an end to the causes of persecution, e.g. stopping the war in Syria. Since persecution of Christians happens mainly in totalitarian societies, political endeavours to promote democracy and civil society can help to reduce discrimination against and persecution of Christians. With regard to the situation in the Middle East and the rapidly declining number of Christians in several countries there, the conflicting nature of two actions to support the suffering churches was noted.

The choices are to help Christians to stay and maintain their churches' presence in the region where Christianity was born, or to assist those who are leaving because of the persecution and helping them to retain their Christian identity in their new environment.

One group raised concern regarding assistance with legal action. Often churches or church leaders who are confronted with discrimination and want to dispute a charge do not have the ability to engage a lawyer or lack access to the necessary expertise. A case was mentioned in Central Asia where a well-intentioned person offered to help, but the person's expertise was outdated and in the end hurt the case more than it helped. The group felt that capacity building for churches in this regard should be given more attention. In addition, training of emerging churches in communications and reporting was encouraged, to help them deal with situations that can become contentious and be construed as provocative. Religious Liberty Partnerships was mentioned as an organization that does training on site, and Advocates International and Human Rights Watch were specifically recommended as sources of guidance and legal assistance. This group also emphasized the need for caution in terms of language when speaking about discrimination and persecution. For example, if a Muslim choses to convert to Christianity and is ostracized by his or her family, this is not persecution at a national level. It would be good to produce a glossary on best practices in use of language, to aid in defining terminology.

To help other churches walk alongside the persecuted church, one group proposed that "religious freedom watch" reports from many global Christian organizations and other international research groups should be circulated widely. The items shared could also include statements denouncing persecution and violence affecting church communities. Another proposal suggested that the Global Christian Forum could play the role of conveying solidarity and journeying with the persecuted churches through statements and visits. One participant stated that "This consultation has given us the opportunity to look for creative solutions" in walking with the suffering church.

United response

Just as churches facing discrimination or persecution in a given local, national or regional context should be united and support each other, churches from outside that want to accompany them in their suffering should also engage in united action. The need for a united response to discrimination, persecution and martyrdom was affirmed in numerous comments. One participant declared, "Regardless of our different denominations and backgrounds, we are looked upon by people outside our faith as Christians, as one. We are following Christ together; let us work and speak with one voice." The cooperation of the Orthodox, Catholic and Evangelical churches in Albania was cited as an example. It was also suggested that churches that find themselves on opposite sides of the fault line of discrimination or persecution should seek reconciliation and healing. One participant referred in this regard to a powerful event of Turkish–Armenian Christian reconciliation that took place in Izmir, Turkey and wondered how Christians could foster reconciliation in Ukraine through demonstrating unity in Christ. "The ecumenical movement is a precious gift because it allows churches to get together", this person stated. Another comment was that divisions and diversity help us to seek communion and live it out. In that sense, diversity can also be seen as a gift. Bangladesh was cited as an example; there the Catholic Church, the National Council of Churches and the National Christian Fellowship (Evangelical) each have their national committee and also come together in a loose forum structure that helps them to abide by some rules and regulations. Common understanding around issues that are crucial for all three church families is considered essential.

Solidarity with all who suffer

Discrimination, persecution and martyrdom happen to followers of all religions, not just Christians. Muslims and Hindus are also victims in many contexts. Churches should raise their voice not only for Christians but for all who are persecuted because of their faith, so that the love of Christ can break through boundaries. This will also make the cause of Christians more acceptable to friends of other religions. A typical comment, echoed in other groups as well, was that

"We have a mission to represent all religions, not only Christians. We need to respect all people with different faiths as members of society." As religious persecution around the world is increasing, solidarity with persecuted minorities should not be restricted to Christians but must include all other religious communities, in the name of religious freedom and universal human rights. "For me, is it important to talk about all people who are suffering, regardless of religion", one participant said. Similarly, a leader of an agency working with refugees and displaced persons noted the importance of listening to the voices of victims of discrimination and persecution from around the world, whatever their faith.

Religious freedom and human rights

"Religious freedom is not just the cornerstone of a democratic, civil society; it is the foundation." This statement reflected an overall sentiment regarding human rights and, in particular, religious freedom, called the "mother of all rights" in one group's report. It involves freedom of thought, conscience, religion and belief, which is basic to all human beings, not only *homo religiosus*. Another group affirmed that the approach to human rights was a blessing for many participants, giving them new tools to deal with persecution in their approach to governments in their countries.

Several groups underscored the need for churches to work closely with institutions related to the United Nations when championing the cause of persecuted Christians and other communities. The issue of religious freedom is high on the UN's agenda. The suggestion was made that global church organizations, such as the WCC, that have official status at the United Nations should engage with the Universal Periodic Review mechanism (UPR) to bring up cases of violation of religious freedom. They should work with national groups, asking them what to report to UPR on their behalf. Another very important UN procedure to use is that of the Special Rapporteur on Freedom of Religion and Belief. The current occupant of that position, it was indicated, is a Catholic theologian. In addition to inviting him to conduct country visits (pending an official invitation from the country in question), other ways of engaging with the Special Rapporteur and making sure that violations of religious freedom are reported to the UN exist. It is also important to cooperate with secular organizations such as Human Rights Watch, which often have much more experience in engaging with international and regional human rights mechanisms than churches and have larger audiences.

One group member reported on contacts with the World Bank, stating that it was also essential to press the issue of religious freedom with economic institutions like this one because religious liberty and economic development go hand in hand. This fact has been increasingly recognized at the global level, contrary to the trend in Europe to confine religion to the private sphere.

With regard to human rights, two perspectives were reflected in the group reports. One was that human rights are fundamentally based in the Bible, and that Christians should allow for differing understandings of human rights by Muslims and other communities that do not adhere to biblical teaching. The other view was that human rights are based on natural law, which is no longer generally observed, and that today new basic laws are being passed that contradict and harm Christian values and belief. In this respect, one participant commented that from a western European perspective, there is a need at all levels—political, media, academia, clergy, lay—to spell out a proper understanding of freedom of religion and belief.[1] Christians should learn to register their objections when secular societies pass laws or institute social practices that violate this basic human right.

Secularism

In reaction to the stories of suffering, some participants from highly secularized societies pointed out that secularism was their greatest problem, and perhaps even an alternative form of persecution. In Australia, for instance, the churches are now dealing with a cultural shift towards hard-line secularism, strongly influenced by media and supported by government. The question was raised whether in some such situations one could speak of discrimination. Do Christians living in a secular society experience discrimination? Where is the voice

---

1   "Freedom of religion and belief" is a technical term of the UN, with "belief" referring to a non-religious worldview.

of Christ in countries that call themselves free and democratic? Some Christian communities in Europe claim that they are persecuted as they endeavour to evangelize. Another prominent concern regarding Western countries was their spiritual emptiness, which can be a bigger danger than persecution. On the other hand, examples of civil organizations in Europe assisting refugees were mentioned as a source of hope, as their representatives do seek to focus on the meaning of life.

Christian–Muslim and interfaith relations

The issue of relations between Christianity and Islam emerged as a major theme in several group discussions. Using the term "struggle", one group asked if Islam should be considered inherently anti-Christian and evil, or to what extent it is possible to work with moderate Muslims who want to live in peace. One participant noted the long-standing presence of conflict: "Going back to Abraham and his two sons Isaac and Ishmael, we have to accept that there is hatred between brothers; it is our responsibility to start with self-examination before we ask others to do so." In response to this approach, a participant from Syria stated that violence will continue if Christians opt for a position of power. He underscored the importance of freedom of conscience, pluralism, interreligious dialogue and ecumenism. Christians should not support fighting between Sunnis and Shias, and they should not encourage conflicts in the hope that they might destroy Islam from inside. Christians have to be a model of charity, reconciliation and wisdom, not viewing Islam as evil or violent. "We have to find the way of life, leave the door open, and not be in an attitude of condemnation, because it will cause violence that will never end", one participant stated. Pointing to the action of Christian militias in Syria, another participant questioned the option of military resistance against violent Muslim radicalism.

Other group members from the Middle East spoke in the same spirit. They said that in spite of the long experience of persecution, Christians in the Holy Land and in the Middle East in general have shown their resilience and countered torment with good works in the name of Christ. Christian witness is best expressed through acts of love and compassion. Christians in the Middle East realize that their commitment to the faith gains respect from Muslims, however averse the latter are to Christian evangelization. Many Muslims are beginning to see Christians' deep convictions and capacity for compassion, grounded in their faith in Christ. The need for the churches to work together across denominational lines was also affirmed.

Another participant observed that interreligious violence has given Islam a bad name. Christians in the Middle East know that problems of fundamentalism also exist in Christianity, and that passages in all scriptures, including the Bible, can be misused to legitimize violence against members of other religious communities.

From Africa, it was reported that for some time now, trust has been developed between Christian and Muslim leaders at the regional level. Whenever there is a threat to peace, or also on topics of mutual concern such as climate change, they come together. Today in Africa, many families can be found of which half the members are Christian and the other half are Muslim. In South Africa, interreligious dialogue is broad and has resulted in positive and often interesting outcomes. For example, several Muslim participants end up embracing ecumenical positions, which completely confuses the outside observer but delivers a strong message. In Nigeria, Muslims bent on destroying churches are touched by the responses of Christians to persecution and are impressed by the love and compassion of Christians. The number of "secret Christians" among Muslims is growing. On the other hand, some Muslims in Nigeria are encouraging intermarriage as a means of trapping Christians. When a Christian marries a Muslim woman who converts, all her rights to guardianship and property are taken away from her.

On a more general level, the benefit of finding allies in the Muslim community was highlighted. Christians should not act alone. They should connect with others in working for peace and justice. Of course, there are differences between Christians and Muslims but God's good name should be made known to all: "We don't need to lock ourselves up in a fortress to honour God!" The vital importance of interfaith cooperation was also affirmed from a western European perspective, specifically an Anglican church working with different ethnic and religious groups in London. A participant from Africa said that he was impressed by how churches in the West provide chaplaincies for Muslims in universities.

Some comments on Christian–Muslim relations were of a more political nature. It was noted that a group like ISIS cannot operate without international help. Nations supplying weapons that feed the wars are lacking clear policies. Before the wars in Iraq and Syria the churches had good relations with the Muslims. This harmony has evaporated because of the intervention of the USA and other Western powers. It was suggested that the churches should support leaders in the Arab world such as King Abdullah II of Jordan, who encourages Christians to speak out with one consolidated voice against discrimination, persecution and martyrdom of Christians in Egypt, Iraq and Syria. Reference was made to the congress on "The Challenges Facing Arab Christians", held in September 2013 in Jordan, at which Christian leaders from the Arab countries gathered to speak about their situation, in the context of increasing threats to their existence in the Middle East.

It was also reported that African political leaders are starting to realize the value of working closely with the Arab Muslim countries in finding solutions together. The churches can play an important role in bringing nations closer to one another. "We need to support leaders who oppose all forms of discrimination and persecution and promote peace and tolerance", one participant said.

Evangelism, conversion and proselytism
One group discussed evangelism, conversion and proselytism. Evangelism was seen as integral to Christianity. China was mentioned as a country where local Christians are spreading the faith and the church is experiencing great revival. The church in China is manifesting a post-denominational Christianity. The Chinese government, however, does not allow evangelism among the Kazakhs and the Ugurs, who are Muslims. Conversion is understood as a faith commitment, but it can be interpreted negatively. Muslim accusations of Christian proselytism need to be addressed with clarification about the true nature of evangelism. The conclusion in the group was that evangelization,

proselytism and conversion remain problematic issues when we are dealing with the issue of persecution.

In another group the document *Christian Witness in a Multi-Religious World*, jointly published by the Catholic Church, the WEA and the WCC, was referred to. It was suggested that this encouraging paper should be widely disseminated and promoted.

The European refugee crisis

Although the refugee crisis in Europe was not directly on the consultation agenda, one group reported that it should be taken into consideration in discourse on discrimination and persecution, and several groups spent time discussing it. A participant who grew up under the communist regime of the former Soviet Union testified to the challenges he faced when his country became free and democratic. He expressed concern about how to address the needs of refugees who have suffered discrimination and persecution when they arrive in democratic societies where there is freedom of worship.

The flow of refugees fleeing the Middle East to European secular societies was seen as an indication of how much people are fearing the rising tide of fanatical Islam. This influx of refugees was seen as exacerbating problems between Christians and Muslims in Europe. A participant from outside Europe wondered if the people of Sweden and Germany recognized that Muslims will negatively impact their countries: "Do they not see the red warning flag?" Of course, one can also be more open and hope that the Muslims coming to Europe will become Christian! Another participant, from the Middle East, said that Christians should open their homes to fellow Christians as a first priority and only secondarily to Muslims. This position was opposed by a voice from Europe who defended the principle of accepting refugees regardless of their religion, whether Christian or Muslim. In a similar comment, the decision of German Chancellor Angela Merkel to receive a million refugees was called a Christian act. "Never forget the origins of the European Union, a peace project based on the Christian faith", said one group member. With regard to the fear of Muslim impact in countries where Christians are the overwhelming majority, it was noted that the same dynamic can be observed in both Europe and some African countries such as Kenya.

Beyond the need to welcome the refugees, groups considered whether the problems causing the crisis could be resolved. How can the war in Syria be stopped? One element of the response was that the situation would return to normal if the West, especially the USA, were determined to bring an end to the war. It was also suggested that Middle Eastern countries should close their borders so that no more persons could escape.

An encouraging tone was expressed from Jordan, where the presence of a large number of refugees has had substantial effects on the country. Christian denominations should work closely with government institutions to create educational programs promoting tolerance. They should offer services through their local churches to reach all groups of the community, including both refugees and locals. Another interesting testimony referred to the reception of refugees from Russia in Latin America in the 1930s. They were well received, integrated well and prospered. The question was raised whether such experiences from a very different historical and cultural context can contribute positively to solving the current crisis. "Are we prepared to accept the challenges and responsibilities, to open our doors and welcome the refugees when they knock at our borders?"

Church, state and society
Only two groups discussed the issue of relations between the church, the state and society. It was observed that how Christians view the state differs according to different traditions, and that various models of church–state relations exist in different countries. Experiences shared in one of the two groups ranged from complete freedom of religion to situations of serious discrimination, while some came from churches that hold a privileged position in their country. It was observed that Christians in the Middle East seem confused about how they should view the state. A warning was raised against extrapolating models of democracy that function in some countries to other countries and churches where they may not work. Instead, churches should

accept a kind of "political ecumenism" that allows for different forms of governmental and organizational structures.

Another comment was that the relationships of Christians with their society also vary considerably in different countries, and that this in turn has an impact on how those societies view Christians. The experience of Christians in relation to their society is influenced by the type of culture or the varieties of multiculturalism shaping that particular society. The relationships also depend on each church's tradition; e.g. the Orthodox and Catholic traditions of relating to society differ from how the newer evangelical and Pentecostal churches situate themselves with regard to society and culture. In addition, churches have different internal cultures even though they may share the same beliefs. In some contexts, specific theological commitments impact the church's position on cultural or political concerns.

These observations were illustrated by the Israeli-Palestinian situation. How Israel is interpreted theologically influences how some churches respond to events in the Middle East. Some argued that the problems faced by evangelical Christians in Israel/Palestine in relating to the traditional churches are caused by their support of the Israeli occupation, not by their different ways of expressing their faith.

Process of the meeting and gender balance

The group reports reflected unanimous appreciation and gratitude for the consultation and the unique opportunity provided to address discrimination, persecution and martyrdom in a gathering representative of all Christian traditions.

Some specific comments were reported concerning the process of the meeting and representation. One group explicitly noted the lack of gender balance, calling this a serious concern because women are very often the ones who suffer most from discrimination and persecution. The obvious under-representation of women among the speakers, panellists and voices of suffering churches was seen as detrimental to the integrity of the consultation. Another group member asked why the United Nations had not been invited to send a representative. In the first round of group discussions there was criticism that little or no time was made available for interaction from the floor with the speakers. On the other hand, the fact that a participant from Sudan, who was not part of a panel, could give a spontaneous testimony from the floor was warmly welcomed: "It was a moment of sharing the pain and sharing peace with the Christians of that country."

Screen capture, 'Persecution, Discrimination, Martyrdom: Following Christ Together' video.

CONSULTATION MESSAGE

04 November 2015

"If one member suffers, all suffer together; if one member is honoured, all rejoice together." (1 Corinthians 12:26)

1. For the first time in the modern history of Christianity high level leaders and representatives of the various Church traditions gathered together to listen to, learn from, and stand with discriminated and persecuted Churches and Christians in the world today.

2. This global gathering of 145 people took place from 2 – 4 November, 2015, in Tirana, Albania, a country that was declared by its constitution to be an atheist state in 1967, and now has flourishing churches in a framework of religious freedom even though some discrimination may remain.

3. The Consultation, entitled **Discrimination, Persecution, Martyrdom: Following Christ Together**, was convened by the Global Christian Forum together with the Pontifical Council for Promoting Christian Unity (Roman Catholic Church), the Pentecostal World Fellowship, the World Evangelical Alliance, and the World Council of Churches. It was organized in close

collaboration with the Orthodox Autocephalous Church of Albania, the Albanian Bishops' Conference, and the Evangelical Alliance of Albania.

4. We have come together because discrimination, persecution and martyrdom among Christians and people of other faiths in the contemporary world are growing due to a complex variety of factors in different realities and contexts.

5. As we follow Christ, Christians can be exposed to any form of persecution, suffering and martyrdom, because the sinful world is against the Gospel of salvation. But from earliest times Christians experienced the hope and reality of the Resurrection through walking the way of the Cross. Together we follow Christ as we "hunger and thirst for righteousness" (Matthew 5:6) for all.

6. The life of the Church for centuries has been a constant witness in two ways: the proclamation of the Gospel of Christ, and the testimony through the shedding of the martyr's blood. The 21st century is full of moving stories of faithful people who have paid for their dedication to Christ through suffering, torture and execution. Christian martyrs unite us in ways we can hardly imagine.

7. We acknowledge that solidarity among Christian churches is needed to strengthen Christian witness in the face of discrimination, persecution, and martyrdom. In the 21st century, we need to urgently strengthen the solidarity of all Christians, following up on what has been accomplished with insight and discernment from this Consultation.

8. We repent of having at times persecuted each other and other religious communities in history, and ask forgiveness from each other and pray for new ways of following Christ together.

In communion with Christ we commit ourselves:

    (a) **To listen more** to the experiences of Christians, Churches, and of all those who are discriminated against and persecuted, and deepen our engagement with suffering communities.

(b) **To pray more** for Churches, Christians, and for all those suffering discrimination and persecution, as well as for the transformation of those who discriminate and persecute.

(c) **To speak up more** with respect and dignity, with a clear and strong voice together, on behalf of those who are suffering.

(d) **To do more** in mutual understanding to find effective ways of solidarity and support for healing, reconciliation, and for the religious freedom of all oppressed and persecuted people.

9. Listening to the experience of those going through challenging times, praying and discerning together ways of following Christ in these harsh realities, the Consultation calls on:

(a) **All Christians** to include more prominently in their daily prayers those who are discriminated against, persecuted, and suffering for the fulfilment of God's Kingdom.

(b) **All Christian organisations on regional, national and local levels** from various traditions to learn, pray and work together in their localities for the persecuted to ensure they are better supported.

(c) **All Churches** to engage more in dialogue and co-operation with other faith communities, and be "as wise as serpents and innocent as doves" (Matthew 10:16) by remaining vigilant, watchful and fearless in the face of discrimination and persecution.

(d) **All persecutors** who discriminate against and oppress Christians and violate human rights to cease their abuse, and to affirm the right of all human beings to life and dignity.

(e) **All governments** to respect and protect the freedom of religion and belief of all people as a fundamental human right. We also appeal to governments and international organisations to respect and protect Christians and all other people of goodwill from threats and violence committed in the name of religion. In addition, we ask them to work for peace and reconciliation, to seek the settlement of on-going conflicts, and to stop the flow of arms, especially to violators of human rights.

(f) **All media** to report in an appropriate and unbiased way on violations of religious freedom, including the discrimination and persecution of Christians as well as of other faith communities.

(g) **All educational institutions** to develop opportunities and tools to teach young people in particular about human rights, religious tolerance, healing of memories and hostilities of the past, and peaceful means of conflict resolution and reconciliation.

(h) **All people of good will** to work for justice, peace and development, knowing that poverty and disrespect of human dignity are major contributing factors to violence.

10. We recommend that the Global Christian Forum evaluates within two years the work of this event, and reports to all four bodies for their follow up.

May God the Father who created us equal by His grace, strengthen our efforts to overcome all forms of discrimination and persecution.

May His Holy Spirit guide us in solidarity with all those who seek peace and reconciliation.

May He heal the wounds of the persecuted and grant us hope as we look forward to the glorious coming of our Lord Jesus Christ who will make all things new.

Brother Richard (Taizé Community) with stewards.

Participants

Listed alphabetically, by surname. Some names and countries have not been included for security reasons.

Participants

Bishop Ivan Abrahams, World Methodist Council, South Africa

Ms Berit Hagen Agøy, Church of Norway, Norway

Revd Agustín Aguilera Bowyer, National Association of Evangelicals of Bolivia, Bolivia

Dr Clare Amos, World Council of Churches, United Kingdom

H.B. Archbishop Anastasios, Orthodox Autocephalous Church of Albania, Albania

Dr Barakatullo Ashurov

Archbishop Antoine Audo, Chaldean Catholic Diocese of Aleppo, Syria

Most Rev Joseph Bagobiri, Christian Association of Nigeria, Nigeria

H.E. Metr Dr Isaac Barakat, Greek Orthodox Patriarchate of Antioch and All the East, Syria / Germany

Pastor Nordine Benzid, Association of Protestant Churches of Algeria, Algeria

Bishop Leanid Biruk, Church of Christians of Evangelical Faith - Belarus, Belarus

Rev Mansour Borji, Pars Theological Centre / "Article 18", Iran

Mrs Esme Ruth Bowers, Evangelical Alliance of South Africa, South Africa

Dr Ronald Boyd-MacMillan, Open Doors International, United Kingdom

Ms Klaudia Bumci, Radio Vaticana, Italy

Revd Margareta Carlenius, Church of Sweden, Sweden

Archbishop Basilos Georges Casmoussa, Syrian Catholic Patriarchate, Iraq

H.E. Archbishop. Mor Chrysostomos Mikhael Chamoun, Syrian Orthodox Patriarchate of Antioch and All the East, Lebanon

Rev Pierre Cibambo Ntakobajira, Caritas Internationalis, Vatican City

Rev Msgr Duarte da Cunha, Council of European Bishops' Conferences, Portugal

Rev David Das, National Council of Churches Bangladesh, Bangladesh

Dr Julia Duchrow, Bread for the World - Protestant Development Service, Germany

Mr Feije Duim, Kerk in Actie / Protestant Church in the Netherlands, Netherlands

Bishop Vassilii Evchik, Church of Christians of Evangelical Faith - Russia, Russia

Rev Serge Fornerod, Federation of Swiss Protestant Churches, Switzerland

Bishop George Frendo, o.p., Catholic Archdiocese of Tiranë-Durrës / Pontifical Council for Interreligious Dialogue, Albania

Rev César García, Mennonite World Conference, Colombia

Dr Willfried Gasser, World Evangelical Alliance, Switzerland

H.E. Metr Prof Dr Gennadios of Sassima, Ecumenical Patriarchate / World Council of Churches, Turkey

Rev Refat Fathy Roman Gergis, Evangelical Presbyterian Church of Egypt - Synod of the Nile, Egypt

Bishop Dodë Gjergji, Apostolic Administration of Prizren, Kosovo

Pastor Rhode Gloria González Zorrilla, Cuban Council of Churches, Cuba

Rev Dr Robert Gribben, World Methodist Council, Australia

Rev Dr Gabriel Hachem, Middle East Council of Churches, Lebanon

Bishop John Saw Yaw Han, Catholic Archdiocese of Yangon, Myanmar

Mr Kevin Hartigan, Catholic Relief Services, USA

Rev Dr A. R. Hashmat, Assemblies of God Pakistan, Pakistan

Ms Andrea Hattler Bramson, Foundations and Donors Interested in Catholic Activities, USA

Dr Thomas Heine-Geldern, Aid to the Church in Need, Austria

Dr Philipp W. Hildmann, World Evangelical Alliance, Germany

Archbishop Stanislav Hočevar, Pontifical Council for Promoting Christian Unity, Slovenia

Dr Daniel Hoffman, Middle East Concern, United Kingdom

The Rt Rev Dr Michael Ipgrave, Anglican Communion Network for Inter Faith Concerns, United Kingdom

Rev Lawrence Iwuamadi, Pontifical Council for Promoting Christian Unity / Ecumenical Institute at Bossey, Nigeria

The Most Rev Dr Michael Jackson, Anglican Communion Network for Inter Faith Concerns, Ireland

Mrs Rosangela Jarjour, Fellowship of Middle East Evangelical Churches, Syria / Lebanon

Rev Dr Riad Jarjour, Forum for Development Culture and Dialogue, Syria / Lebanon

Dr Thomas K. Johnson, World Evangelical Alliance, Czech Republic

Dr Munir Kakish, Council of Local Evangelical Churches in the Holy Land, Palestinian Territories

Pastor Ali Kalkandelen, Alliance of Protestant Churches in Turkey, Turkey

Revd Dr Andre Karamaga, All Africa Conference of Churches, Kenya

H.E. Metr Prof Dr Vasilios Karayiannis, Church of Cyprus, Cyprus

Rev Dr Tomi Karttunen, Evangelical Lutheran Church of Finland, Finland

H.E. Archbishop Mor Dionysus Jean Kawak, Syrian Orthodox Patriarchate of Antioch and All the East, Syria

Mrs Consolata Kivuti, Evangelical Alliance of Kenya, Kenya

Cardinal Kurt Koch, Pontifical Council for Promoting Christian Unity, Vatican City

Prof Dr Dimitra Koukoura, Ecumenical Patriarchate / World Council of Churches, Greece

Pastor Nikë Krasniqi, Kosova Protestant Evangelical Church, Kosovo

Pastor Artur Krasniqi, Kosova Protestant Evangelical Church, Kosovo

Rev Ali Kurti, Evangelical Alliance of Albania, Albania

Rev Vijayesh Lal, Evangelical Fellowship of India, India

Mr Rauli Lehtonen, Swedish Pentecostal movement / Light for the Nations, Sweden

Rev Dr Guy Liagre, Conference of European Churches, Belgium

Rev Henrek Lokra, Communion of Churches in Indonesia, Indonesia

Rev Nicta Lubaale, Organisation of African Instituted Churches, Uganda

Archbishop Felix A. Machado, Catholic Diocese of Vasai, India

Pastor Serhiy Manelyuk, Kiev Bible Institute, Ukraine

Very Rev Fr Housig Mardirossian, Armenian Catholicosate of Cilicia, Lebanon

Bishop Azad Marshall, Anglican Diocese of Iran

Rev Obed Erelio Martínez Lima, Cuba Christian Forum, Cuba

Archbishop Angelo Massafra, O.F.M., Catholic Episcopal Conference of Albania / Archdiocese of Shkodër-Pult, Albania

H.G. Bishop Andon Merdani, Orthodox Autocephalous Church of Albania, Albania

Pastor César Augusto Mermejo Pérez, Evangelical Council of Venezuela, Venezuela

Archbishop Rrok Kola Mirdita, Catholic Archdiocese of Tiranë-Durrës, Albania

Rev Kristin Molander, Church of Sweden, Sweden

Archbishop Ramiro Moliner Inglés, Apostolic Nunciature of Albania, Albania

Bishop Dr Panti Filibus Musa, Lutheran World Federation / Lutheran Church of Christ in Nigeria, Nigeria

Dr Farhana Nazir, Gujranwala Theological Seminary / Presbyterian Church of Pakistan, Pakistan

Dr Nikolay Nedelchev, Evangelical Alliance Bulgaria, Bulgaria

Dr Alfred Neufeld, World Evangelical Alliance, Paraguay

Mr Brian O'Connell, Religious Liberty Partnership, USA

Bishop Dr Chibuzo Raphael Opoko, Methodist Church Nigeria, Nigeria

Rev Akil Pano, Evangelical Alliance of Albania, Albania

Dr James Payton, Christian Reformed Church in North America, Canada

Rev Dr Anthony Peck, Baptist World Alliance / European Baptist Federation, United Kingdom

Bishop Ragnar Persenius, Church of Sweden, Sweden

Rev Prof Andrzej Perzyński, Catholic University in Warsaw, Poland

Rev Jerry Pillay, World Communion of Reformed Churches, South Africa

Ms Elona Prroj, Evangelical Alliance of Albania, Albania

Ms Amela Puljek-Shank, Mennonite Central Committee, Bosnia

Bishop Cesar Vicente P. Punzalan III, World Evangelical Alliance, Philippines

Ms Yamini Ravindran, National Christian Evangelical Alliance of Sri Lanka, Sri Lanka

Prof Dr Andrea Riccardi, Community of Sant'Egidio, Italy

Mr David Rihani, Jordan Evangelical Council, Jordan

Prof Dr Teresa Francesca Rossi, Centro Pro Unione, Italy

Prof Dr Rainer Rothfuss, University Tübingen / International Society for Human Rights, Germany

Mr Antoine Saad, Middle East Council of Churches, Lebanon

Rev Fr Dmitry Safonov, Moscow Patriarchate - Russian Orthodox Church, Russia

H.E. Archbishop Sebouh Sarkissian, Armenian Prelacy Diocese of Tehran - Holy See of Cilicia, Iran

Rev Dr Hermen Shastri, Council of Churches of Malaysia, Malaysia

Pastor Potifar Souina, Evangelical Alliance Chad, Chad

Dr Brian Stiller, World Evangelical Alliance, Canada

Rev Karna Bahadur Tamang, National Churches Fellowship of Nepal, Nepal

Prof Dr Georges Tamer, Friedrich-Alexander University - Oriental Philology and Islamic Studies, Germany

Mr Üllas Tankler, United Methodist Church - General Board of Global Ministries, Estonia

Mr Jeff Taylor, Open Doors International, USA

Bishop Efraim Tendero, World Evangelical Alliance, Philippines

Dr Mervyn Thomas, Religious Liberty Partnership, United Kingdom

Rev Dr Tshewang, Bhutan Evangelical Alliance, Bhutan

Rev Dr Olav Fykse Tveit, World Council of Churches, Norway

Msgr Dr Joris Vercammen, Old Catholic Churches of the Union of Utrecht, Netherlands

Ms Zahra Vieneuve, Under Caesar's Sword, USA

Rev Dr David Wells, Pentecostal World Fellowship, Canada

Rev Dr Ibrahim Wushishi Yusuf, Christian Council of Nigeria, Nigeria

Msgr Basel Yaldo, Chaldean Catholic Patriarchate of Babylon, Iraq

Rev Dr Godfrey Yogarajah, World Evangelical Alliance / Evangelical Alliance Sri Lanka, Sri Lanka

Planning Group

Rev Dr Andrzej Choromanski, Pontifical Council for Promoting Christian Unity / Global Christian Forum, Poland

Rev Ingolf Ellsell, Pentecostal World Fellowship, Germany

Archpriest Mikhail Goundiaev, Moscow Patriarchate - Russian Orthodox Church / Global Christian Forum, Russia

Rev Dr Arto Hämäläinen, Pentecostal World Fellowship, Finland

Rev Dr Richard Howell, Asia Evangelical Alliance / Evangelical Fellowship in India / Global Christian Forum, India

Rev Dr Pirjo-Liisa Penttinen, World Young Women's Christian Association / Global Christian Forum, Finland

Prof Dr Christof Sauer, World Evangelical Alliance / International Institute for Religious Freedom, Germany

Prof Dr Thomas Schirrmacher, World Evangelical Alliance / International Institute for Religious Freedom, Germany

Rev Dr Hielke Wolters, World Council of Churches, Netherlands

Observers

Mr Ernst Bergen, Mennonite Brethren Church in Paraguay, Paraguay

Mrs Lucy Bergen, Mennonite Brethren Church in Paraguay, Paraguay

Rev Dr Sangdo Choi, Global Forum for the Future of World Christianity, Korea

Dr Joel Edwards, Christian Solidarity Worldwide, United Kingdom

Dr Leonardo Emberti Gialloreti, Community of Sant'Egidio, Italy

Fr Marco Gnavi, Community of Sant'Egidio, Italy

Mrs Susan Gribben, Anglican Church of Australia, Australia

Mrs Jacqueline Gundersen, Epaphroditus Foundation, USA

Rev Carl Gundersen, Epaphroditus Foundation, USA

Mrs Sharon Dee Kakish, Council of Local Evangelical Churches in the Holy Land, Palestinian Territories

Mrs Abla Maalouf-Tamer, Orthodox, Germany

Mrs Wilma Neufeld, Mennonite Brethren Church in Paraguay, Paraguay

Mr Birger Nygaard, Evangelical Lutheran Church in Denmark, Denmark

Mr Mikael Stjernberg, Christian Council of Sweden, Sweden

Dr Sierry Tendero, World Evangelical Alliance, Philippines

Rev Geneviève Toilliez, Evangelical Mennnonite Church of Strasboug Illkirch, France

Mrs Maria van Beek, Global Christian Forum, Netherlands/Switzerland

Mr Titus Vogt, International Institute for Religious Freedom, Germany

Local Guests

Mr Robert Andoni, Orthodox Autocephalous Church of Albania, Albania

Ms Joan Baba, Orthodox Autocephalous Church of Albania, Albania

H.G. Bishop Asti Bakalbashi, Orthodox Autocephalous Church of Albania, Albania

Ms Pamela Barksdale, Orthodox Autocephalous Church of Albania, Albania

Ms Arvenola Bekteshi, World Vision Albania, Albania

Fr Anastas Bendo, Orthodox Autocephalous Church of Albania, Albania

Pastor Ylli Beqiraj, Albania Bible Institute IBSH, Albania

Fr Zef Bisha, Catholic Church in Albania, Albania

Mr Miron Çako, Orthodox Autocephalous Church of Albania, Albania

Fr Bernard Caruana, Catholic Church in Albania, Albania

Mr Thoma Çomëni, Orthodox Autocephalous Church of Albania, Albania

Mr Meriton Cungu, Evangelical Alliance of Albania, Albania

Mr Eduart Demo, Illyricum Movement, Albania

Mr Thoma Dhima, Orthodox Autocephalous Church of Albania, Albania

Ms Dora Dietrich, Nehemia Center, Dürres, Albania

Pastor Ueli Dietrich, Nehemia Center, Dürres, Albania

Pastor Ylli Doçi, Cornerstone Church of Tirana, Albania

Pastor Hervin Fushekati, Church of God, Albania

Mr Parashqevi Gega, Orthodox Autocephalous Church of Albania, Albania

Mr Majlind Gegprifti, Evangelical Alliance of Albania, Albania

Don Arben Gilaj, Catholic Church in Albania, Albania

Fr Prel Gjurashaj, Catholic Church in Albania, Albania

Pastor Alfred Golloshi, Liria Church, Albania

Mr Nikola Khodeli, Orthodox Autocephalous Church of Albania, Albania

Mr Ilia Koçi, Orthodox Autocephalous Church of Albania, Albania

Ms Luljeta Lila, Orthodox Autocephalous Church of Albania, Albania

Fr Emanuel Lusha, Orthodox Autocephalous Church of Albania, Albania

Fr Ilia Mazniku, Orthodox Autocephalous Church of Albania, Albania

Rev Msgr Romanus Mbena, Embassy of the Holy See in Albania, Vatican City

Dr Jeffrey McDonald, Orthodox Autocephalous Church of Albania, Albania

Ms Joan Meni, Orthodox Autocephalous Church of Albania, Albania

Ms Dana Molla, Betesda, Albania

Pastor Fitor Muça, Rilindja Church, Albania

H.E. Metr Nathanail, Orthodox Autocephalous Church of Albania, Albania

Dr Albert Nikolla, Catholic Church in Albania, Albania

Pastor Barry Odgen, International Protestant Assembly, Albania

Ms Lindita Pano, Gospel Christ Church, Albania

Mr Josh Parker, Evangelical Alliance of Albania, Albania

Fr Grigor Pelushi, Orthodox Autocephalous Church of Albania, Albania

Mr Vlash Plepi, Orthodox Autocephalous Church of Albania, Albania

Pastor Gentian Proseku, Word of Life Church, Albania

Mr Dhimitër Qosja, Orthodox Autocephalous Church of Albania, Albania

Mr Paolo Rago, Community of Sant'Egidio, Albania

Mr Pellumb Ranxha, Albania Bible Institute IBSH, Albania

Mr Andi Rembeci, Orthodox Autocephalous Church of Albania, Albania

Ms Olta Rozgari, Evangelical Alliance of Albania, Albania

Mr Thoma Shkira, Orthodox Autocephalous Church of Albania, Albania

Archim Kozma Sovjani, Orthodox Autocephalous Church of Albania, Albania

Mr Ned Spieker, YWAM Albania, Albania

Pastor Ermir Taja, Church of God Vore, Albania

Mr Nikola Tashi, Orthodox Autocephalous Church of Albania, Albania

Ms Ilia Telo, Orthodox Autocephalous Church of Albania, Albania

Mr Harallamb Terziu, Orthodox Autocephalous Church of Albania, Albania

Pastor Shaun Thomson, Evangelical Church, Gjirokastër, Albania

Spiro Topanxha, Orthodox Autocephalous Church of Albania, Albania

Mr Stavraq Trako, Orthodox Autocephalous Church of Albania, Albania

Archpriest Jani Trebicka, Orthodox Autocephalous Church of Albania, Albania

Ms Majlinda Treska, Joshua Center, Albania

Mr Genti Tupa, Evangelical Alliance of Albania, Albania

Don Henry Veldkamp, Catholic Church in Albania, Albania

Ms Ergerta Xhafa, Evangelical Alliance of Albania, Albania

Nikolin Zharkalli, Orthodox Autocephalous Church of Albania, Albania

National Organising Committee

Mr Nathan Hoppe, Orthodox Autocephalous Church of Albania, Albania

Dr Ariela Mitri, Catholic Church in Albania, Albania

Mr Erion Prendi, Evangelical Alliance of Albania, Albania

Communications Team

Mr Eero Antturi, Keymedia, Finland
Mr Mark Beach, Global Christian Forum, USA
Ms Julia Bicknell, World Watch Monitor, United Kingdom
Rev Pierre Bou Zeidan, Catholic journalist, Lebanon
Rev Kim Cain, Global Christian Forum, Australia
Rev Vito del Prete, Agenzia Fides (Vatican), Vatican City
Ms Marianne Ejdersten, World Council of Churches, Sweden
Mr Peter Kenny, Ecumenical News, Switzerland
Mrs Terri Miller, Global Christian Forum, United Kingdom
Mr Juan Diego Ortube Padilla, Net for God / Chemin Neuf Community, Bolivia
Ms Naveen Qayyum, World Council of Churches, Pakistan
Fr Gabriel Roussineau, Net for God / Chemin Neuf Community, France
Mr Coetzee Zietsman, Meropa Visual, South Africa

Staff

Mr Vincenzo Cortese, Interpreter, Italy
Mrs Joy Lee, Global Christian Forum, Korea / USA
Mr Fation Losha, ABC Health Center, Albania
Ms Christine Méar, Interpreter, France
Mr Forenc Mene, Interpreter, Albania
Rev Dr Larry Miller, Global Christian Forum, France
Mrs Eleanor Miller, Global Christian Forum, France
Mr Zefjan Nikolla, Interpreter, Albania
Rev Dr Carlos Sintado, Interpreter, Switzerland
Mr Niko Solihin, Global Christian Forum, Indonesia
Ms Vinjola Tave, ABC Health Center, Albania
Ms Francesca Turi, Interpreter, Italy
Mr Hubert van Beek, Global Christian Forum, Netherlands/ Switzerland

Mrs Marie-Noëlle von der Recke, Interpreter, France

Mr Martin Warnecke, International Institute for Religious Freedom, Germany

Brother Richard, Taizé Community, France

Steward Leaders

Ms Ana Baba, Orthodox Autocephalous Church of Albania, Albania

Ms Ingrida Bida, Orthodox Autocephalous Church of Albania, Albania

Mr Priam Dautaj, Evangelical Alliance of Albania, Albania

Mr Elidon Dodaj, Caritas Albania, Albania

Stewards

Mr Henri Berisha, Catholic Church in Albania, Albania

Mr Kostandin Beshiri, Orthodox Autocephalous Church of Albania, Albania

Ms Lorena Bida, Orthodox Autocephalous Church of Albania, Albania

Ms Fizjona Comani, Evangelical Alliance of Albania, Albania

Ms Aurel Dema, Catholic Church in Albania, Albania

Ms Gentjana Dema, Catholic Church in Albania, Albania

Ms Jolanda Dema, Catholic Church in Albania, Albania

Mr Denis Dervishi, Orthodox Autocephalous Church of Albania, Albania

Ms Kostandina Dusha, Orthodox Autocephalous Church of Albania, Albania

Motër File Gështenja, Catholic Church in Albania, Albania

Ms Ershela Gjoni, Catholic Church in Albania, Albania

Mr Reald Halili, Evangelical Alliance of Albania, Albania

Ms Gabriela Kola, Orthodox Autocephalous Church of Albania, Albania

Ms Maria Kola, Orthodox Autocephalous Church of Albania, Albania

Ms Vasiliqi Lloci, Orthodox Autocephalous Church of Albania, Albania

Ms **Diella Marku**, Catholic Church in Albania, Albania

Ms **Greta Marku**, Catholic Church in Albania, Albania

Ms **Jani Meni**, Orthodox Autocephalous Church of Albania, Albania

Ms **Elpiniqi Merkuri**, Catholic Church in Albania, Albania

Mr **Ervin Mihali**, Orthodox Autocephalous Church of Albania, Albania

Ms **Maria Mihali**, Orthodox Autocephalous Church of Albania, Albania

Ms **Laert Miraku**, Orthodox Autocephalous Church of Albania, Albania

Ms **Valbona Palaj**, Catholic Church in Albania, Albania

Ms **Zoj Palaj**, Catholic Church in Albania, Albania

Ms **Krisild Pepkolaj**, Catholic Church in Albania, Albania

Mr **Alban Petro**, Orthodox Autocephalous Church of Albania, Albania

Ms **Kostandina Petro**, Orthodox Autocephalous Church of Albania, Albania

Mr **Defrim Shehi**, Evangelical Alliance of Albania, Albania

Mr **Adi Shimplaku**, Orthodox Autocephalous Church of Albania, Albania

Ms **Elisabeta Shqau**, Orthodox Autocephalous Church of Albania, Albania

Ms **Elena Sinani**, Orthodox Autocephalous Church of Albania, Albania

Mr **Amarildo Tashi**, Orthodox Autocephalous Church of Albania, Albania

Ms **Angjelina Vaso**, Orthodox Autocephalous Church of Albania, Albania

Mr **Ergys Vladi**, Evangelical Alliance of Albania, Albania

Ms **Arvela Vukaj**, Catholic Church in Albania, Albania

Ms **Diljana Vukzaj**, Catholic Church in Albania, Albania

Mr **Martin Ziu**, Orthodox Autocephalous Church of Albania, Albania

www.ingramcontent.com/pod-product-compliance
Lightning Source LLC
Chambersburg PA
CBHW060311240426
43661CB00059B/2721